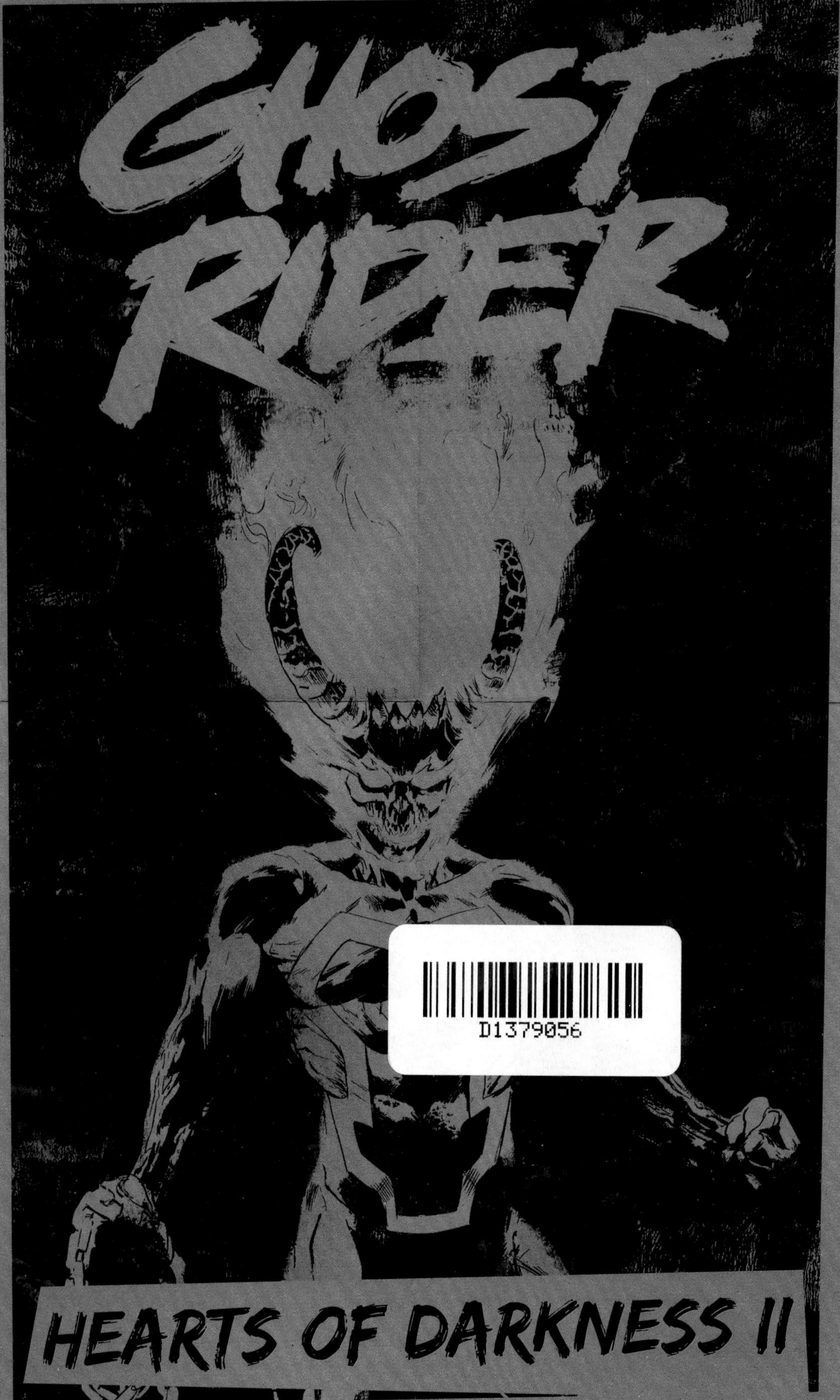
GHOST
RIDER
HEARTS OF DARKNESS II

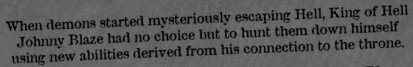

When demons started mysteriously escaping Hell, King of Hell Johnny Blaze had no choice but to hunt them down himself using new abilities derived from his connection to the throne.

Fearing that the staggering power of Hell was driving Blaze mad, his brother, Danny Ketch, went to a different nether realm known as Limbo and was bonded to the Spirit of Corruption, a supernatural entity strong enough to exterminate Ghost Riders.

Meanwhile, Lilith, Mother of Demons, gathers demon followers from the shadows!

COLLECTION EDITOR: Jennifer Grünwald
ASSISTANT MANAGING EDITOR: Maia Loy
ASSISTANT MANAGING EDITOR: Lisa Montalbano
EDITOR, SPECIAL PROJECTS: Mark D. Beazley

VP PRODUCTION & SPECIAL PROJECTS: Jeff Youngquist
BOOK DESIGNER: Adam Del Re
SVP PRINT, SALES & MARKETING: David Gabriel
EDITOR IN CHIEF: C.B. Cebulski

GHOST RIDER VOL. 2: HEARTS OF DARKNESS II. Contains material originally published in magazine form as SPIRITS OF GHOST RIDER: MOTHER OF DEMONS (2020) #1, GHOST RIDER (2019) #5-7 and GHOST RIDER 2099 (2019) #1. First printing 2020. ISBN 978-1-302-92006-7. Published by MARVEL WORLDWIDE, INC., a subsidiary of MARVEL ENTERTAINMENT, LLC. OFFICE OF PUBLICATION: 1290 Avenue of the Americas, New York, NY 10104. © 2020 MARVEL No similarity between any of the names, characters, persons, and/or institutions in this magazine with those of any living or dead person or institution is intended, and any such similarity which may exist is purely coincidental. Printed in Canada. KEVIN FEIGE, Chief Creative Officer; DAN BUCKLEY, President, Marvel Entertainment; JOHN NEE, Publisher; JOE QUESADA, EVP & Creative Director; TOM BREVOORT, SVP of Publishing; DAVID BOGART, Associate Publisher & SVP of Talent Affairs; Publishing & Partnership; DAVID GABRIEL, VP of Print & Digital Publishing; JEFF YOUNGQUIST, VP of Production & Special Projects; DAN CARR, Executive Director of Publishing Technology; ALEX MORALES, Director of Publishing Operations; DAN EDINGTON, Managing Editor; SUSAN CRESPI, Production Manager; STAN LEE, Chairman Emeritus. For information regarding advertising in Marvel Comics or on Marvel.com, please contact Vit DeBellis, Custom Solutions & Integrated Advertising Manager, at vdebellis@marvel.com. For Marvel subscription inquiries, please call 888-511-5480. Manufactured between 7/17/2020 and 8/18/2020 by SOLISCO PRINTERS, SCOTT, QC, CANADA.

10 9 8 7 6 5 4 3 2 1

GHOST RIDER

HEARTS OF DARKNESS II

WRITER: **Ed Brisson**

SPIRITS OF GHOST RIDER: MOTHER OF DEMONS

ARTIST: **Roland Boschi** COLOR ARTIST: **Dan Brown**

COVER ART: **Philip Tan & Jay David Ramos**

GHOST RIDER #5-6

ARTIST: **Juan Frigeri**

COLOR ARTISTS: **Jason Keith** with **Dono Sánchez-Almara** (#6)

COVER ART: **Aaron Kuder & Federico Blee**

GHOST RIDER #7

ARTIST: **Aaron Kuder** COLOR ARTIST: **Jason Keith**

COVER ART: **Aaron Kuder & Jason Keith**

GHOST RIDER 2099

ARTIST: **Damian Couceiro**

COLOR ARTIST: **Dono Sánchez-Almara**

COVER ART: **Valerio Giangiordano & Frank D'Armata**

LETTERER: **VC's Joe Caramagna**

EDITOR: **Chris Robinson**

SENIOR EDITOR: **Jordan D. White**

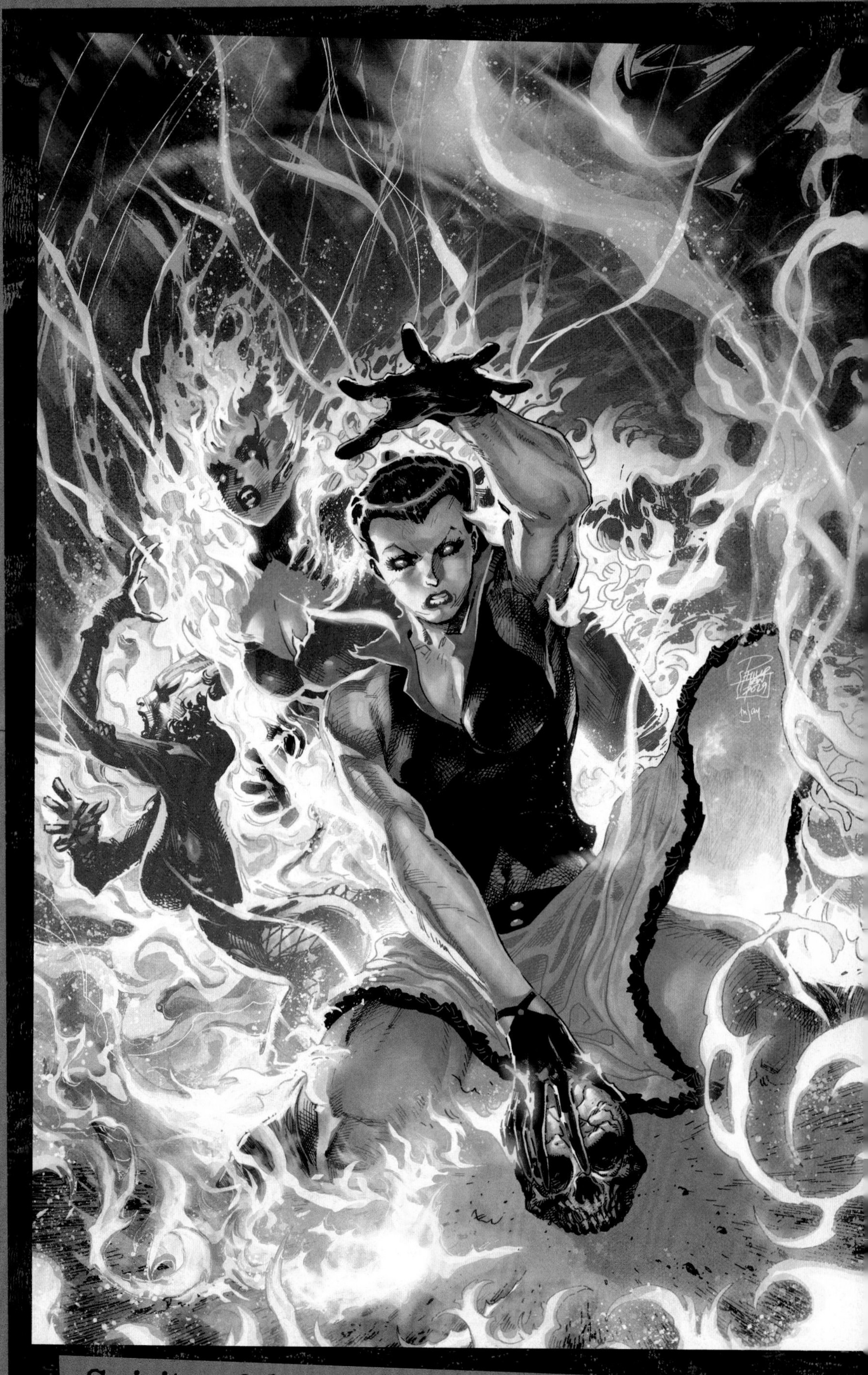

Spirits of Ghost Rider: Mother of Demons

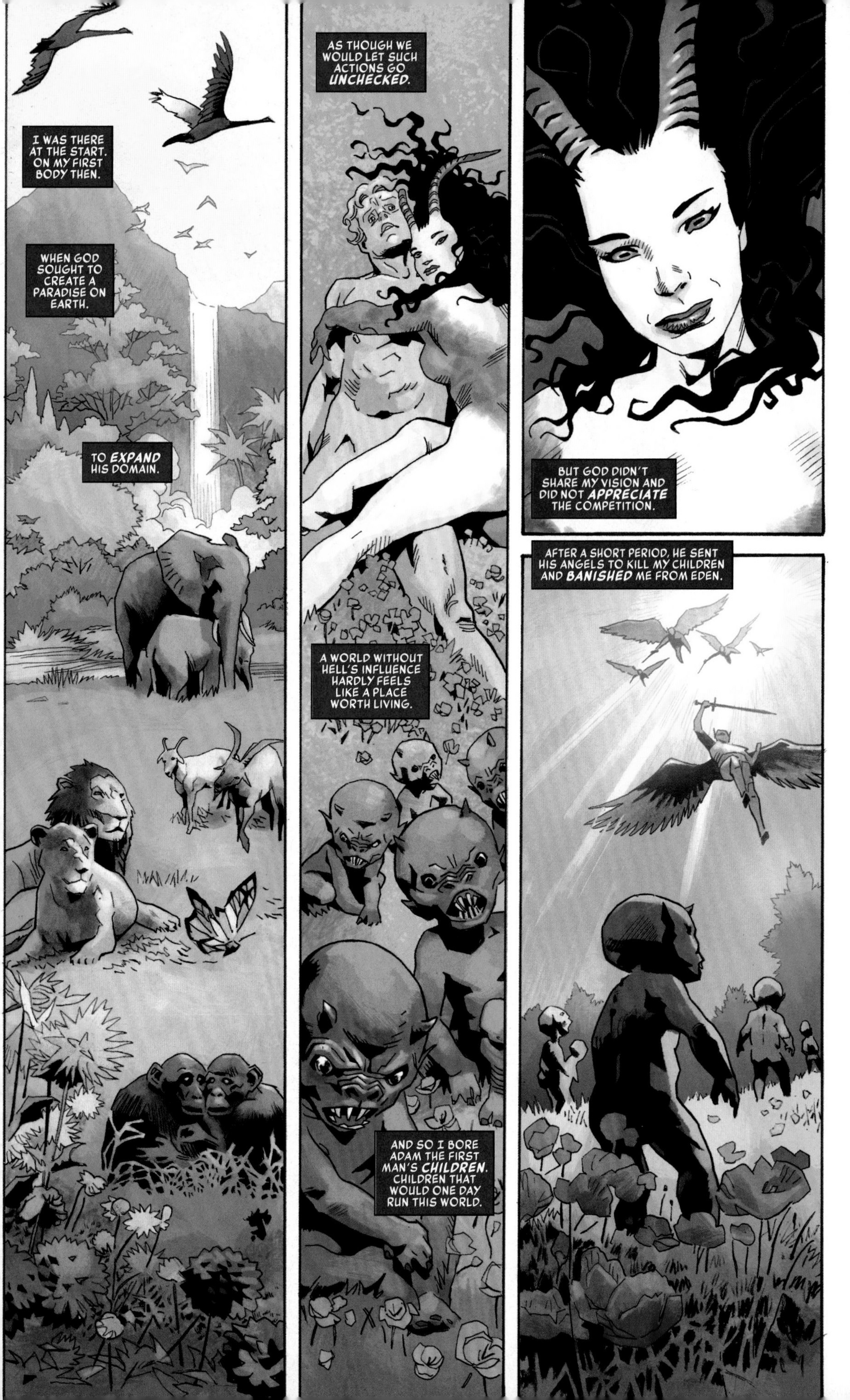
I WAS THERE AT THE START. ON MY FIRST BODY THEN.
WHEN GOD SOUGHT TO CREATE A PARADISE ON EARTH.
TO EXPAND HIS DOMAIN.
AS THOUGH WE WOULD LET SUCH ACTIONS GO UNCHECKED.
A WORLD WITHOUT HELL'S INFLUENCE HARDLY FEELS LIKE A PLACE WORTH LIVING.
AND SO I BORE ADAM THE FIRST MAN'S CHILDREN. CHILDREN THAT WOULD ONE DAY RUN THIS WORLD.
BUT GOD DIDN'T SHARE MY VISION AND DID NOT APPRECIATE THE COMPETITION.
AFTER A SHORT PERIOD, HE SENT HIS ANGELS TO KILL MY CHILDREN AND BANISHED ME FROM EDEN.

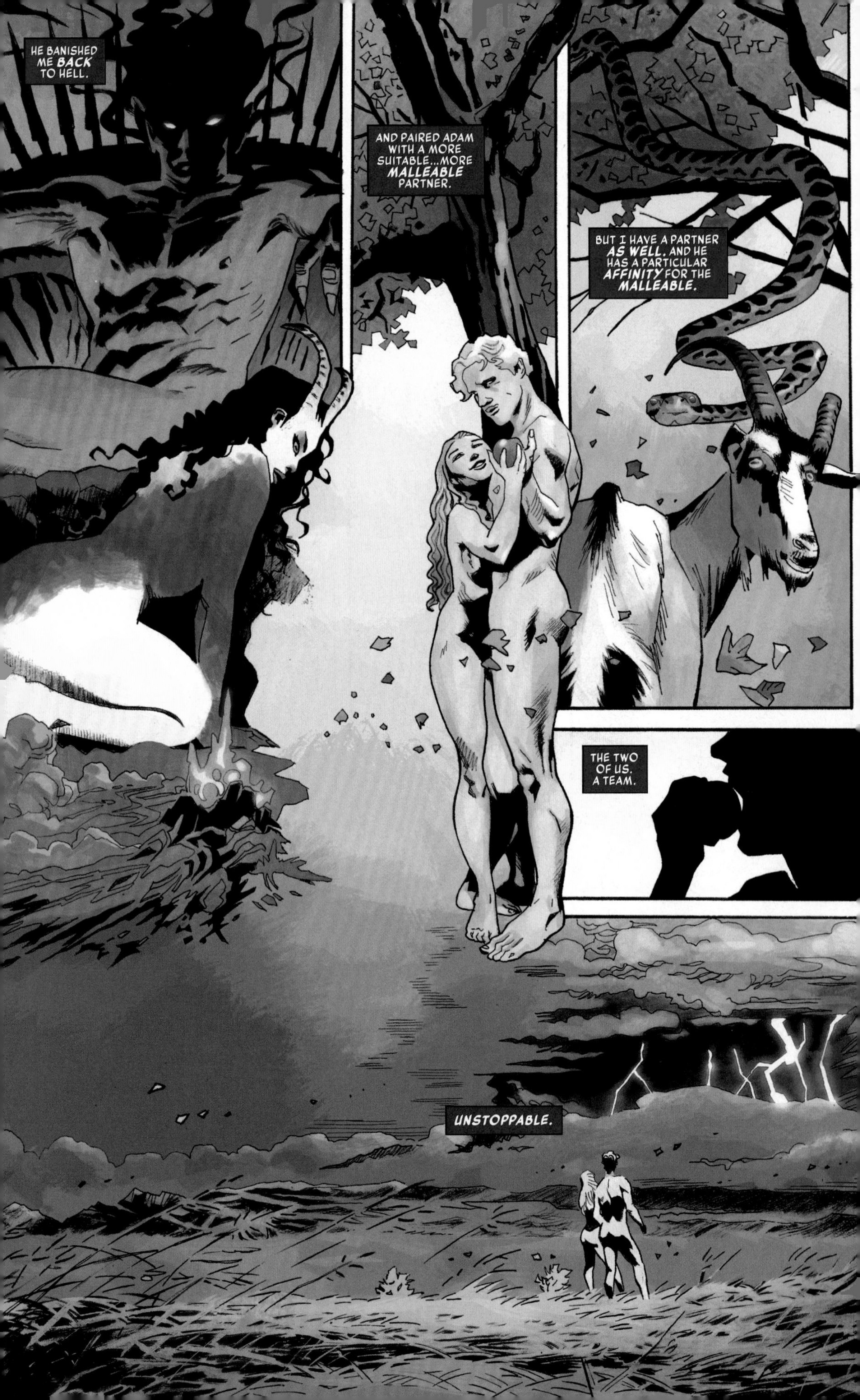
HE BANISHED ME BACK TO HELL.
AND PAIRED ADAM WITH A MORE SUITABLE...MORE MALLEABLE PARTNER.
BUT I HAVE A PARTNER AS WELL. AND HE HAS A PARTICULAR AFFINITY FOR THE MALLEABLE.
THE TWO OF US. A TEAM.
UNSTOPPABLE.

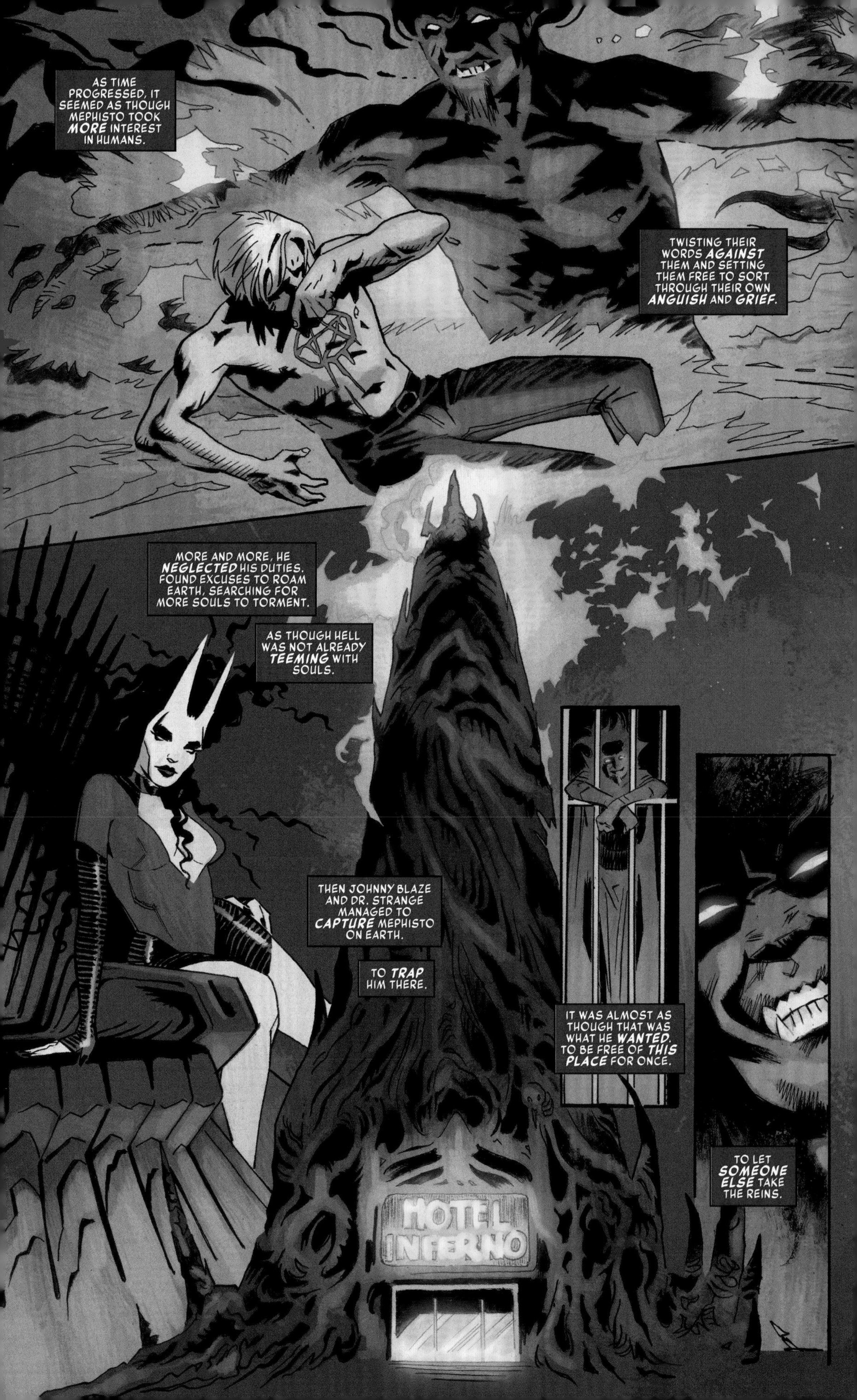
AS TIME PROGRESSED, IT SEEMED AS THOUGH MEPHISTO TOOK MORE INTEREST IN HUMANS.
TWISTING THEIR WORDS AGAINST THEM AND SETTING THEM FREE TO SORT THROUGH THEIR OWN ANGUISH AND GRIEF.
MORE AND MORE, HE NEGLECTED HIS DUTIES. FOUND EXCUSES TO ROAM EARTH, SEARCHING FOR MORE SOULS TO TORMENT.
AS THOUGH HELL WAS NOT ALREADY TEEMING WITH SOULS.
THEN JOHNNY BLAZE AND DR. STRANGE MANAGED TO CAPTURE MEPHISTO ON EARTH.
TO TRAP HIM THERE.
IT WAS ALMOST AS THOUGH THAT WAS WHAT HE WANTED. TO BE FREE OF THIS PLACE FOR ONCE.
TO LET SOMEONE ELSE TAKE THE REINS.
HOTEL INFERNO

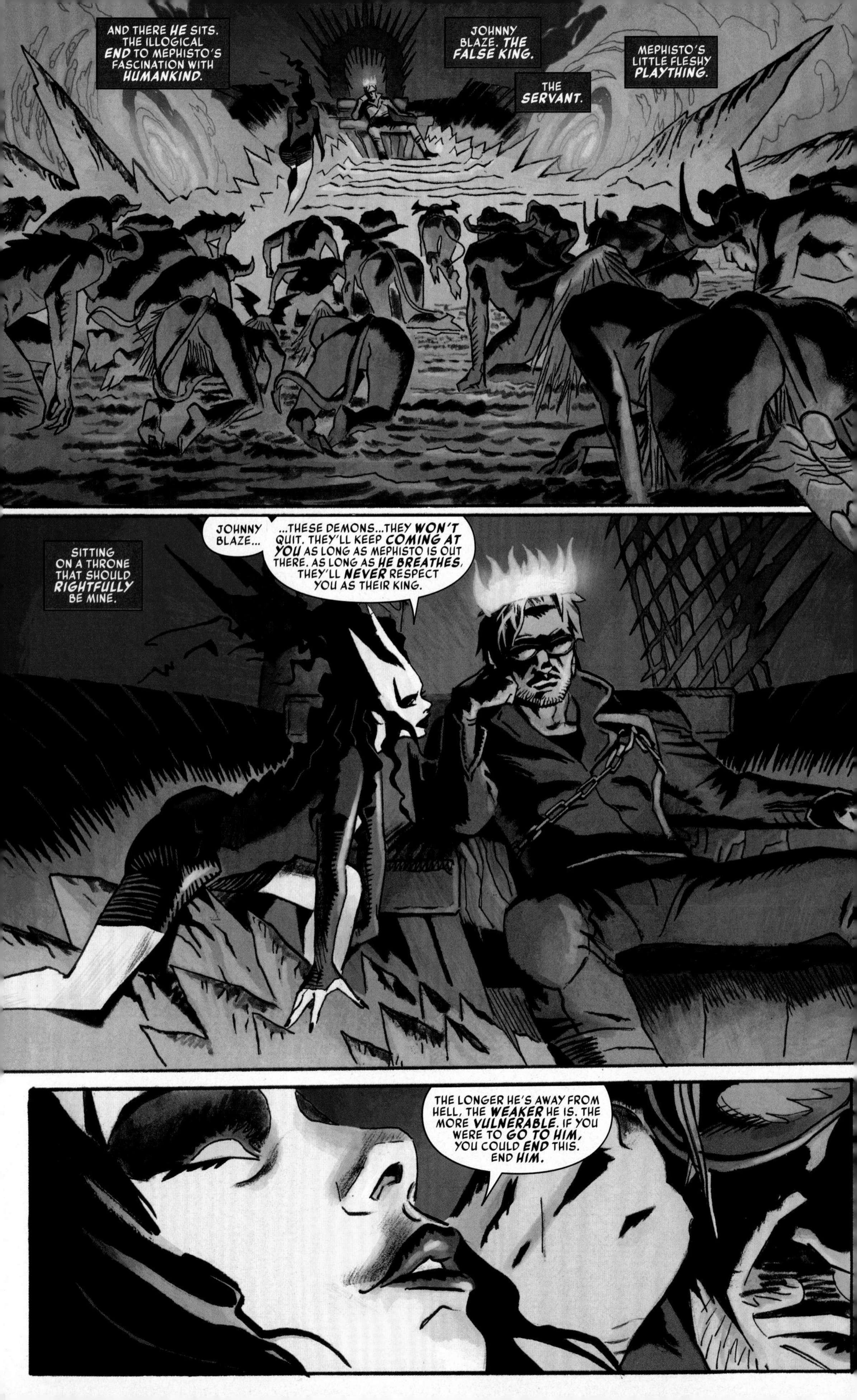
AND THERE HE SITS. THE ILLOGICAL END TO MEPHISTO'S FASCINATION WITH HUMANKIND.
JOHNNY BLAZE. THE FALSE KING.
THE SERVANT.
MEPHISTO'S LITTLE FLESHY PLAYTHING.
SITTING ON A THRONE THAT SHOULD RIGHTFULLY BE MINE.
JOHNNY BLAZE...
...THESE DEMONS...THEY WON'T QUIT. THEY'LL KEEP COMING AT YOU AS LONG AS MEPHISTO IS OUT THERE. AS LONG AS HE BREATHES, THEY'LL NEVER RESPECT YOU AS THEIR KING.
THE LONGER HE'S AWAY FROM HELL, THE WEAKER HE IS. THE MORE VULNERABLE. IF YOU WERE TO GO TO HIM, YOU COULD END THIS. END HIM.

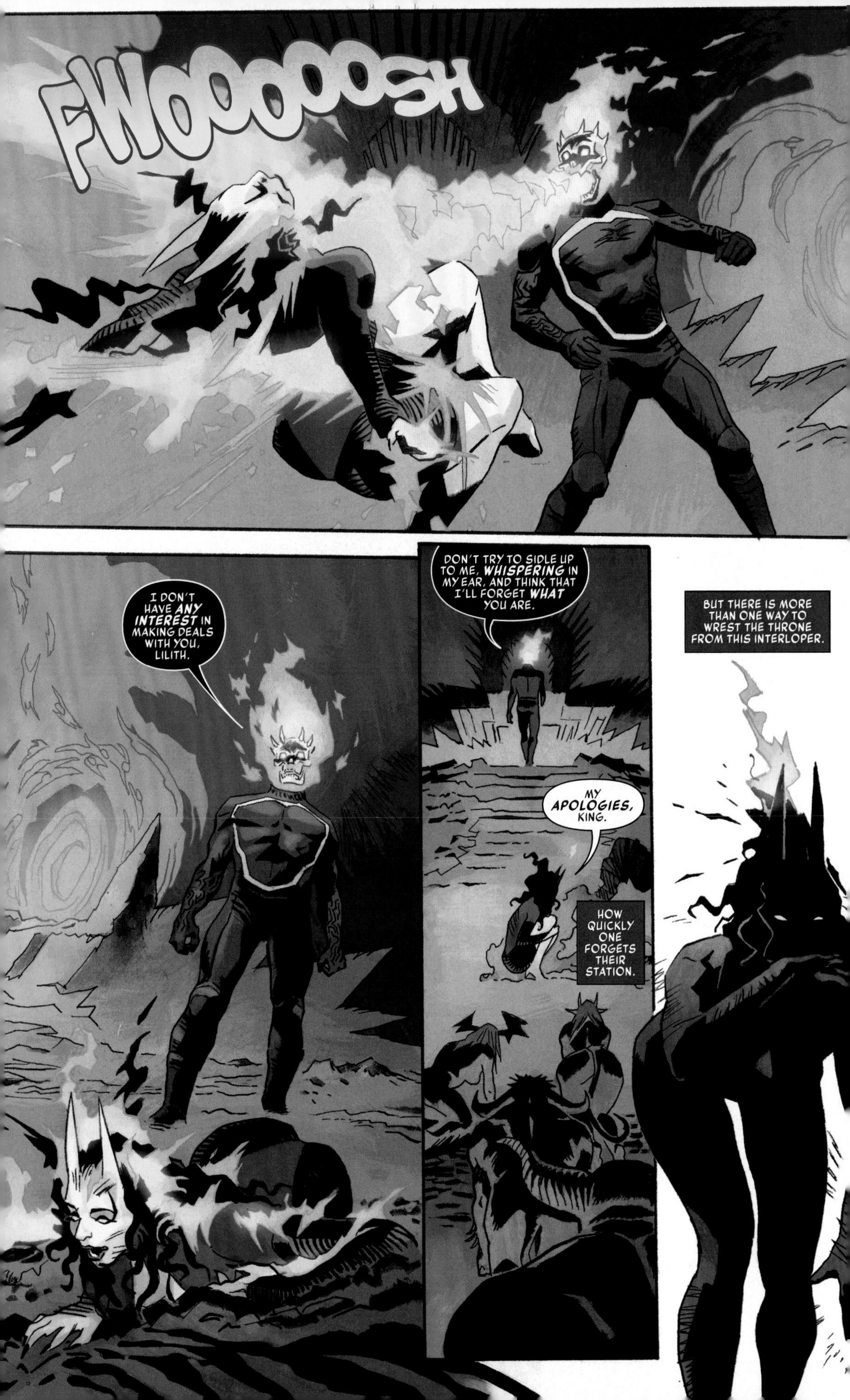
FWOOOOOOSH
I DON'T HAVE ANY INTEREST IN MAKING DEALS WITH YOU, LILITH.
DON'T TRY TO SIDLE UP TO ME, WHISPERING IN MY EAR, AND THINK THAT I'LL FORGET WHAT YOU ARE.
MY APOLOGIES, KING.
HOW QUICKLY ONE FORGETS THEIR STATION.
BUT THERE IS MORE THAN ONE WAY TO WREST THE THRONE FROM THIS INTERLOPER.

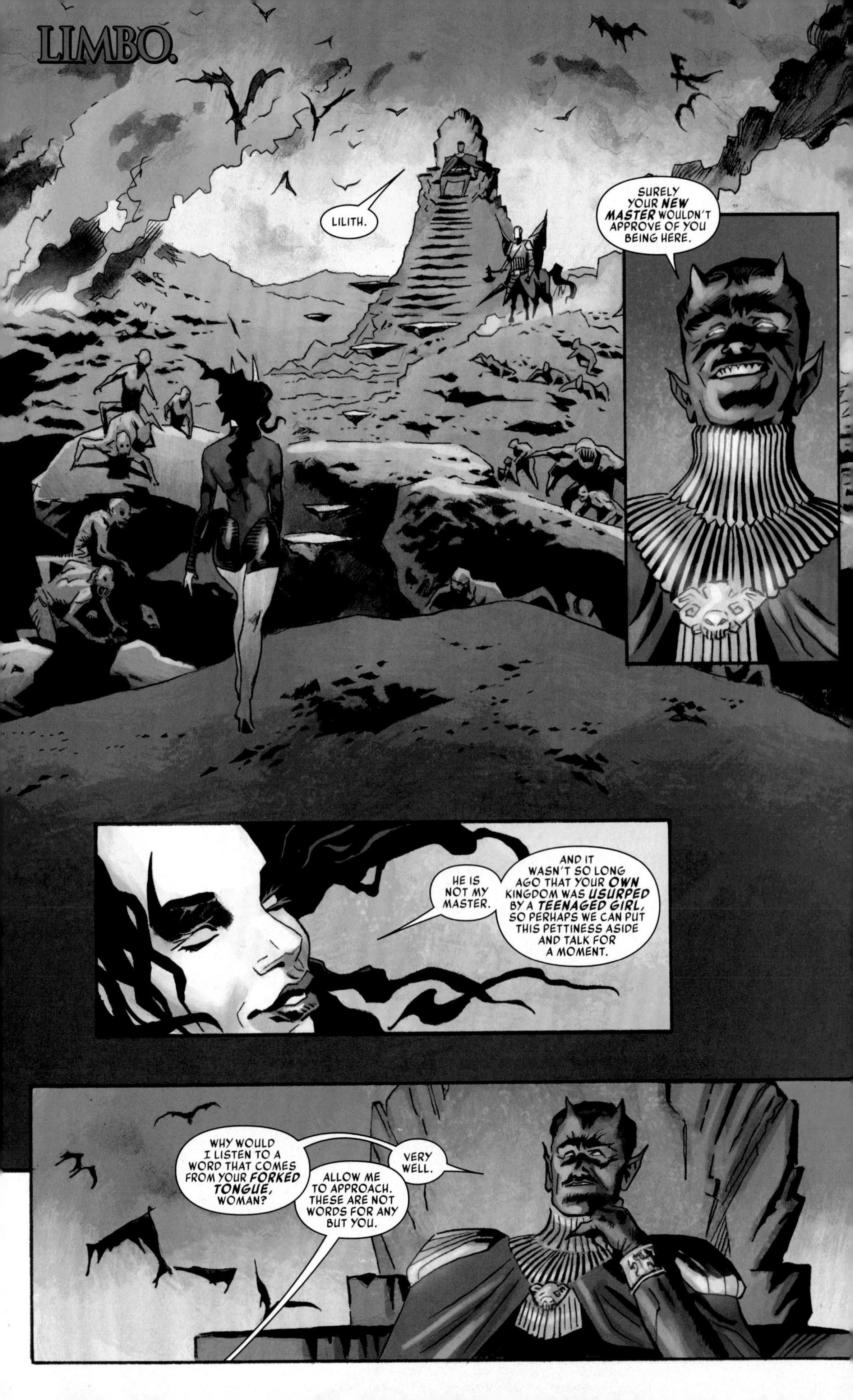
LIMBO.
LILITH.
SURELY YOUR NEW MASTER WOULDN'T APPROVE OF YOU BEING HERE.
HE IS NOT MY MASTER.
AND IT WASN'T SO LONG AGO THAT YOUR OWN KINGDOM WAS USURPED BY A TEENAGED GIRL, SO PERHAPS WE CAN PUT THIS PETTINESS ASIDE AND TALK FOR A MOMENT.
WHY WOULD I LISTEN TO A WORD THAT COMES FROM YOUR FORKED TONGUE, WOMAN?
ALLOW ME TO APPROACH. THESE ARE NOT WORDS FOR ANY BUT YOU.
VERY WELL.

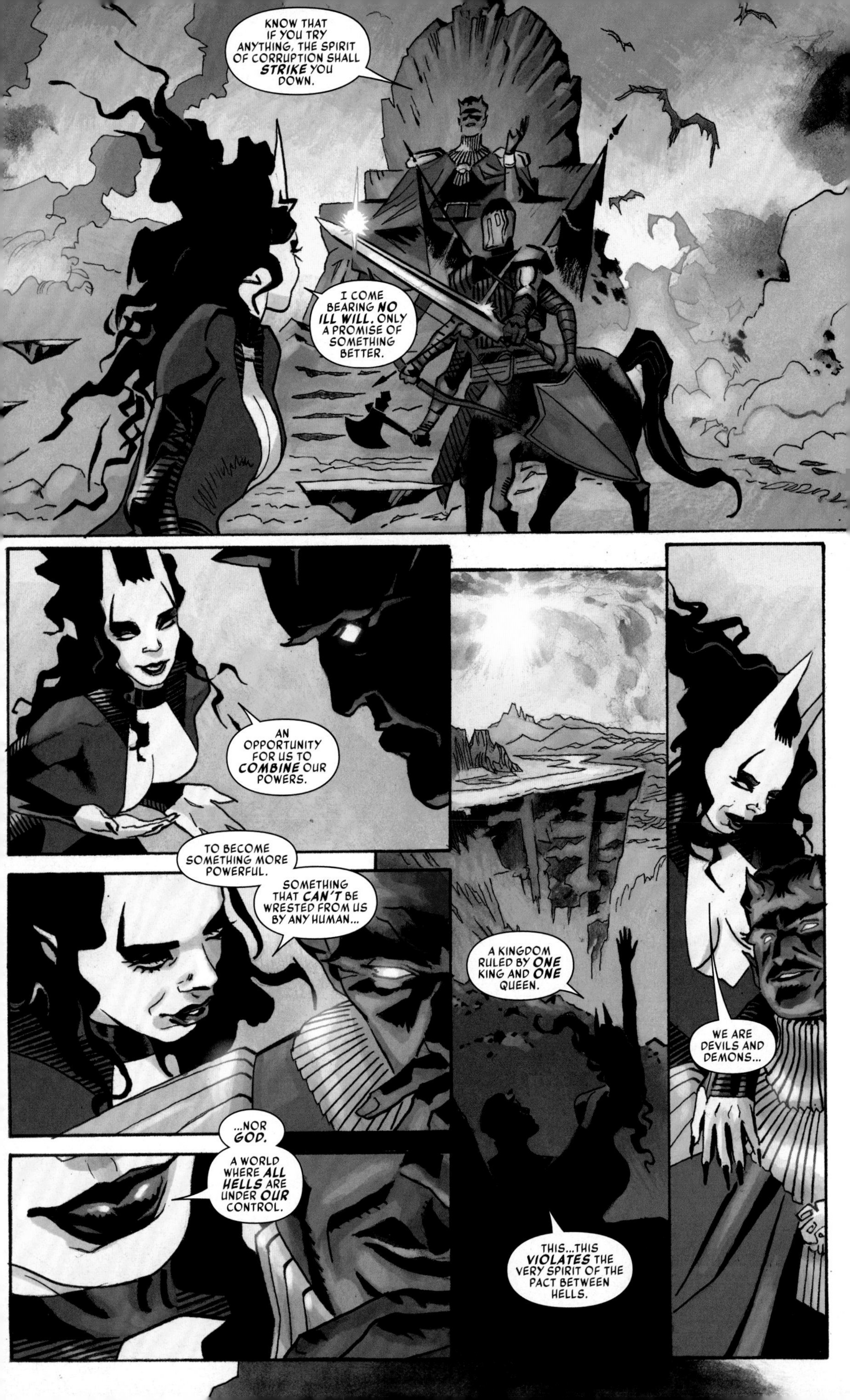
KNOW THAT IF YOU TRY ANYTHING, THE SPIRIT OF CORRUPTION SHALL STRIKE YOU DOWN.
I COME BEARING NO ILL WILL. ONLY A PROMISE OF SOMETHING BETTER.
AN OPPORTUNITY FOR US TO COMBINE OUR POWERS.
TO BECOME SOMETHING MORE POWERFUL.
SOMETHING THAT CAN'T BE WRESTED FROM US BY ANY HUMAN...
...NOR GOD.
A WORLD WHERE ALL HELLS ARE UNDER OUR CONTROL.
A KINGDOM RULED BY ONE KING AND ONE QUEEN.
THIS...THIS VIOLATES THE VERY SPIRIT OF THE PACT BETWEEN HELLS.
WE ARE DEVILS AND DEMONS...

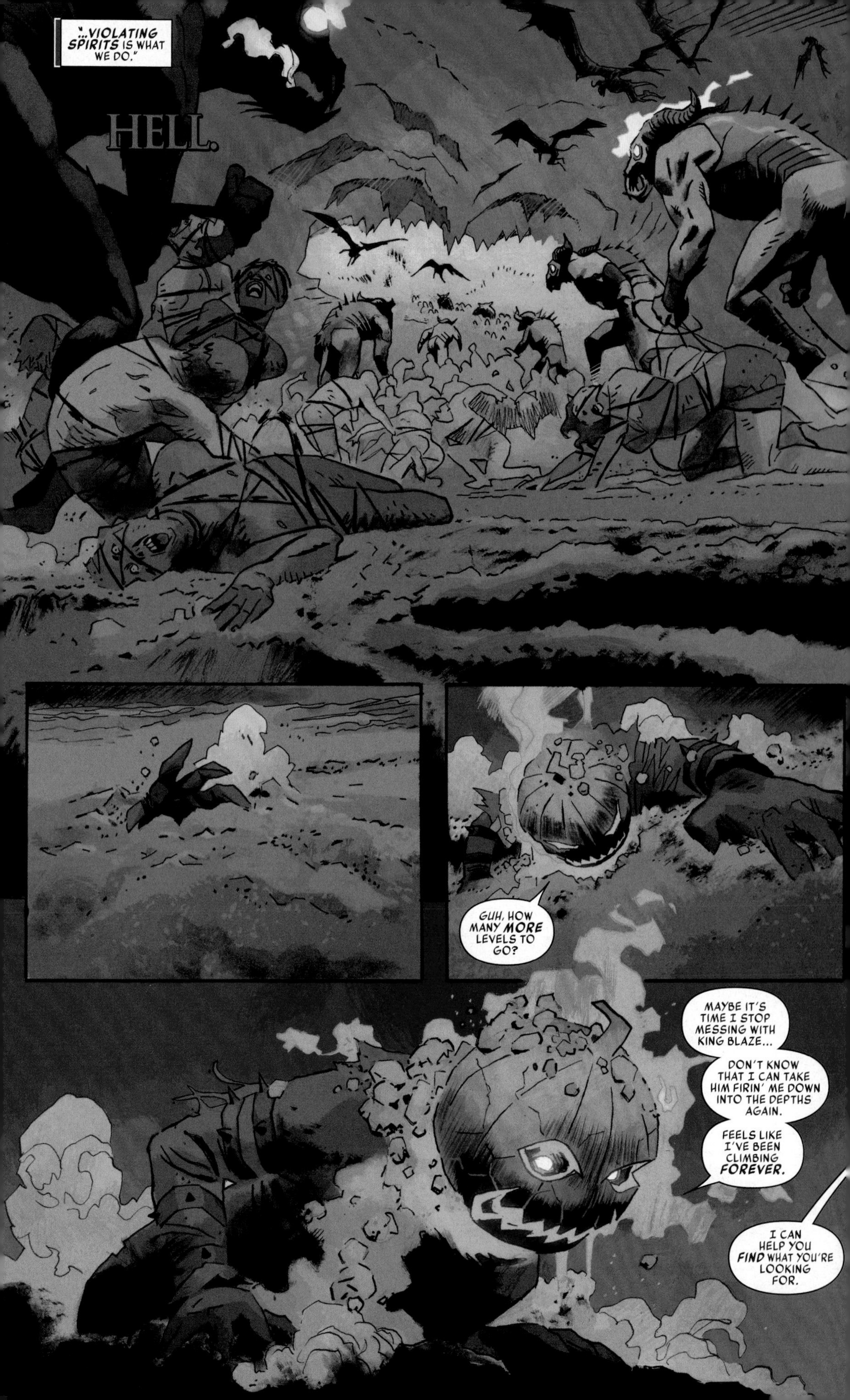
"...VIOLATING SPIRITS IS WHAT WE DO."
HELL.
GUH, HOW MANY MORE LEVELS TO GO?
MAYBE IT'S TIME I STOP MESSING WITH KING BLAZE...
DON'T KNOW THAT I CAN TAKE HIM FIRIN' ME DOWN INTO THE DEPTHS AGAIN.
FEELS LIKE I'VE BEEN CLIMBING FOREVER.
I CAN HELP YOU FIND WHAT YOU'RE LOOKING FOR.

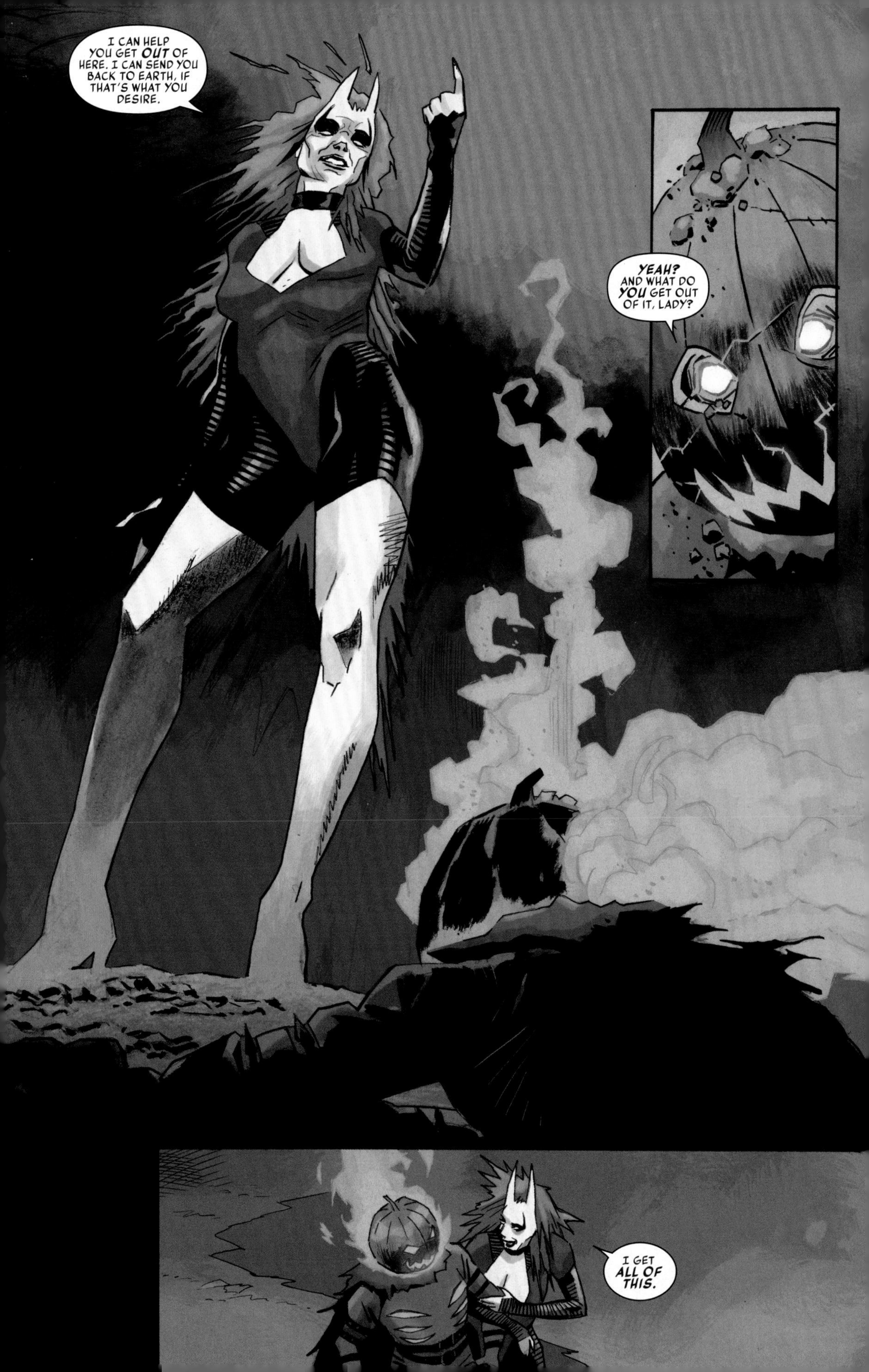
I CAN HELP YOU GET OUT OF HERE. I CAN SEND YOU BACK TO EARTH, IF THAT'S WHAT YOU DESIRE.
YEAH? AND WHAT DO YOU GET OUT OF IT, LADY?
I GET ALL OF THIS.

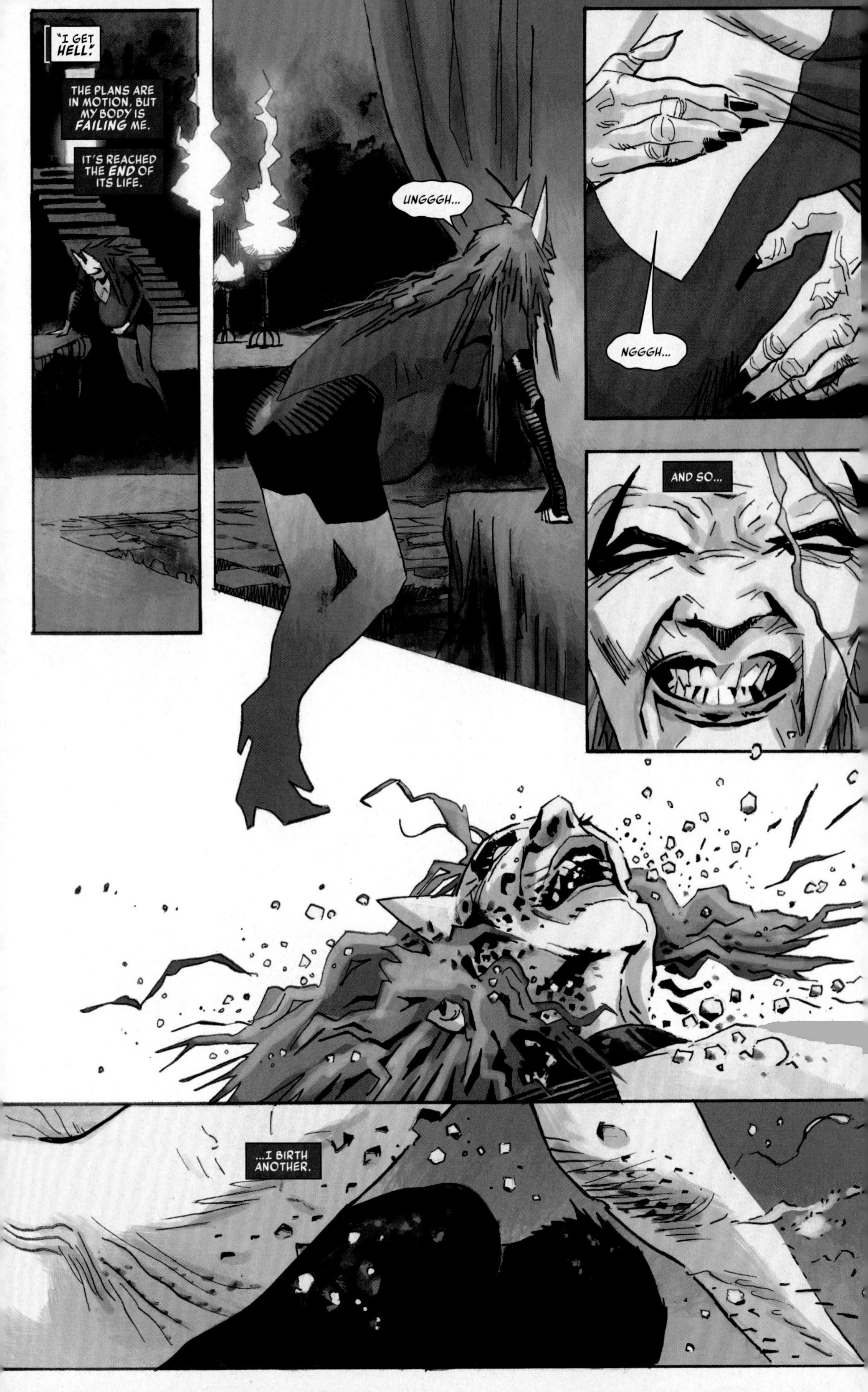
"I GET HELL."
THE PLANS ARE IN MOTION, BUT MY BODY IS FAILING ME.
IT'S REACHED THE END OF ITS LIFE.
UNGGGH...
NGGGH...
AND SO...
...I BIRTH ANOTHER.

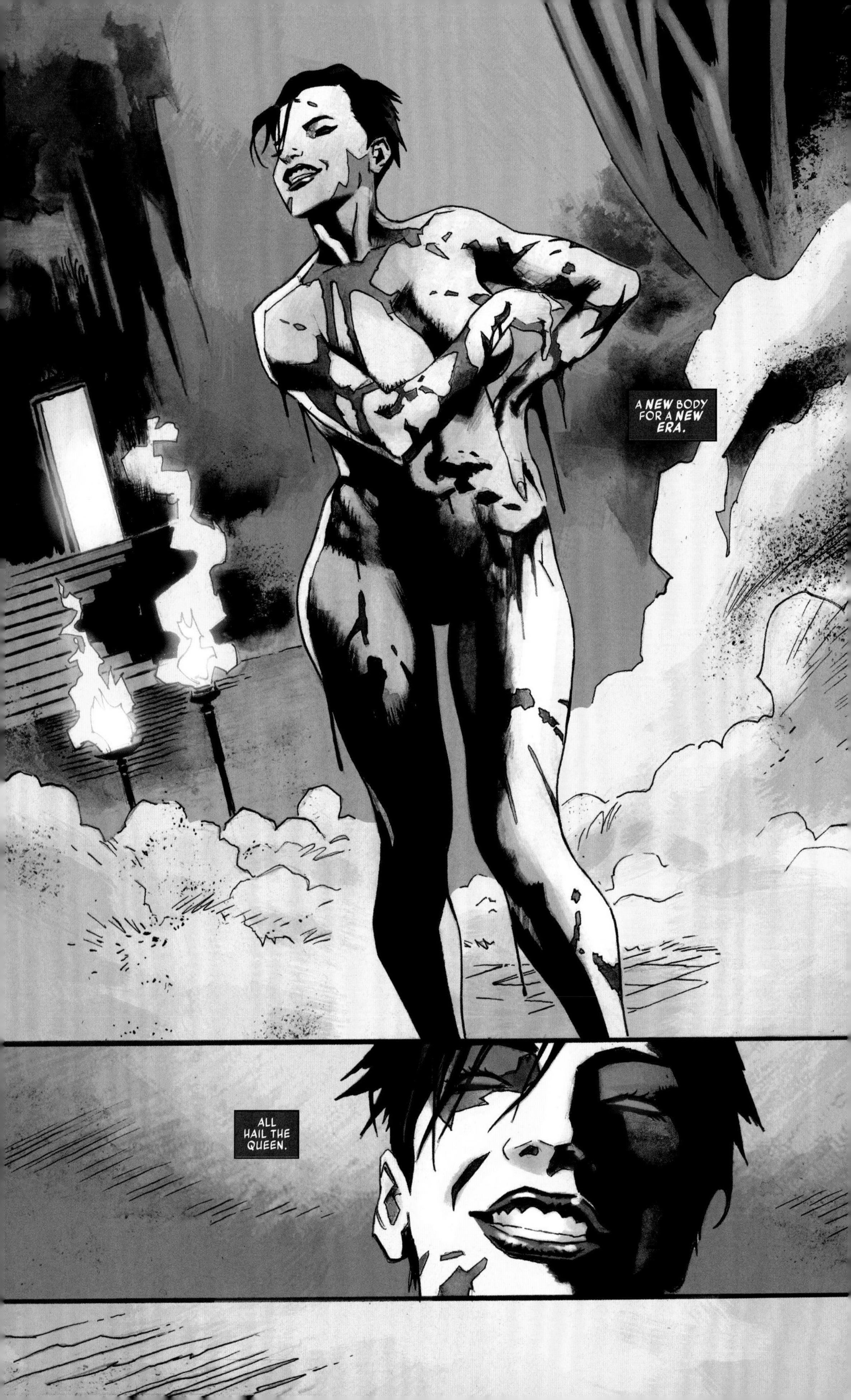
A NEW BODY FOR A NEW ERA.
ALL HAIL THE QUEEN.

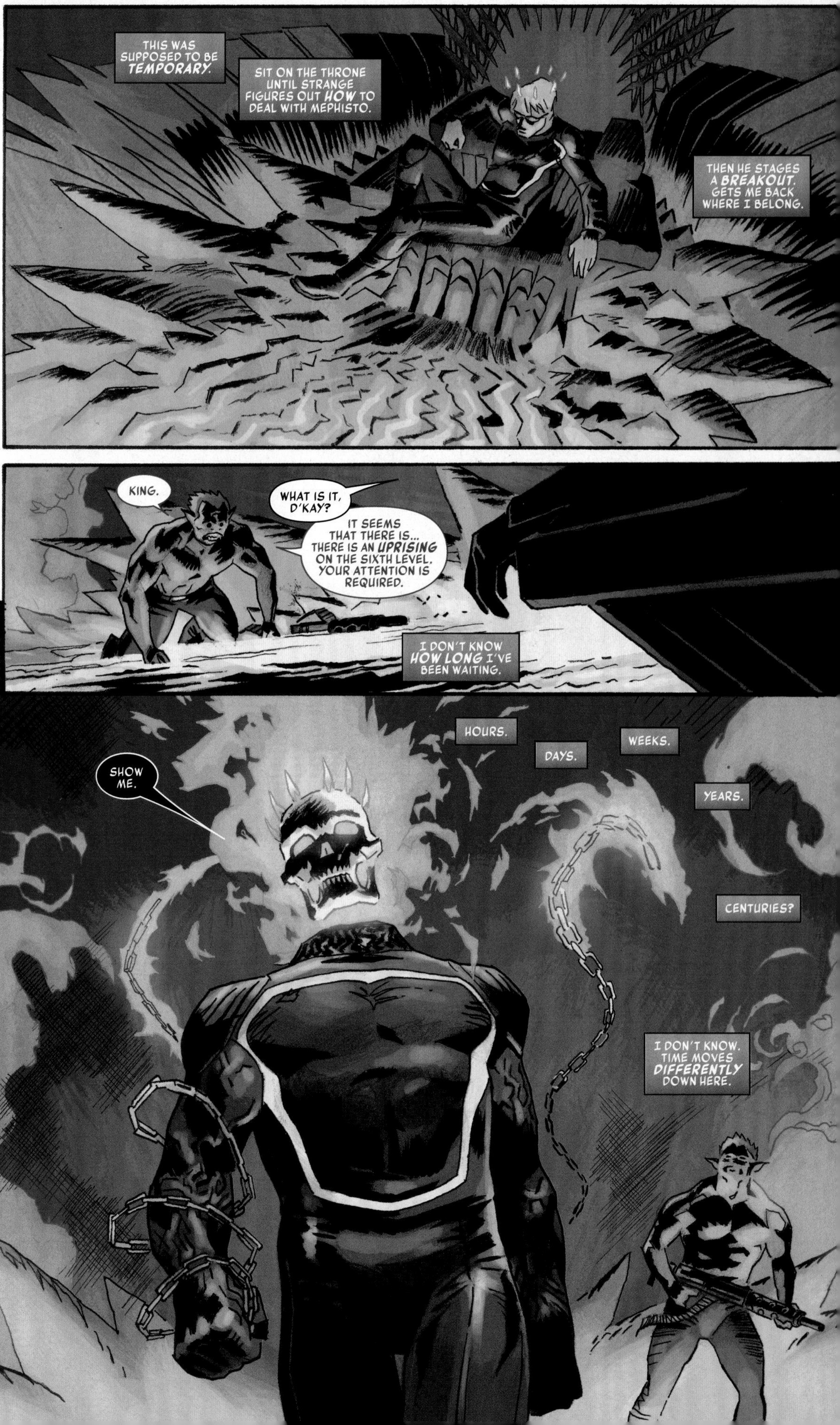
THIS WAS SUPPOSED TO BE TEMPORARY.
SIT ON THE THRONE UNTIL STRANGE FIGURES OUT HOW TO DEAL WITH MEPHISTO.
THEN HE STAGES A BREAKOUT. GETS ME BACK WHERE I BELONG.
KING.
WHAT IS IT, D'KAY?
IT SEEMS THAT THERE IS... THERE IS AN UPRISING ON THE SIXTH LEVEL. YOUR ATTENTION IS REQUIRED.
I DON'T KNOW HOW LONG I'VE BEEN WAITING.
SHOW ME.
HOURS.
DAYS.
WEEKS.
YEARS.
CENTURIES?
I DON'T KNOW. TIME MOVES DIFFERENTLY DOWN HERE.

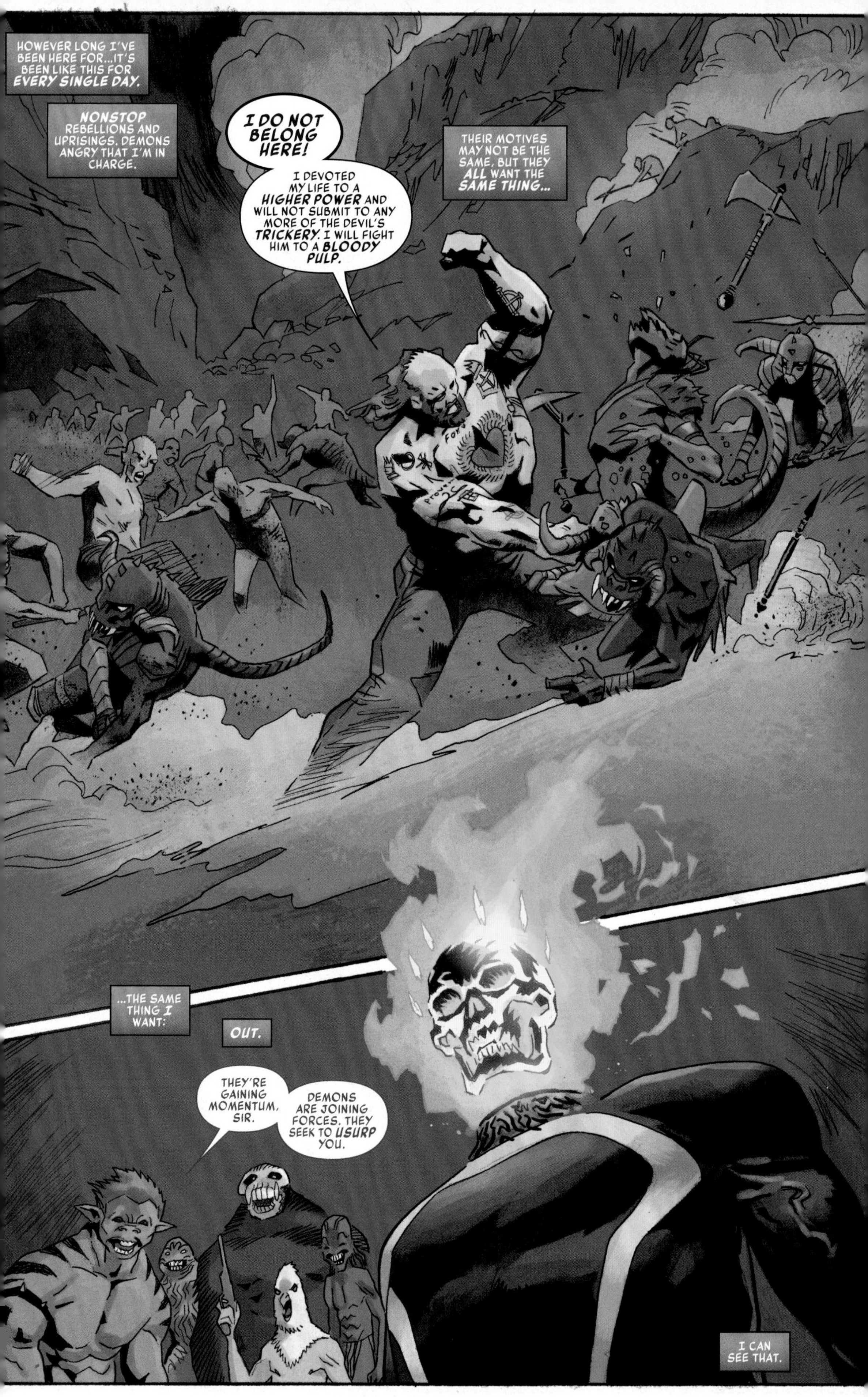

HOWEVER LONG I'VE BEEN HERE FOR...IT'S BEEN LIKE THIS FOR EVERY SINGLE DAY.
NONSTOP REBELLIONS AND UPRISINGS. DEMONS ANGRY THAT I'M IN CHARGE.
I DO NOT BELONG HERE!
I DEVOTED MY LIFE TO A HIGHER POWER AND WILL NOT SUBMIT TO ANY MORE OF THE DEVIL'S TRICKERY. I WILL FIGHT HIM TO A BLOODY PULP.
THEIR MOTIVES MAY NOT BE THE SAME, BUT THEY ALL WANT THE SAME THING...
...THE SAME THING I WANT:
OUT.
THEY'RE GAINING MOMENTUM, SIR.
DEMONS ARE JOINING FORCES. THEY SEEK TO USURP YOU.
I CAN SEE THAT.

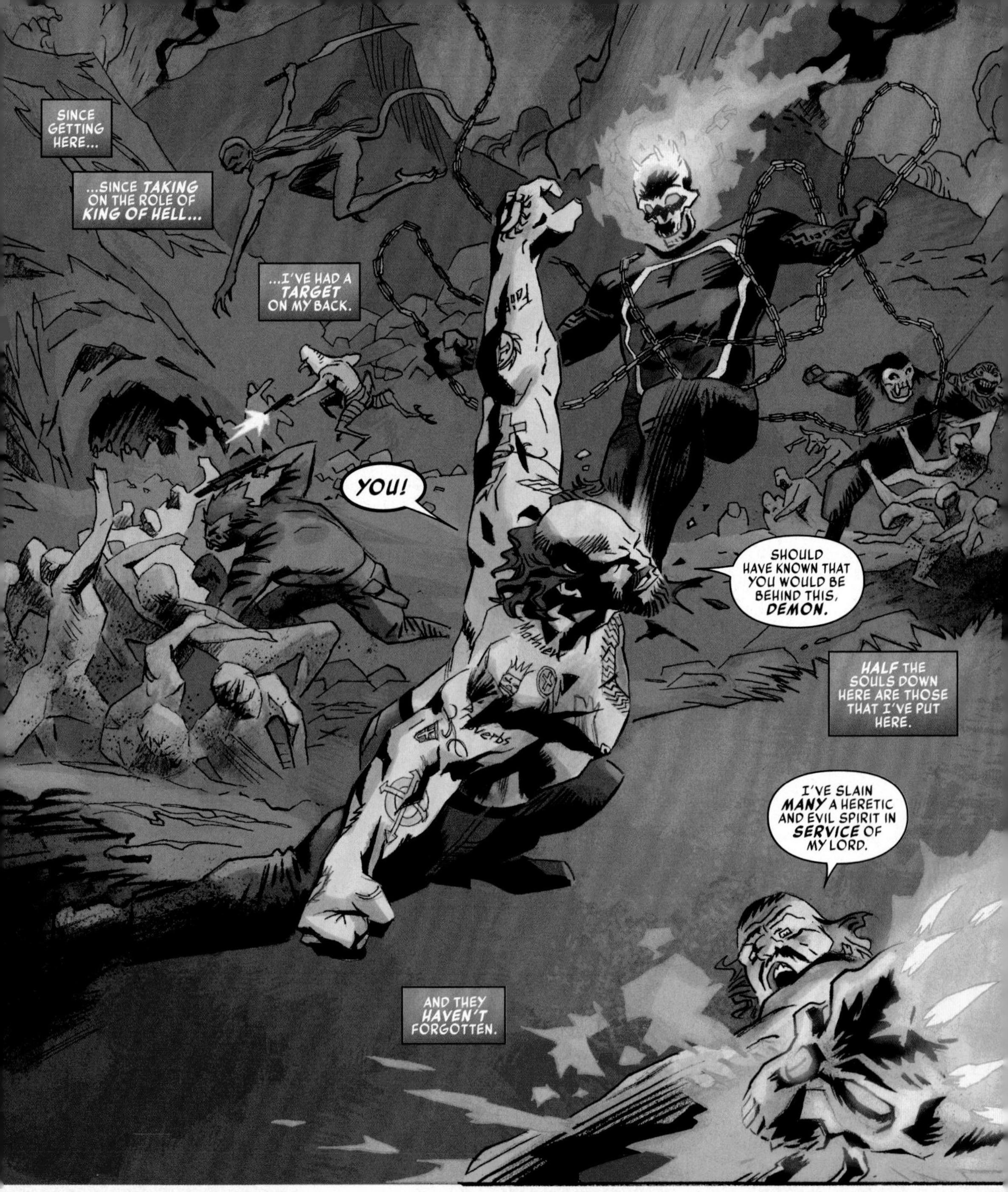
SINCE GETTING HERE...
...SINCE TAKING ON THE ROLE OF KING OF HELL...
...I'VE HAD A TARGET ON MY BACK.
YOU!
SHOULD HAVE KNOWN THAT YOU WOULD BE BEHIND THIS, DEMON.
HALF THE SOULS DOWN HERE ARE THOSE THAT I'VE PUT HERE.
I'VE SLAIN MANY A HERETIC AND EVIL SPIRIT IN SERVICE OF MY LORD.
AND THEY HAVEN'T FORGOTTEN.

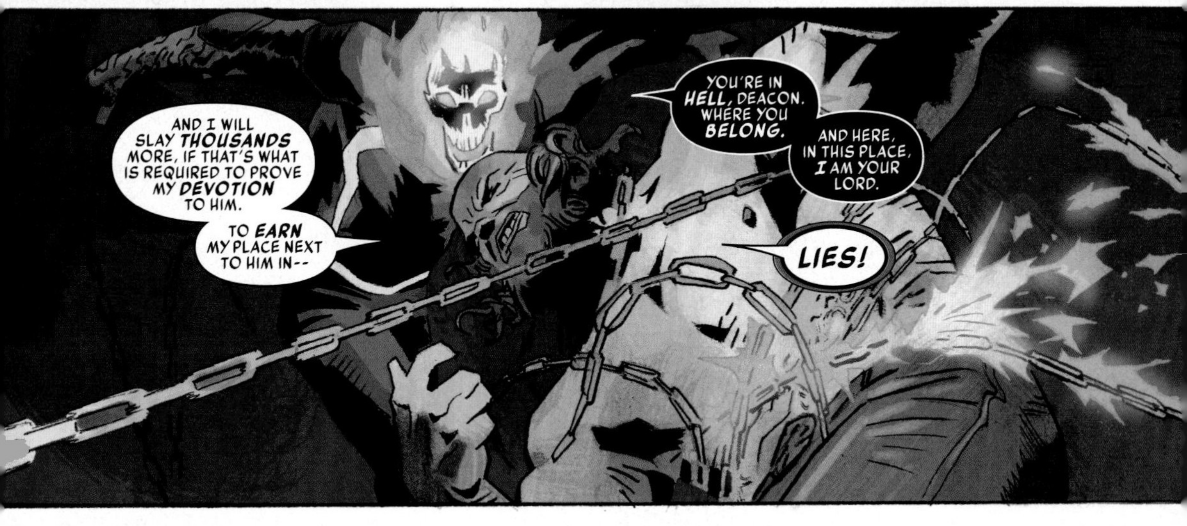
AND I WILL SLAY THOUSANDS MORE, IF THAT'S WHAT IS REQUIRED TO PROVE MY DEVOTION TO HIM.
TO EARN MY PLACE NEXT TO HIM IN--
YOU'RE IN HELL, DEACON. WHERE YOU BELONG.
AND HERE, IN THIS PLACE, I AM YOUR LORD.
LIES!

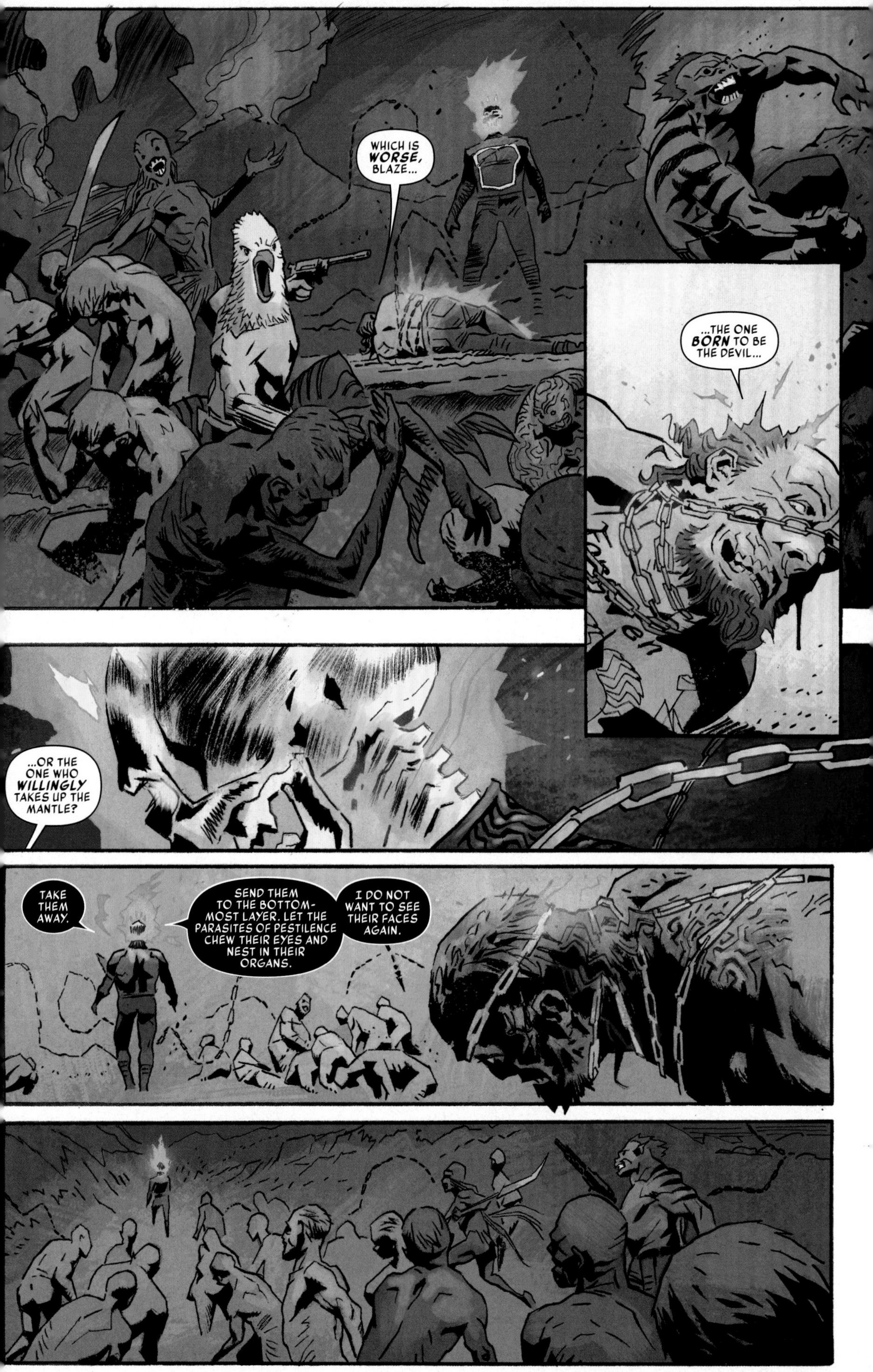
WHICH IS WORSE, BLAZE...
...THE ONE BORN TO BE THE DEVIL...
...OR THE ONE WHO WILLINGLY TAKES UP THE MANTLE?
TAKE THEM AWAY.
SEND THEM TO THE BOTTOM-MOST LAYER. LET THE PARASITES OF PESTILENCE CHEW THEIR EYES AND NEST IN THEIR ORGANS.
I DO NOT WANT TO SEE THEIR FACES AGAIN.

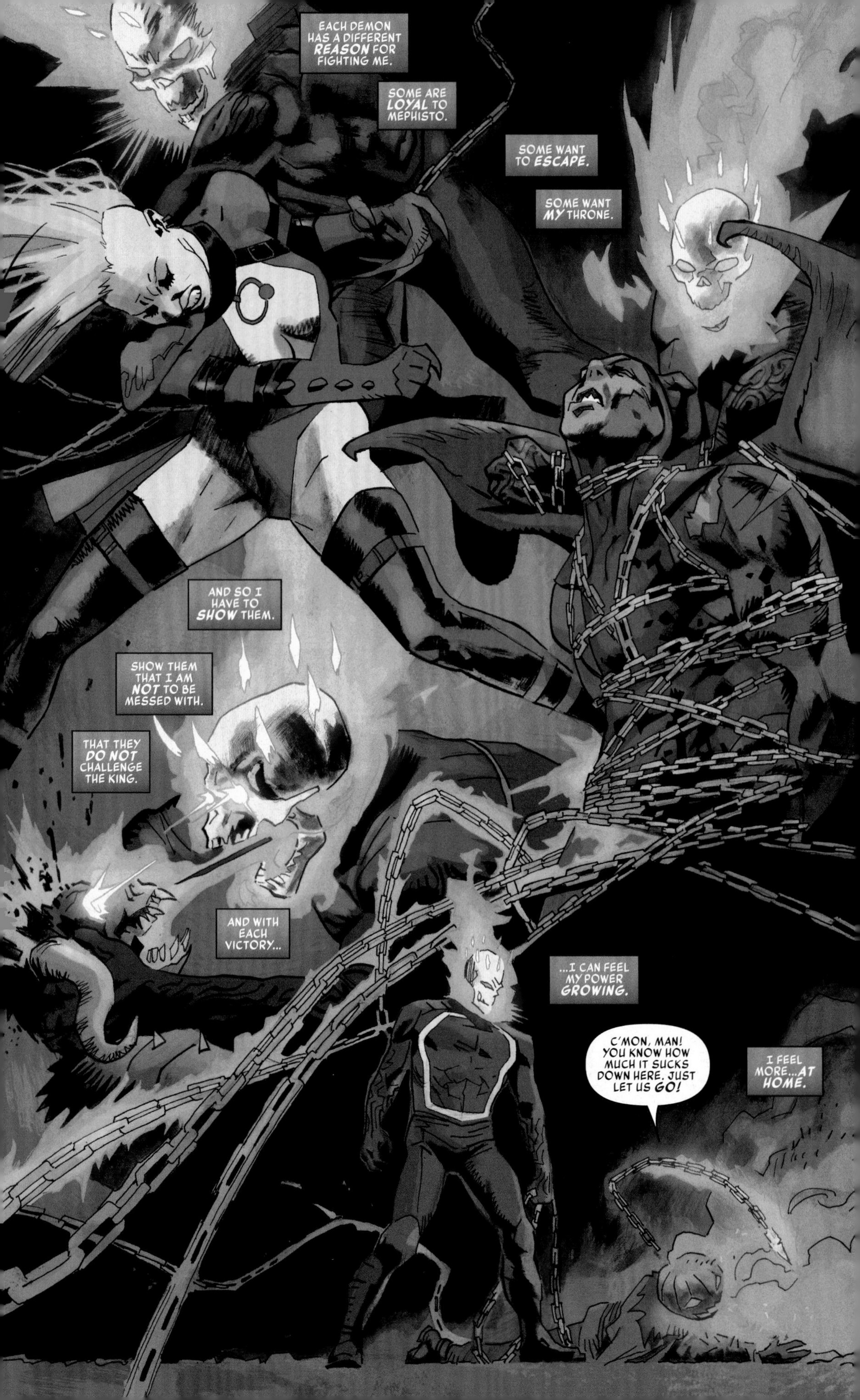
EACH DEMON HAS A DIFFERENT REASON FOR FIGHTING ME.
SOME ARE LOYAL TO MEPHISTO.
SOME WANT TO ESCAPE.
SOME WANT MY THRONE.
AND SO I HAVE TO SHOW THEM.
SHOW THEM THAT I AM NOT TO BE MESSED WITH.
THAT THEY DO NOT CHALLENGE THE KING.
AND WITH EACH VICTORY...
...I CAN FEEL MY POWER GROWING.
C'MON, MAN! YOU KNOW HOW MUCH IT SUCKS DOWN HERE. JUST LET US GO!
I FEEL MORE...AT HOME.

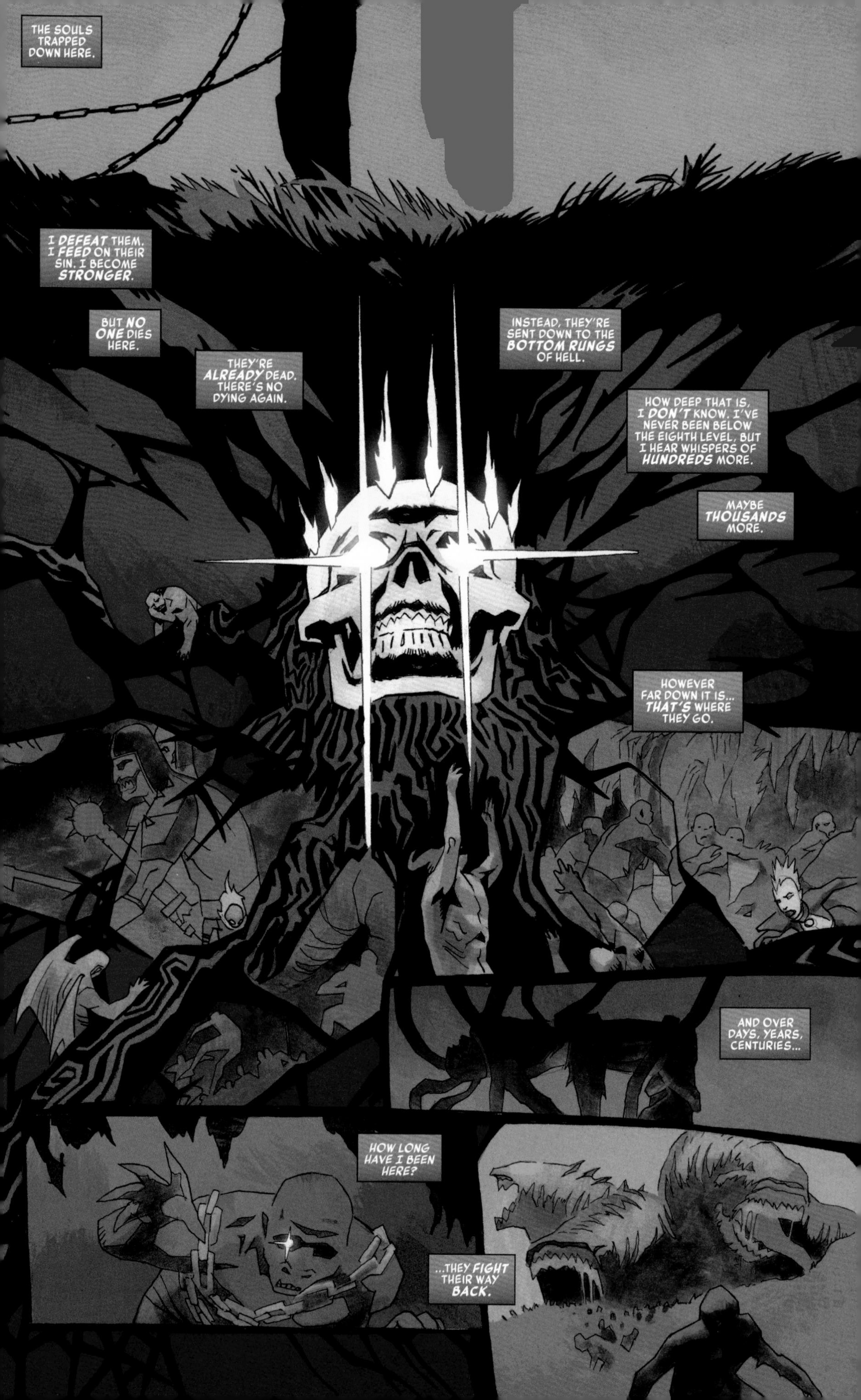
THE SOULS TRAPPED DOWN HERE.
I DEFEAT THEM. I FEED ON THEIR SIN. I BECOME STRONGER.
BUT NO ONE DIES HERE.
THEY'RE ALREADY DEAD. THERE'S NO DYING AGAIN.
INSTEAD, THEY'RE SENT DOWN TO THE BOTTOM RUNGS OF HELL.
HOW DEEP THAT IS, I DON'T KNOW. I'VE NEVER BEEN BELOW THE EIGHTH LEVEL, BUT I HEAR WHISPERS OF HUNDREDS MORE.
MAYBE THOUSANDS MORE.
HOWEVER FAR DOWN IT IS... THAT'S WHERE THEY GO.
AND OVER DAYS, YEARS, CENTURIES...
HOW LONG HAVE I BEEN HERE?
...THEY FIGHT THEIR WAY BACK.

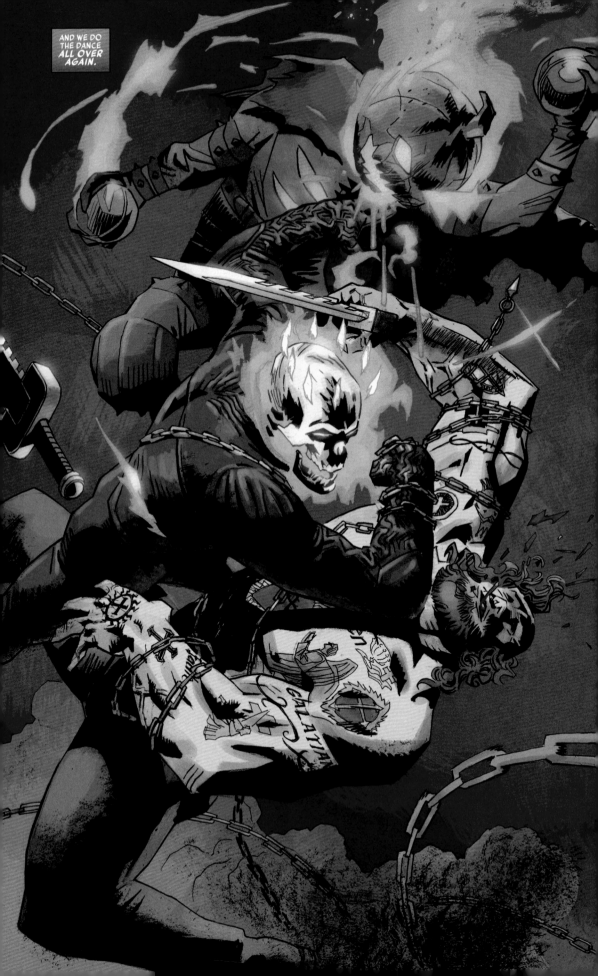

AND WE DO THE DANCE ALL OVER AGAIN.

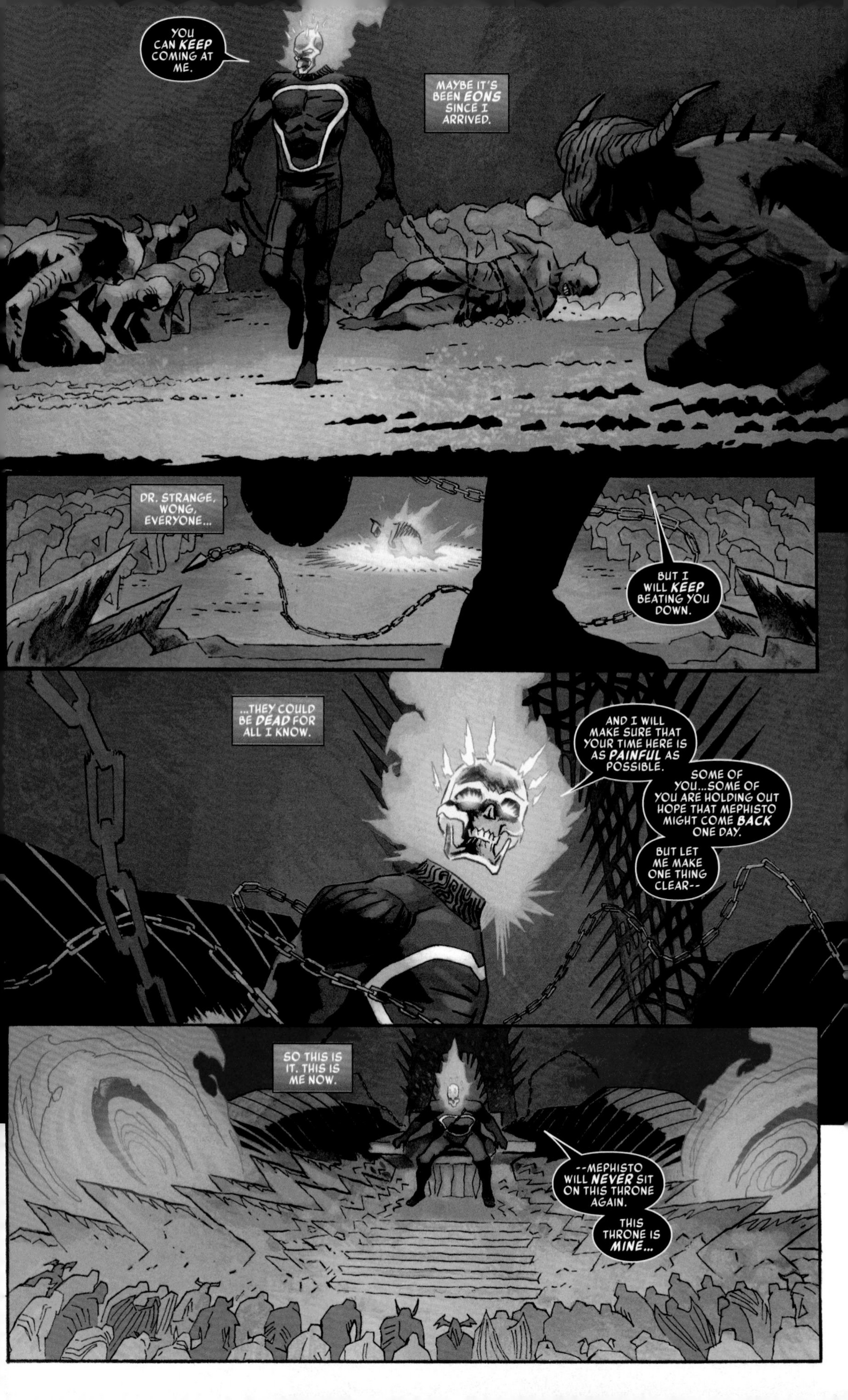
YOU CAN KEEP COMING AT ME.
MAYBE IT'S BEEN EONS SINCE I ARRIVED.
DR. STRANGE, WONG, EVERYONE...
BUT I WILL KEEP BEATING YOU DOWN.
...THEY COULD BE DEAD FOR ALL I KNOW.
AND I WILL MAKE SURE THAT YOUR TIME HERE IS AS PAINFUL AS POSSIBLE.
SOME OF YOU...SOME OF YOU ARE HOLDING OUT HOPE THAT MEPHISTO MIGHT COME BACK ONE DAY.
BUT LET ME MAKE ONE THING CLEAR--
SO THIS IS IT. THIS IS ME NOW.
--MEPHISTO WILL NEVER SIT ON THIS THRONE AGAIN.
THIS THRONE IS MINE...

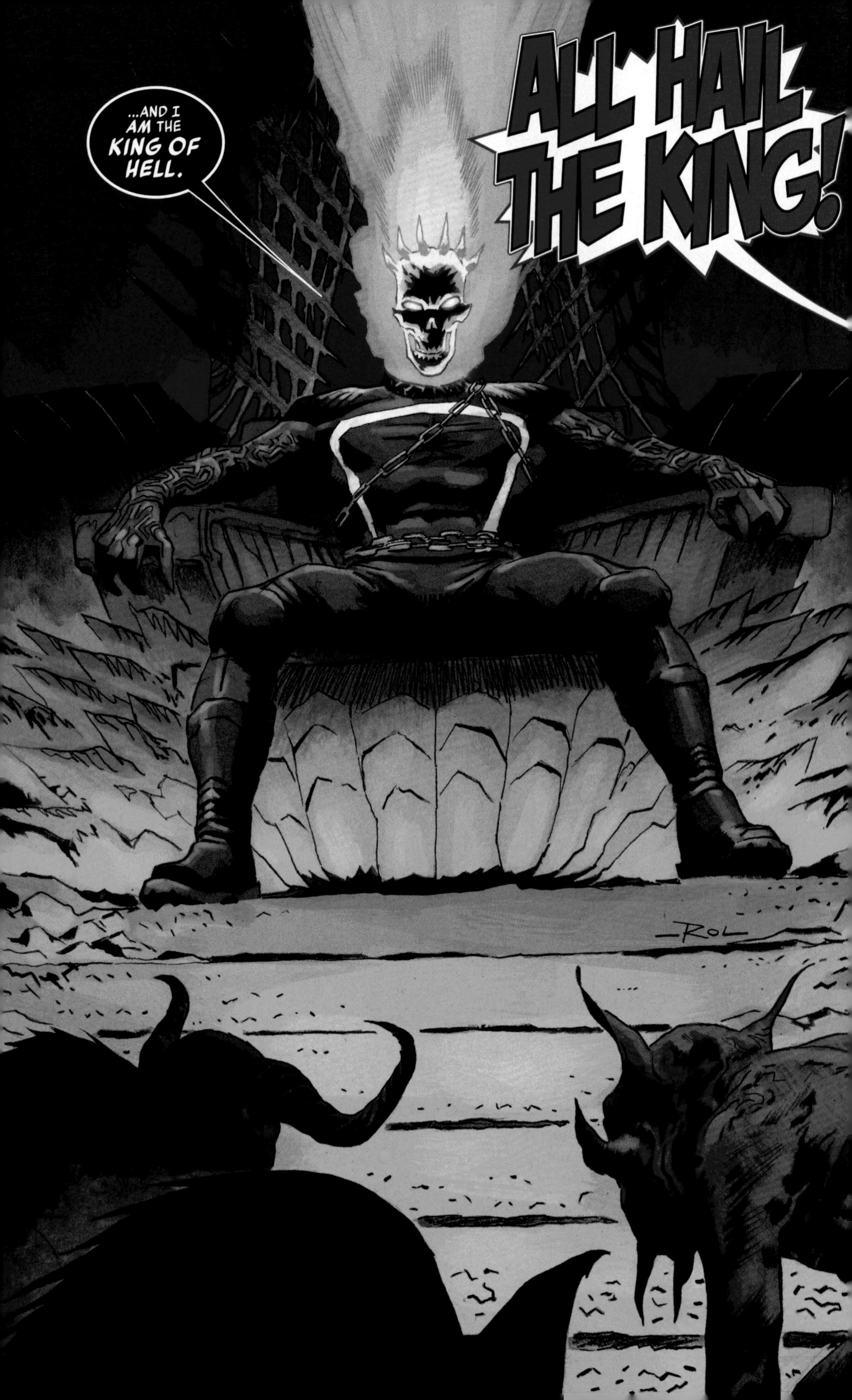
...AND I AM THE KING OF HELL.
ALL HAIL THE KING!
ROL

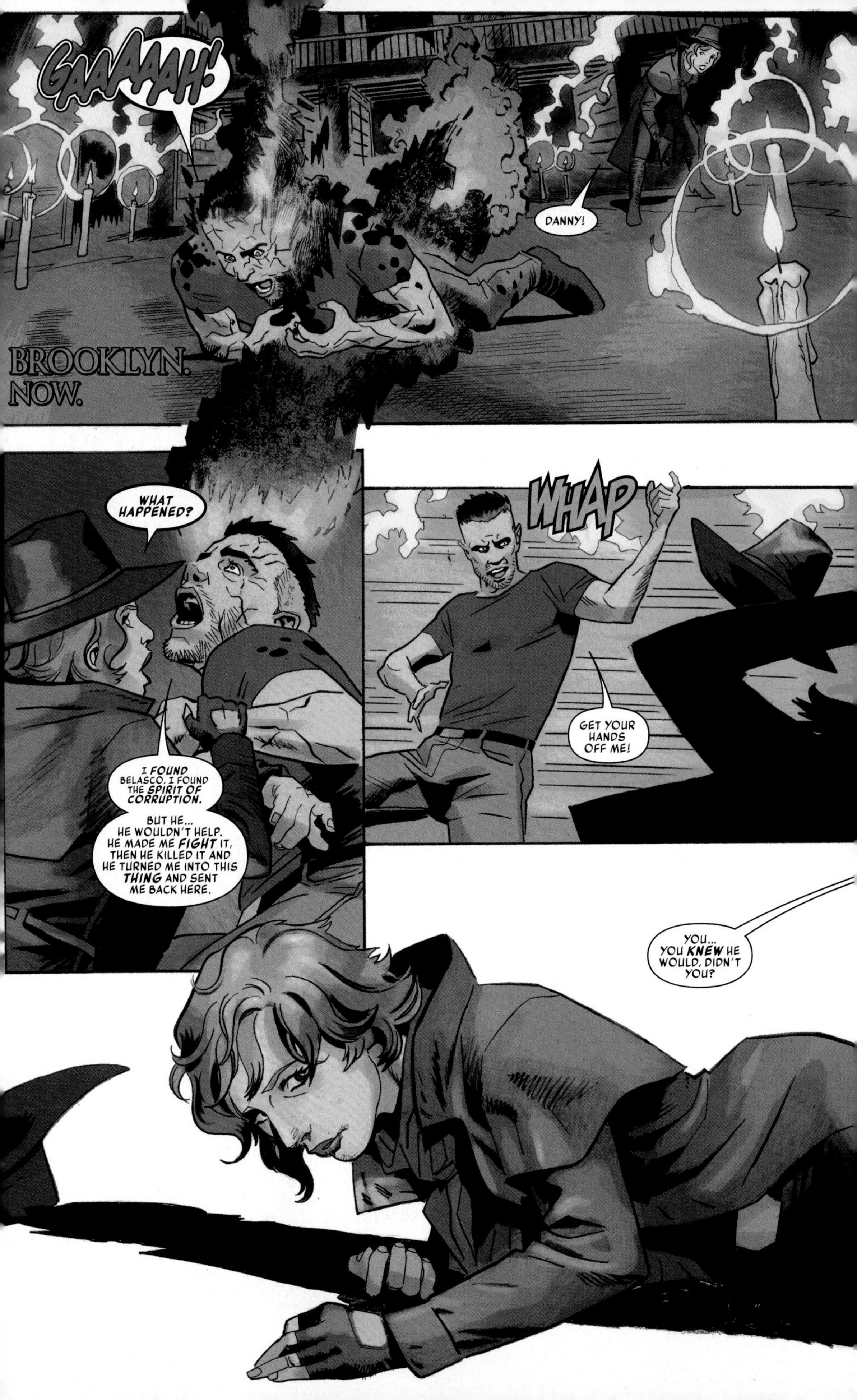
GAAAAAH!
DANNY!
BROOKLYN. NOW.
WHAT HAPPENED?
I FOUND BELASCO. I FOUND THE SPIRIT OF CORRUPTION.
BUT HE... HE WOULDN'T HELP. HE MADE ME FIGHT IT, THEN HE KILLED IT AND HE TURNED ME INTO THIS THING AND SENT ME BACK HERE.
WHAP
GET YOUR HANDS OFF ME!
YOU... YOU KNEW HE WOULD, DIDN'T YOU?

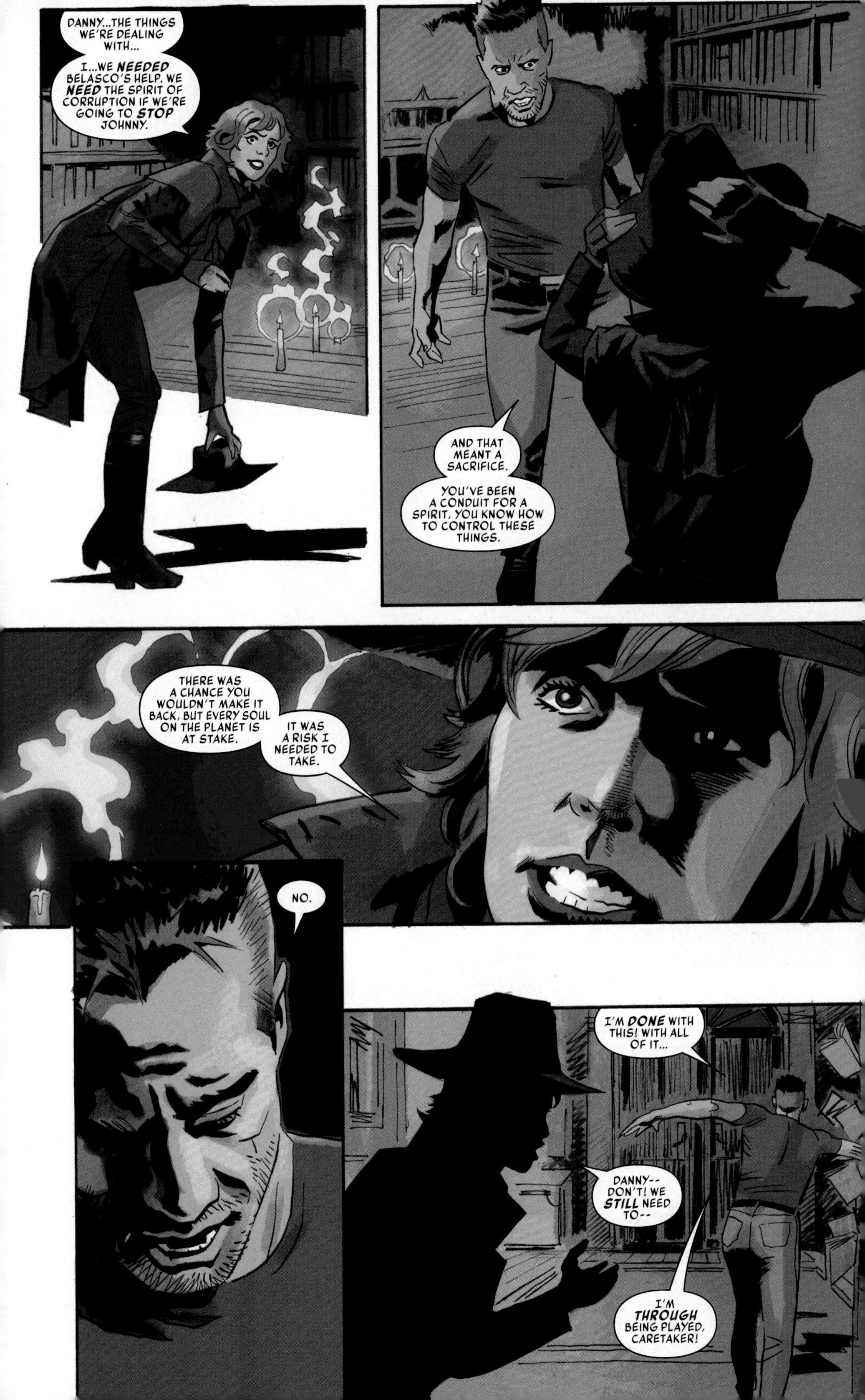
DANNY...THE THINGS WE'RE DEALING WITH...
I...WE NEEDED BELASCO'S HELP. WE NEED THE SPIRIT OF CORRUPTION IF WE'RE GOING TO STOP JOHNNY.
AND THAT MEANT A SACRIFICE.
YOU'VE BEEN A CONDUIT FOR A SPIRIT, YOU KNOW HOW TO CONTROL THESE THINGS.
THERE WAS A CHANCE YOU WOULDN'T MAKE IT BACK, BUT EVERY SOUL ON THE PLANET IS AT STAKE.
IT WAS A RISK I NEEDED TO TAKE.
NO.
I'M DONE WITH THIS! WITH ALL OF IT...
DANNY-- DON'T! WE STILL NEED TO--
I'M THROUGH BEING PLAYED, CARETAKER!

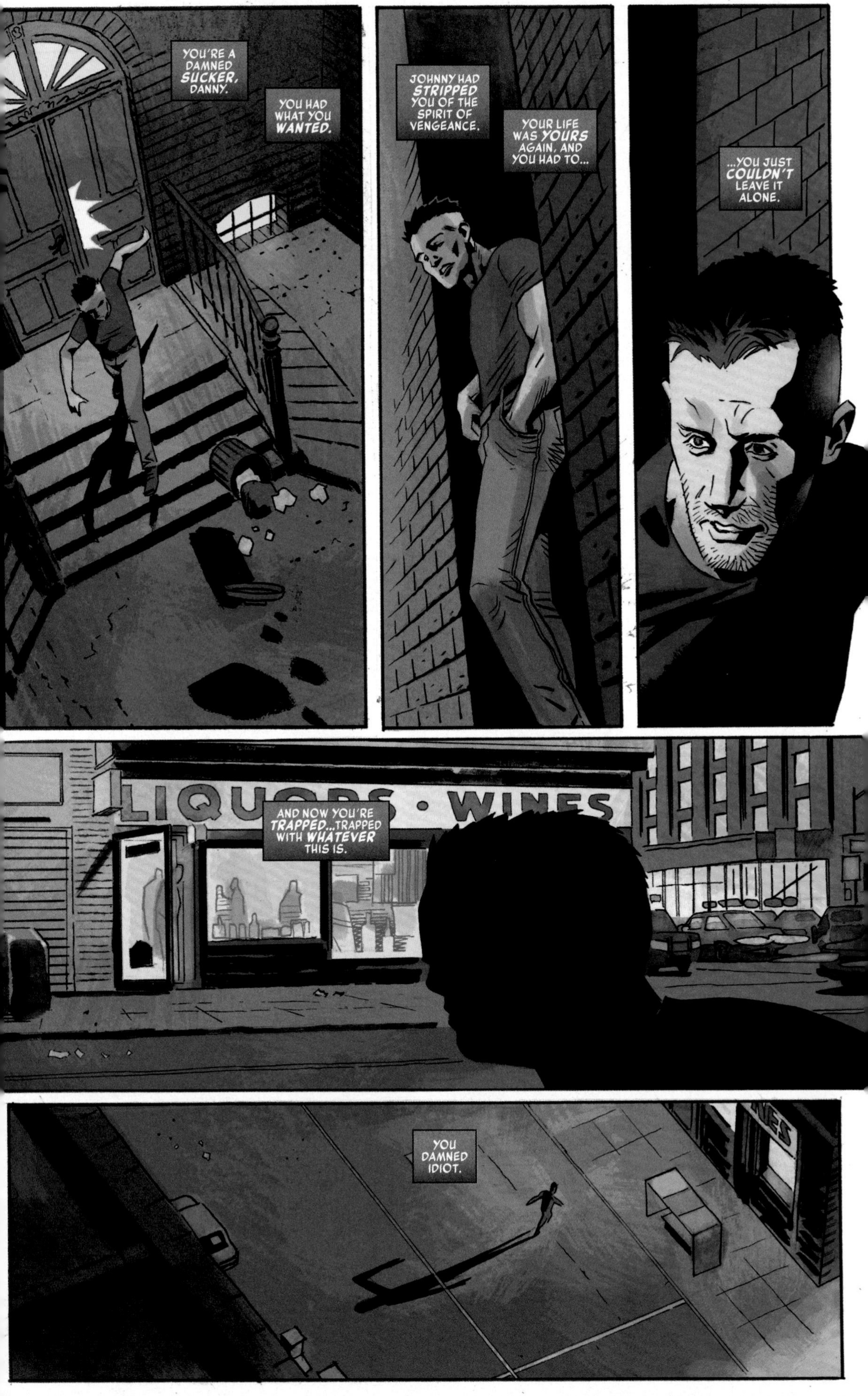
YOU'RE A DAMNED SUCKER, DANNY.
YOU HAD WHAT YOU WANTED.
JOHNNY HAD STRIPPED YOU OF THE SPIRIT OF VENGEANCE.
YOUR LIFE WAS YOURS AGAIN, AND YOU HAD TO...
...YOU JUST COULDN'T LEAVE IT ALONE.
LIQUORS · WINES
AND NOW YOU'RE TRAPPED...TRAPPED WITH WHATEVER THIS IS.
YOU DAMNED IDIOT.

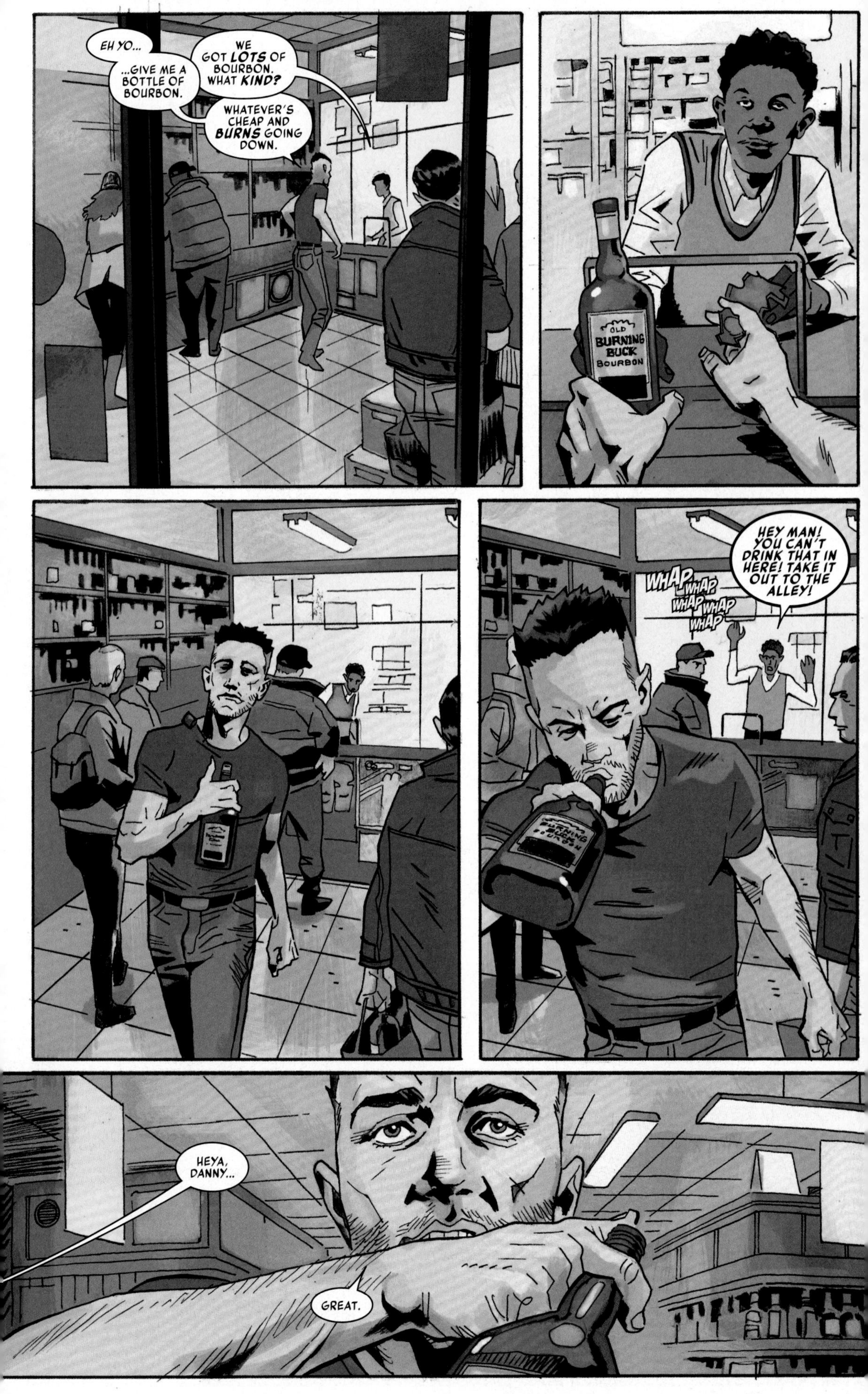
EH YO...
...GIVE ME A BOTTLE OF BOURBON.
WE GOT LOTS OF BOURBON. WHAT KIND?
WHATEVER'S CHEAP AND BURNS GOING DOWN.
OLD BURNING BUCK BOURBON
WHAP WHAP WHAP WHAP WHAP
HEY MAN! YOU CAN'T DRINK THAT IN HERE! TAKE IT OUT TO THE ALLEY!
HEYA, DANNY...
GREAT.

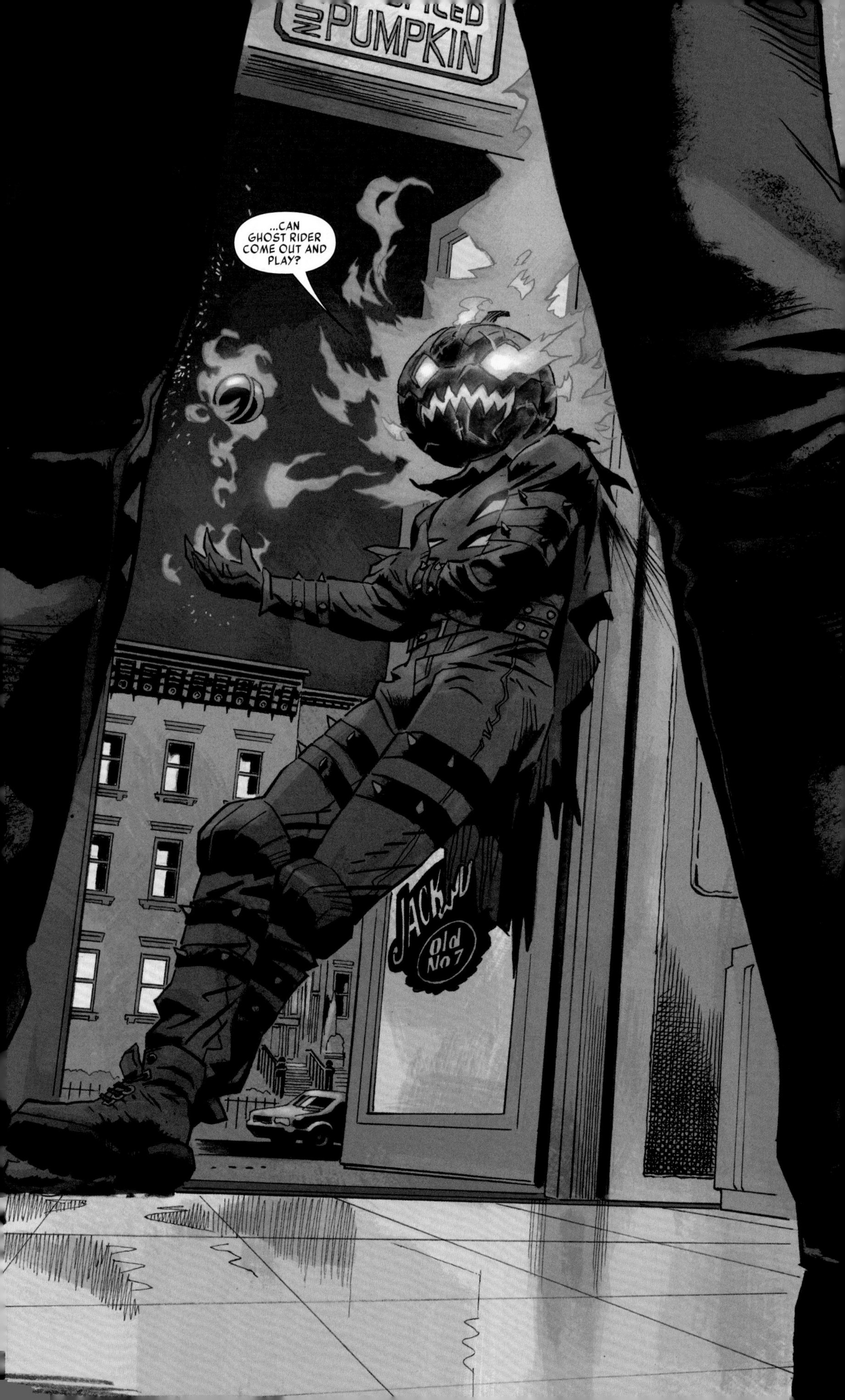
PUMPKIN
...CAN GHOST RIDER COME OUT AND PLAY?
Old No 7

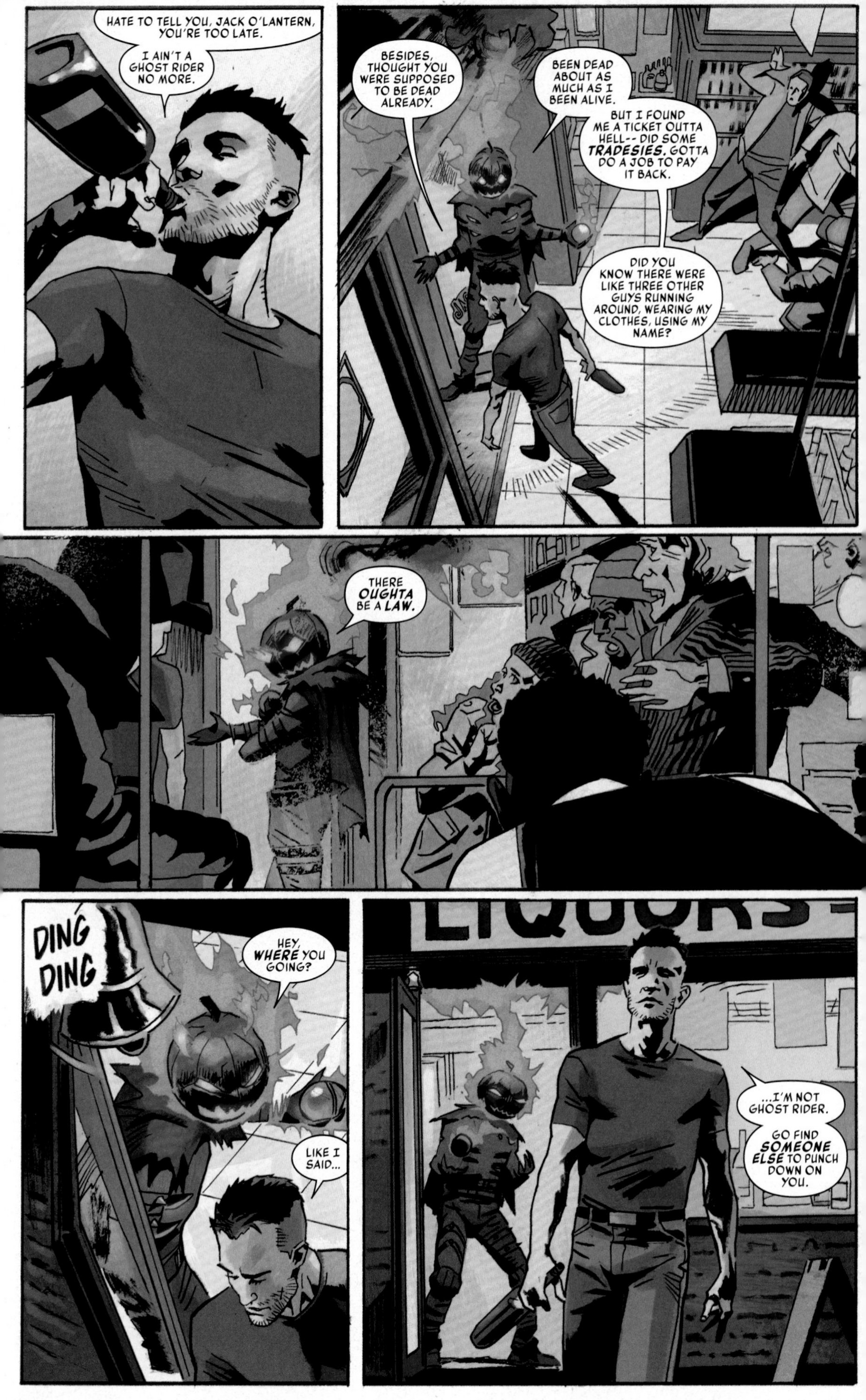
HATE TO TELL YOU, JACK O'LANTERN, YOU'RE TOO LATE.
I AIN'T A GHOST RIDER NO MORE.
BESIDES, THOUGHT YOU WERE SUPPOSED TO BE DEAD ALREADY.
BEEN DEAD ABOUT AS MUCH AS I BEEN ALIVE.
BUT I FOUND ME A TICKET OUTTA HELL-- DID SOME TRADESIES. GOTTA DO A JOB TO PAY IT BACK.
DID YOU KNOW THERE WERE LIKE THREE OTHER GUYS RUNNING AROUND, WEARING MY CLOTHES, USING MY NAME?
THERE OUGHTA BE A LAW.
DING DING
HEY, WHERE YOU GOING?
LIKE I SAID...
LIQUORS
...I'M NOT GHOST RIDER.
GO FIND SOMEONE ELSE TO PUNCH DOWN ON YOU.

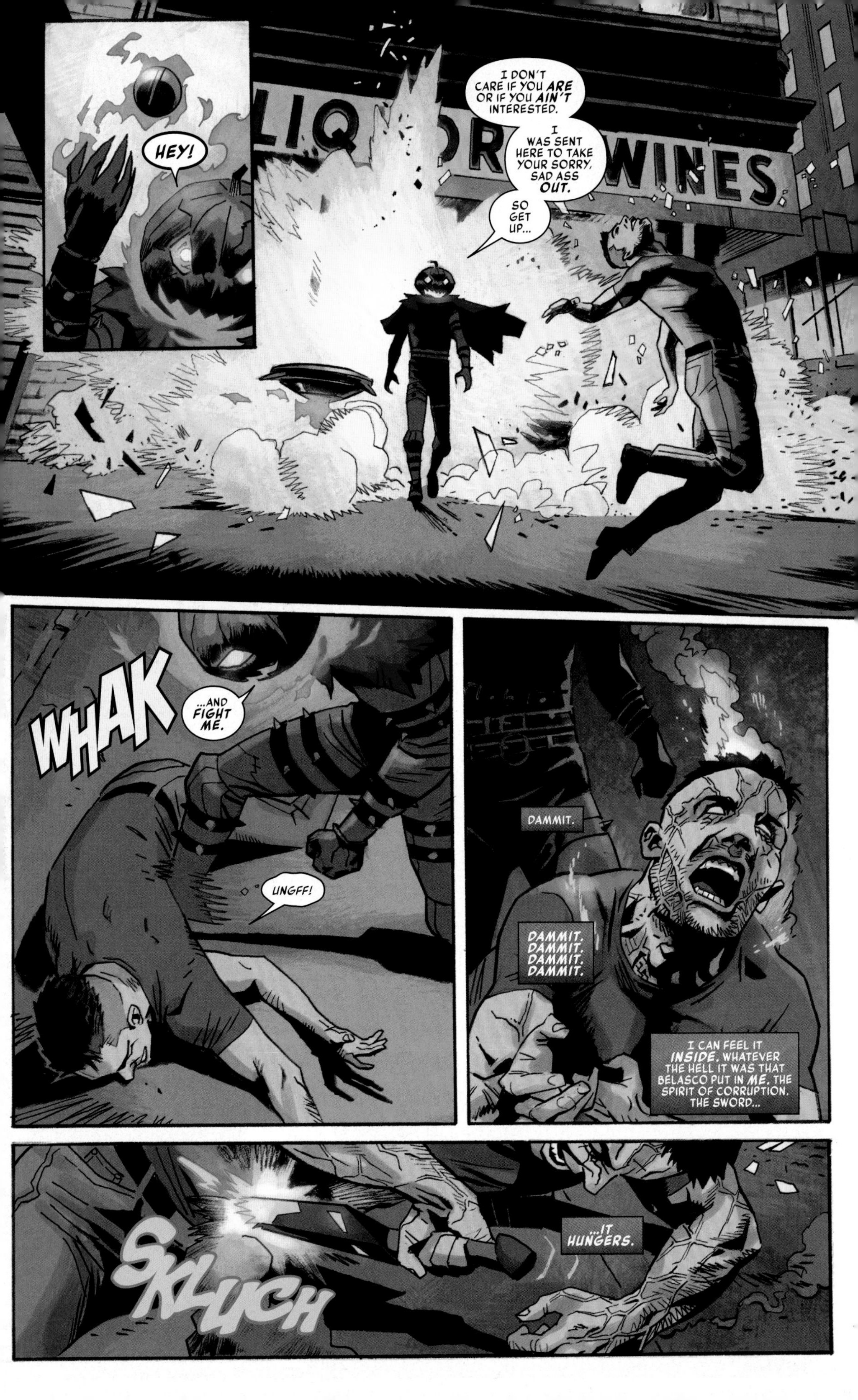
HEY!
LIQ OR WINES
I DON'T CARE IF YOU ARE OR IF YOU AIN'T INTERESTED.
I WAS SENT HERE TO TAKE YOUR SORRY, SAD ASS OUT.
SO GET UP...
WHAK
...AND FIGHT ME.
UNGFF!
DAMMIT.
DAMMIT. DAMMIT. DAMMIT. DAMMIT.
I CAN FEEL IT INSIDE. WHATEVER THE HELL IT WAS THAT BELASCO PUT IN ME. THE SPIRIT OF CORRUPTION. THE SWORD...
SKLUCH
...IT HUNGERS.

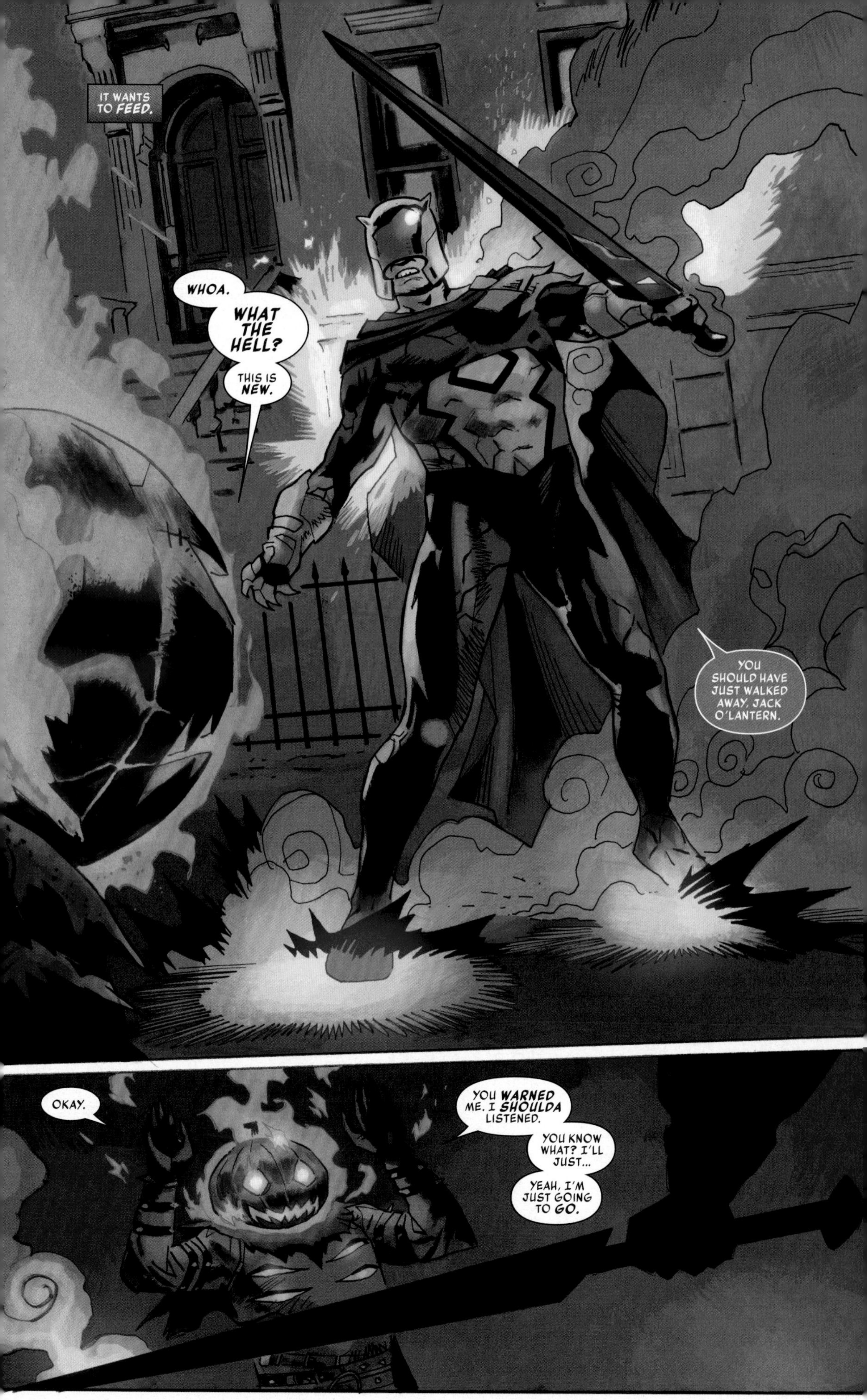
IT WANTS TO FEED.
WHOA.
WHAT THE HELL?
THIS IS NEW.
YOU SHOULD HAVE JUST WALKED AWAY, JACK O'LANTERN.
OKAY.
YOU WARNED ME. I SHOULDA LISTENED.
YOU KNOW WHAT? I'LL JUST...
YEAH, I'M JUST GOING TO GO.

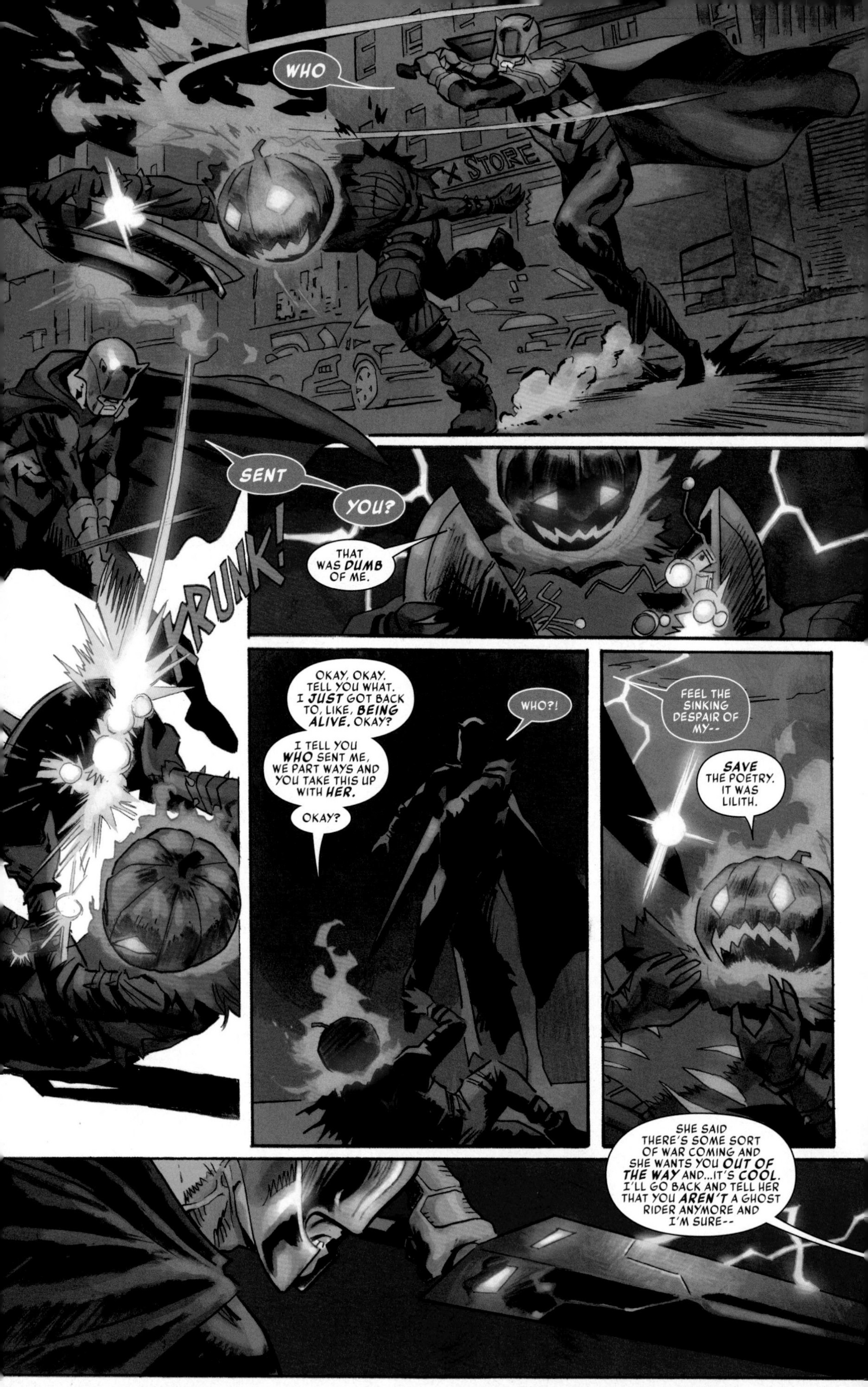
WHO
X STORE
SENT
YOU?
THAT WAS DUMB OF ME.
KRUNK!
OKAY, OKAY. TELL YOU WHAT. I JUST GOT BACK TO, LIKE, BEING ALIVE. OKAY?
I TELL YOU WHO SENT ME, WE PART WAYS AND YOU TAKE THIS UP WITH HER.
OKAY?
WHO?!
FEEL THE SINKING DESPAIR OF MY--
SAVE THE POETRY. IT WAS LILITH.
SHE SAID THERE'S SOME SORT OF WAR COMING AND SHE WANTS YOU OUT OF THE WAY AND...IT'S COOL. I'LL GO BACK AND TELL HER THAT YOU AREN'T A GHOST RIDER ANYMORE AND I'M SURE--

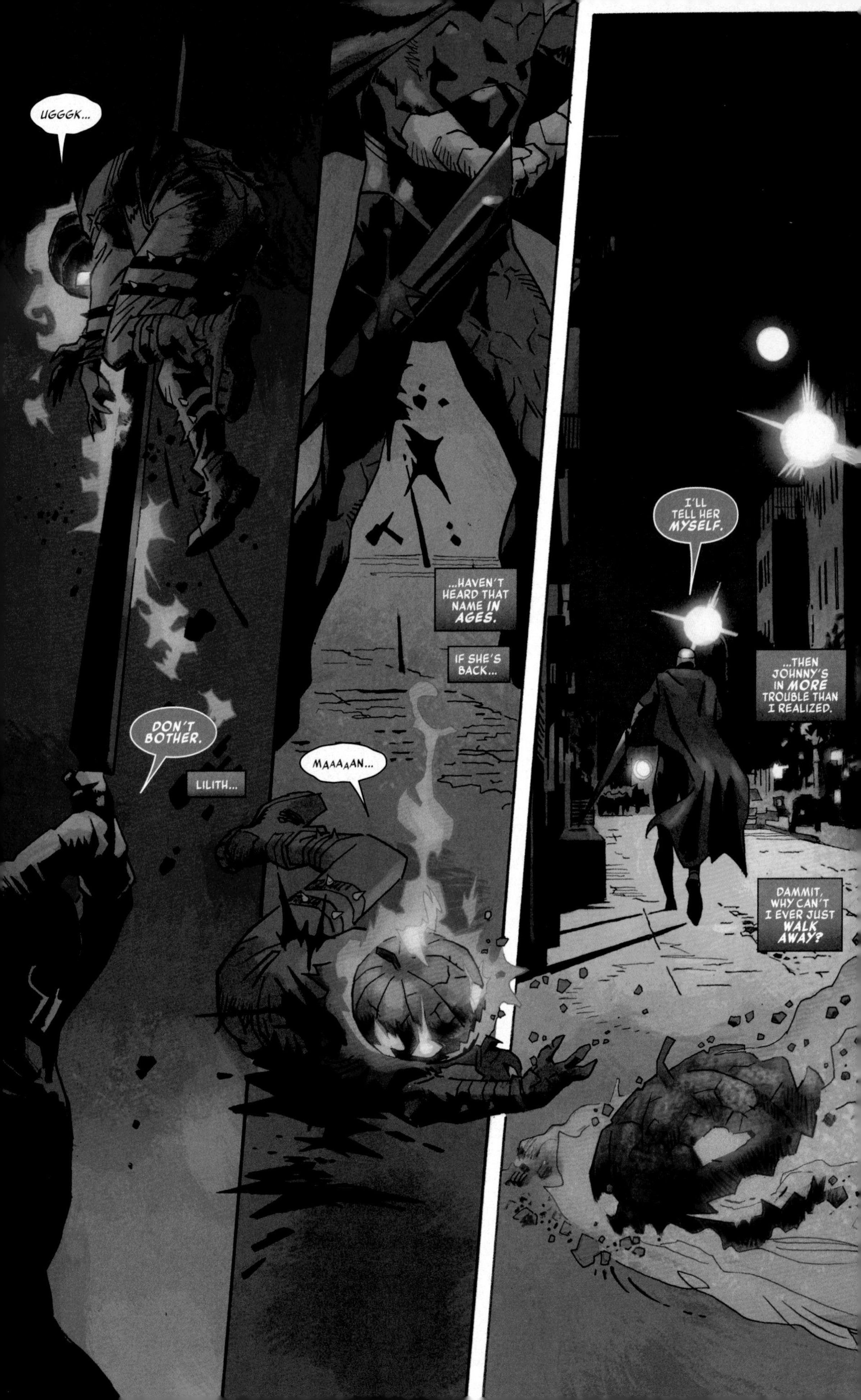
UGGGK...
...HAVEN'T HEARD THAT NAME IN AGES.
IF SHE'S BACK...
DON'T BOTHER.
LILITH...
MAAAAAN...
I'LL TELL HER MYSELF.
...THEN JOHNNY'S IN MORE TROUBLE THAN I REALIZED.
DAMMIT, WHY CAN'T I EVER JUST WALK AWAY?

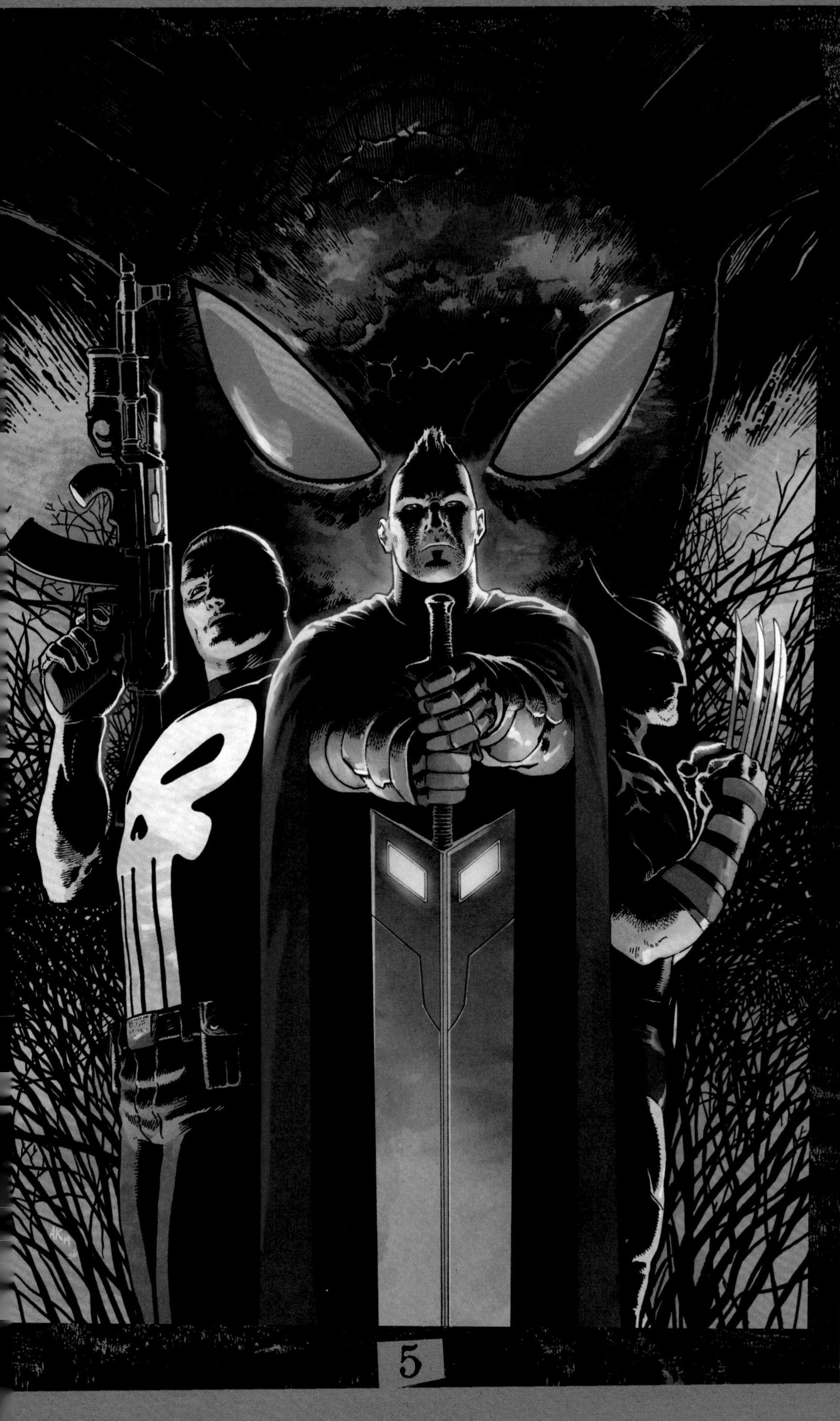
5

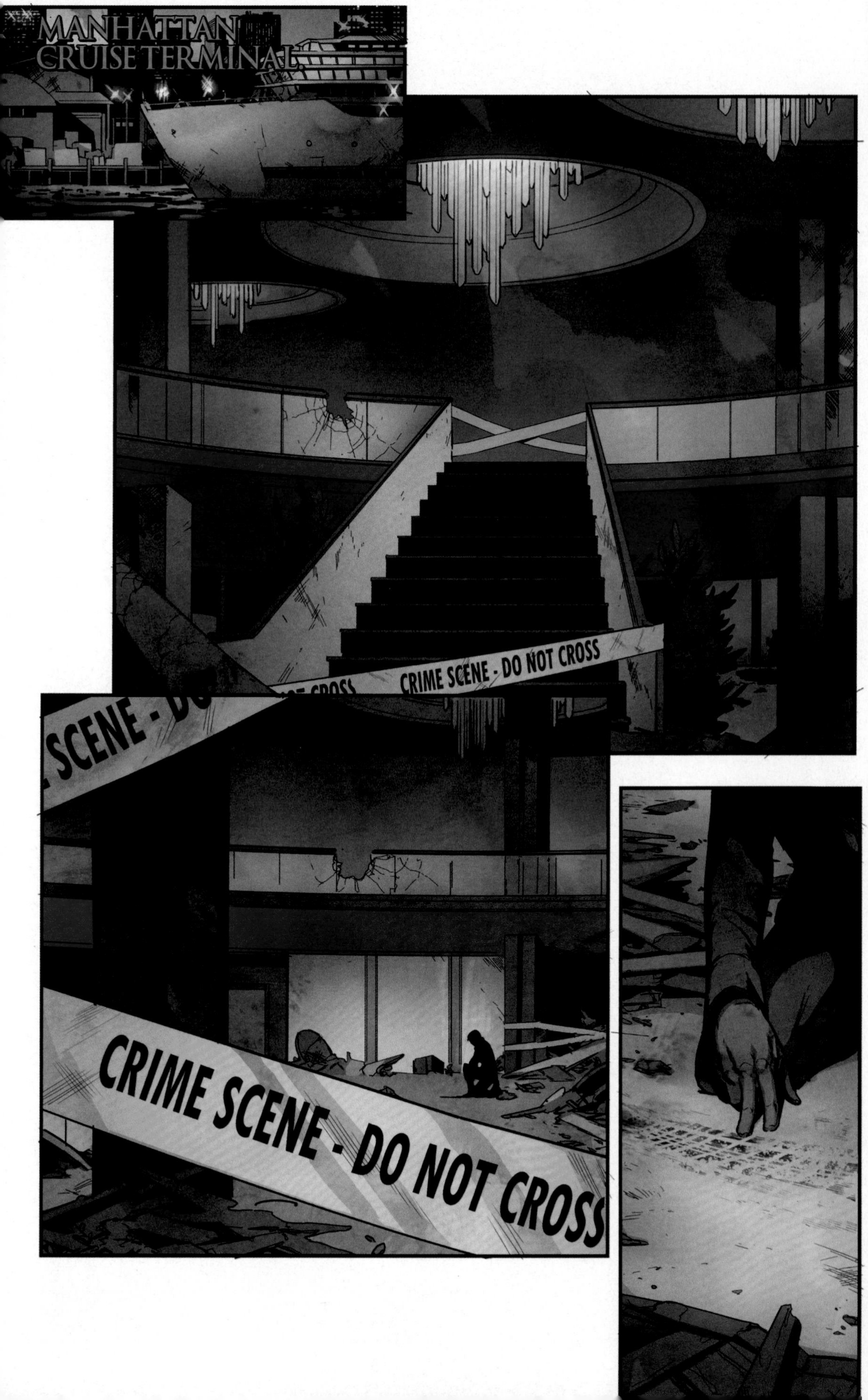
MANHATTAN CRUISE TERMINAL.
CRIME SCENE - DO NOT CROSS
SCENE - DO
CRIME SCENE - DO NOT CROSS

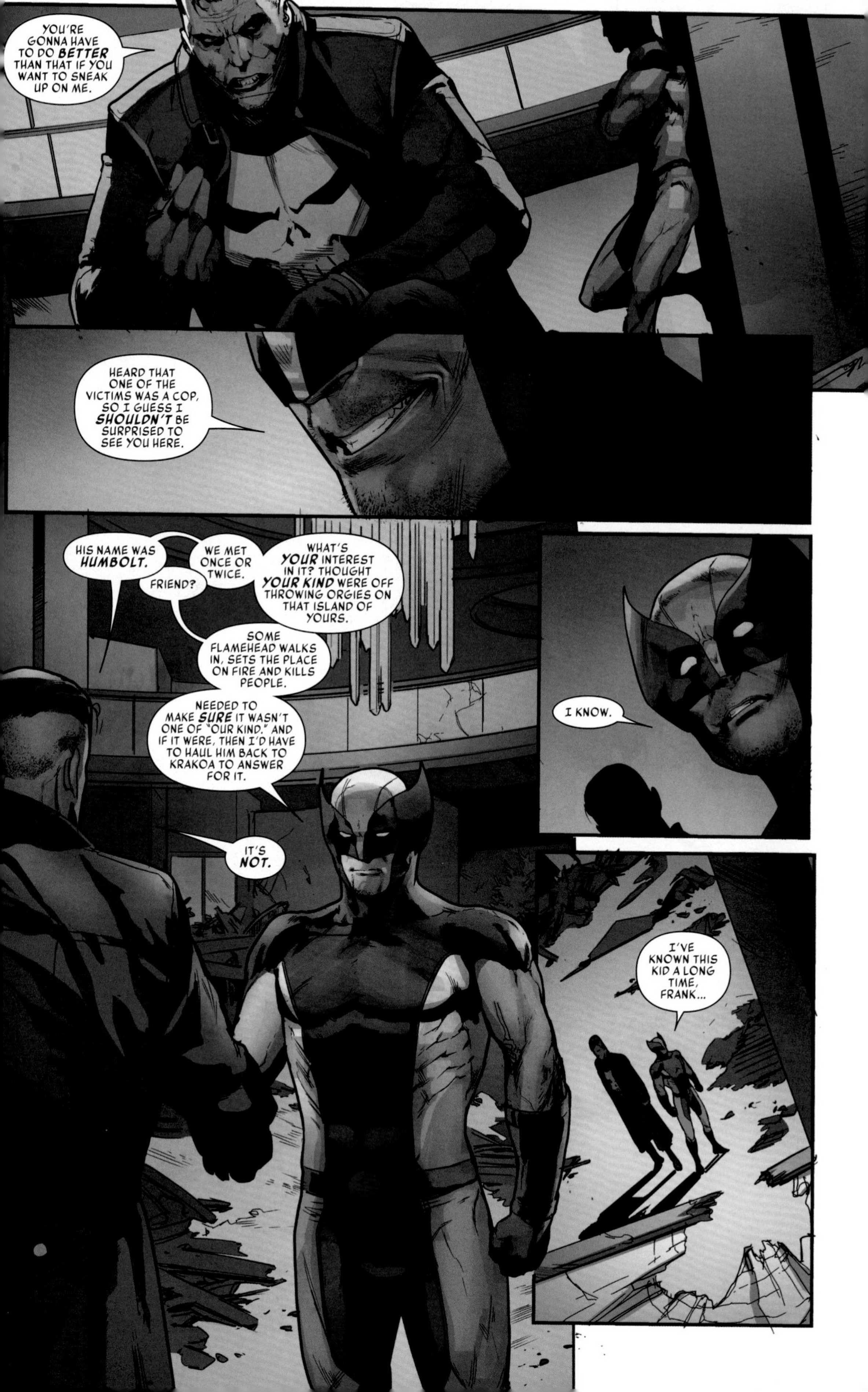
YOU'RE GONNA HAVE TO DO BETTER THAN THAT IF YOU WANT TO SNEAK UP ON ME.
HEARD THAT ONE OF THE VICTIMS WAS A COP, SO I GUESS I SHOULDN'T BE SURPRISED TO SEE YOU HERE.
HIS NAME WAS HUMBOLT.
FRIEND?
WE MET ONCE OR TWICE.
WHAT'S YOUR INTEREST IN IT? THOUGHT YOUR KIND WERE OFF THROWING ORGIES ON THAT ISLAND OF YOURS.
SOME FLAMEHEAD WALKS IN, SETS THE PLACE ON FIRE AND KILLS PEOPLE.
NEEDED TO MAKE SURE IT WASN'T ONE OF "OUR KIND." AND IF IT WERE, THEN I'D HAVE TO HAUL HIM BACK TO KRAKOA TO ANSWER FOR IT.
IT'S NOT.
I KNOW.
I'VE KNOWN THIS KID A LONG TIME, FRANK...

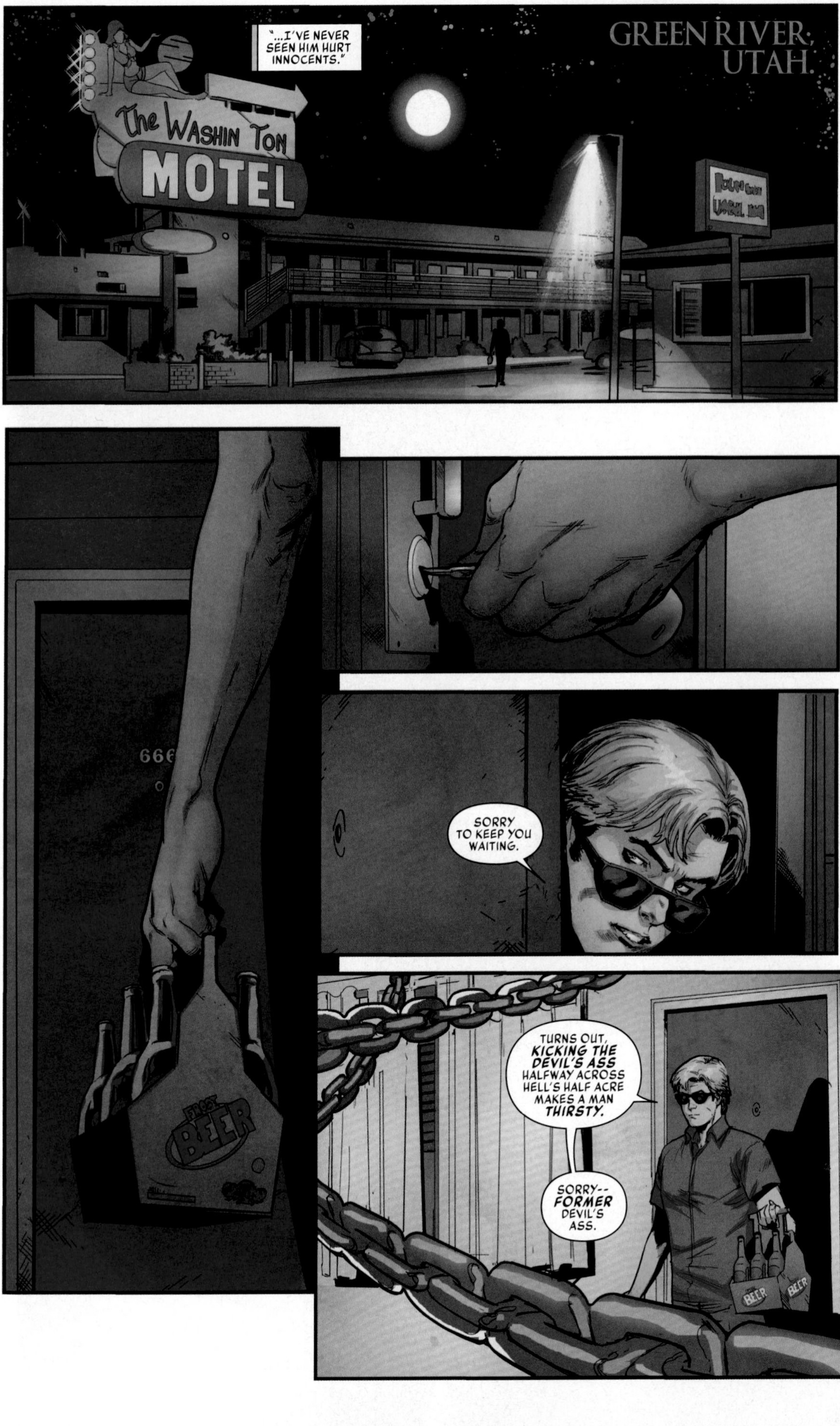
"...I'VE NEVER SEEN HIM HURT INNOCENTS."
GREEN RIVER, UTAH.
The WASHIN TON MOTEL
666
SORRY TO KEEP YOU WAITING.
TURNS OUT, KICKING THE DEVIL'S ASS HALFWAY ACROSS HELL'S HALF ACRE MAKES A MAN THIRSTY.
SORRY-- FORMER DEVIL'S ASS.
BEER

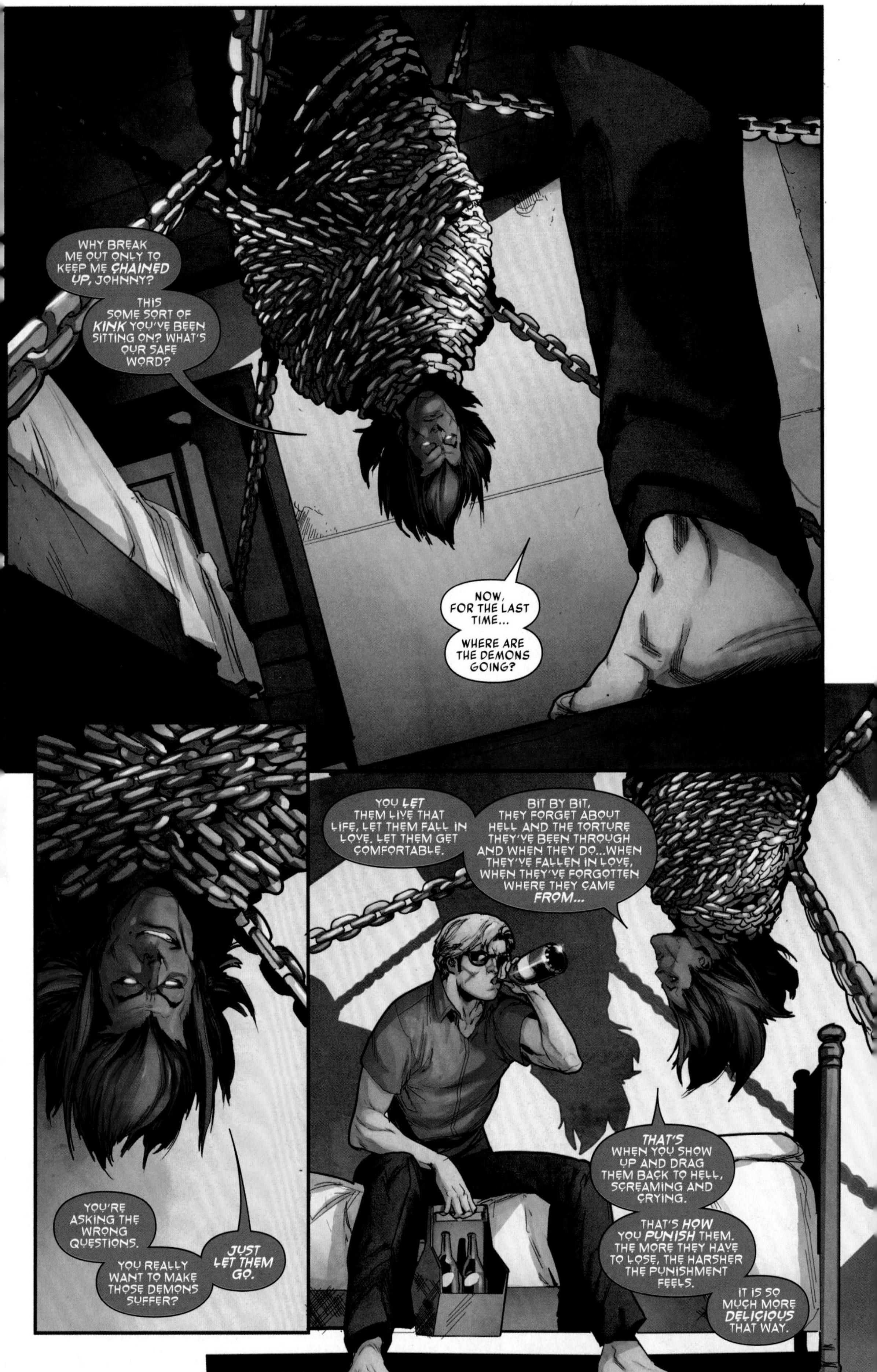
WHY BREAK ME OUT ONLY TO KEEP ME CHAINED UP, JOHNNY?
THIS SOME SORT OF KINK YOU'VE BEEN SITTING ON? WHAT'S OUR SAFE WORD?
NOW, FOR THE LAST TIME...
WHERE ARE THE DEMONS GOING?
YOU'RE ASKING THE WRONG QUESTIONS.
YOU REALLY WANT TO MAKE THOSE DEMONS SUFFER?
JUST LET THEM GO.
YOU LET THEM LIVE THAT LIFE, LET THEM FALL IN LOVE. LET THEM GET COMFORTABLE.
BIT BY BIT, THEY FORGET ABOUT HELL AND THE TORTURE THEY'VE BEEN THROUGH AND WHEN THEY DO...WHEN THEY'VE FALLEN IN LOVE, WHEN THEY'VE FORGOTTEN WHERE THEY CAME FROM...
THAT'S WHEN YOU SHOW UP AND DRAG THEM BACK TO HELL, SCREAMING AND CRYING.
THAT'S HOW YOU PUNISH THEM. THE MORE THEY HAVE TO LOSE, THE HARSHER THE PUNISHMENT FEELS.
IT IS SO MUCH MORE DELICIOUS THAT WAY.

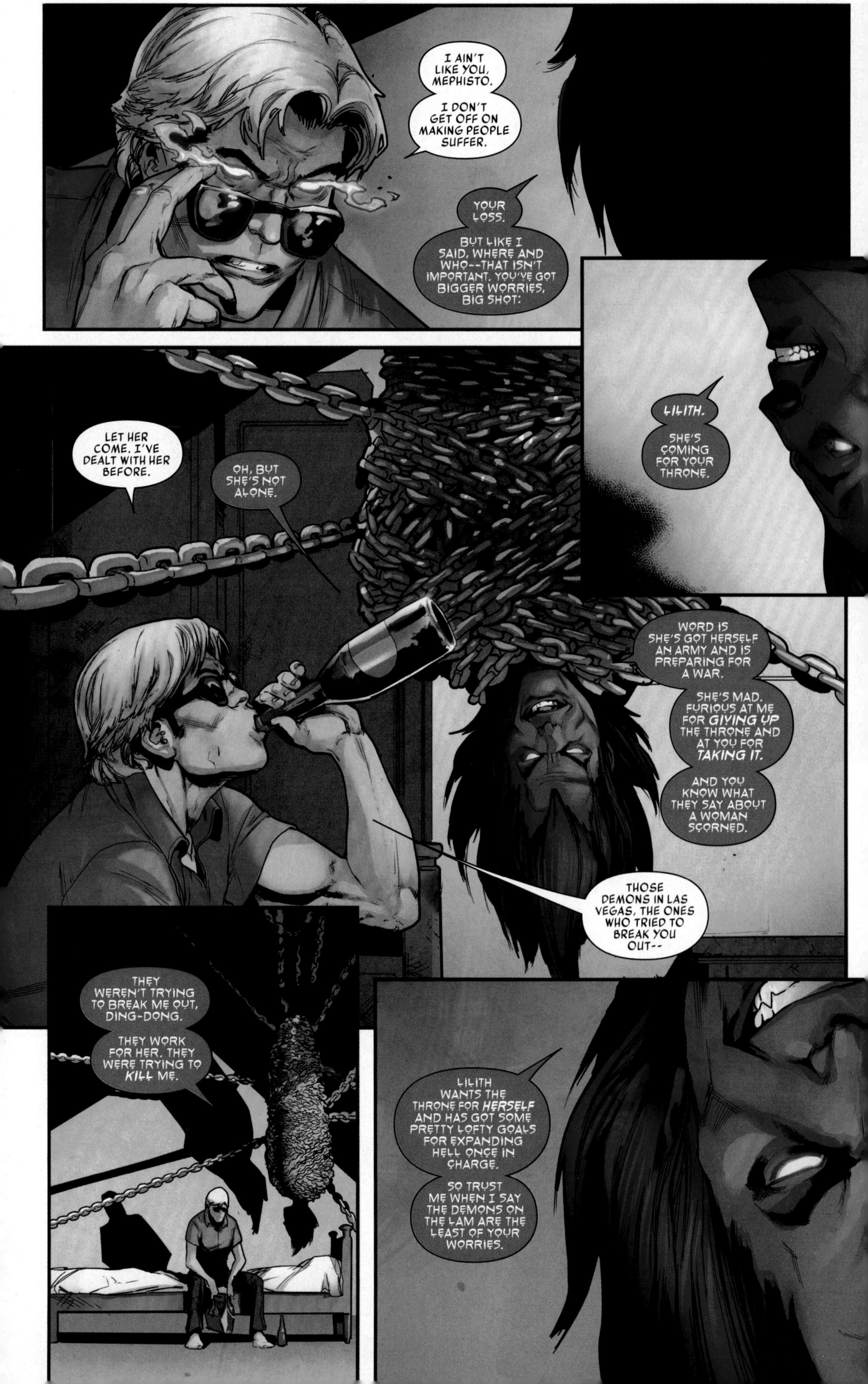

I AIN'T LIKE YOU, MEPHISTO.
I DON'T GET OFF ON MAKING PEOPLE SUFFER.
YOUR LOSS.
BUT LIKE I SAID, WHERE AND WHO--THAT ISN'T IMPORTANT. YOU'VE GOT BIGGER WORRIES, BIG SHOT:
LILITH.
SHE'S COMING FOR YOUR THRONE.
LET HER COME. I'VE DEALT WITH HER BEFORE.
OH, BUT SHE'S NOT ALONE.
WORD IS SHE'S GOT HERSELF AN ARMY AND IS PREPARING FOR A WAR.
SHE'S MAD. FURIOUS AT ME FOR GIVING UP THE THRONE AND AT YOU FOR TAKING IT.
AND YOU KNOW WHAT THEY SAY ABOUT A WOMAN SCORNED.
THOSE DEMONS IN LAS VEGAS, THE ONES WHO TRIED TO BREAK YOU OUT--
THEY WEREN'T TRYING TO BREAK ME OUT, DING-DONG.
THEY WORK FOR HER. THEY WERE TRYING TO KILL ME.
LILITH WANTS THE THRONE FOR HERSELF AND HAS GOT SOME PRETTY LOFTY GOALS FOR EXPANDING HELL ONCE IN CHARGE.
SO TRUST ME WHEN I SAY THE DEMONS ON THE LAM ARE THE LEAST OF YOUR WORRIES.

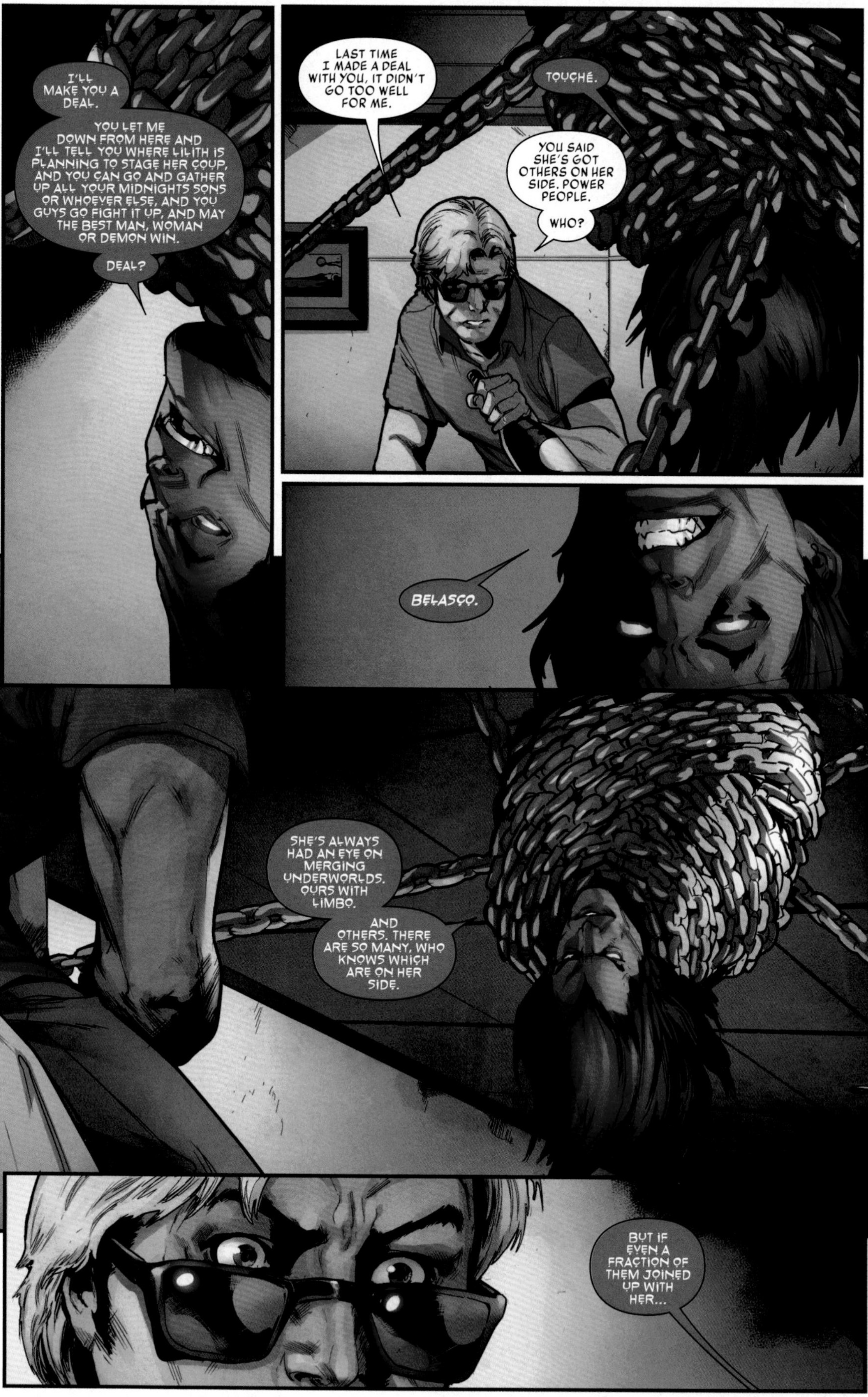
I'LL MAKE YOU A DEAL.
YOU LET ME DOWN FROM HERE AND I'LL TELL YOU WHERE LILITH IS PLANNING TO STAGE HER COUP, AND YOU CAN GO AND GATHER UP ALL YOUR MIDNIGHTS SONS OR WHOEVER ELSE, AND YOU GUYS GO FIGHT IT UP, AND MAY THE BEST MAN, WOMAN OR DEMON WIN.
DEAL?
LAST TIME I MADE A DEAL WITH YOU, IT DIDN'T GO TOO WELL FOR ME.
TOUCHÉ.
YOU SAID SHE'S GOT OTHERS ON HER SIDE. POWER PEOPLE.
WHO?
BELASCO.
SHE'S ALWAYS HAD AN EYE ON MERGING UNDERWORLDS. OURS WITH LIMBO.
AND OTHERS. THERE ARE SO MANY, WHO KNOWS WHICH ARE ON HER SIDE.
BUT IF EVEN A FRACTION OF THEM JOINED UP WITH HER...

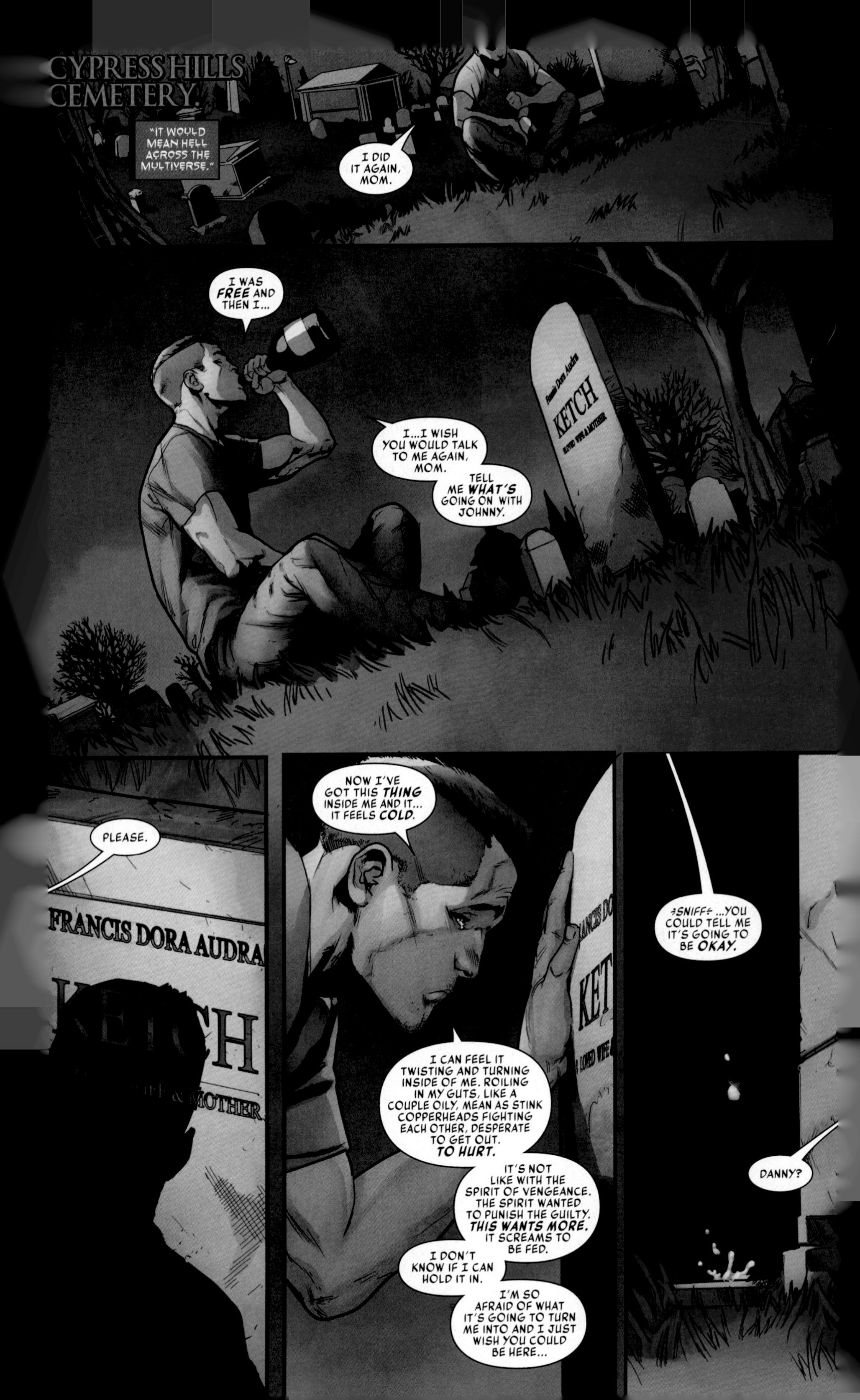
CYPRESS HILLS CEMETERY.
"IT WOULD MEAN HELL ACROSS THE MULTIVERSE."
I DID IT AGAIN, MOM.
I WAS FREE AND THEN I...
I...I WISH YOU WOULD TALK TO ME AGAIN, MOM.
TELL ME WHAT'S GOING ON WITH JOHNNY.
FRANCIS DORA AUDRA KETCH BELOVED WIFE & MOTHER
PLEASE.
FRANCIS DORA AUDRA
KETCH
& MOTHER
NOW I'VE GOT THIS THING INSIDE ME AND IT... IT FEELS COLD.
I CAN FEEL IT TWISTING AND TURNING INSIDE OF ME. ROILING IN MY GUTS, LIKE A COUPLE OILY, MEAN AS STINK COPPERHEADS FIGHTING EACH OTHER, DESPERATE TO GET OUT. TO HURT.
IT'S NOT LIKE WITH THE SPIRIT OF VENGEANCE. THE SPIRIT WANTED TO PUNISH THE GUILTY. THIS WANTS MORE. IT SCREAMS TO BE FED.
I DON'T KNOW IF I CAN HOLD IT IN.
I'M SO AFRAID OF WHAT IT'S GOING TO TURN ME INTO AND I JUST WISH YOU COULD BE HERE...
≠SNIFF≠ ...YOU COULD TELL ME IT'S GOING TO BE OKAY.
DANNY?

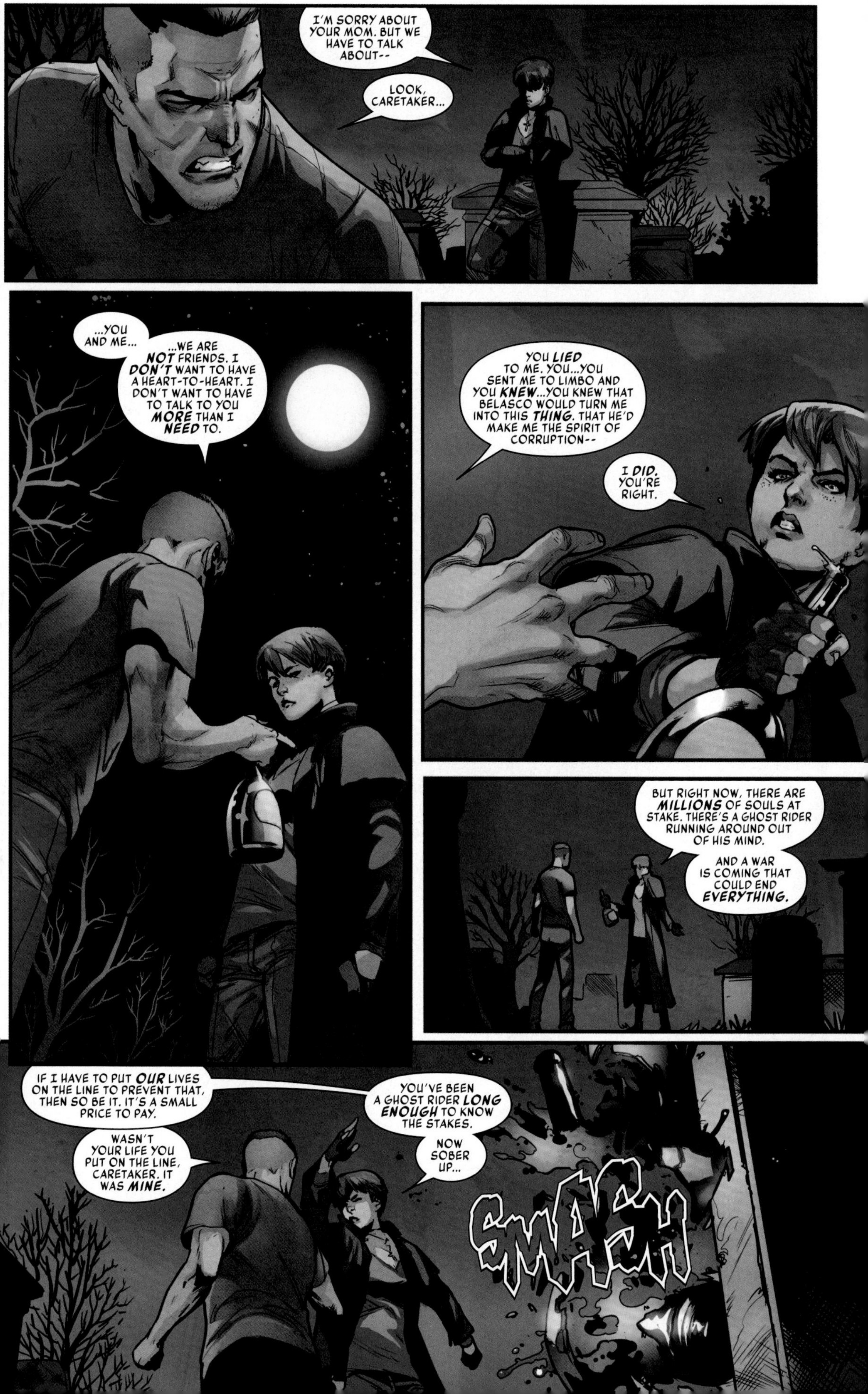

I'M SORRY ABOUT YOUR MOM. BUT WE HAVE TO TALK ABOUT--
LOOK, CARETAKER...
...YOU AND ME...
...WE ARE NOT FRIENDS. I DON'T WANT TO HAVE A HEART-TO-HEART. I DON'T WANT TO HAVE TO TALK TO YOU MORE THAN I NEED TO.
YOU LIED TO ME. YOU...YOU SENT ME TO LIMBO AND YOU KNEW...YOU KNEW THAT BELASCO WOULD TURN ME INTO THIS THING. THAT HE'D MAKE ME THE SPIRIT OF CORRUPTION--
I DID. YOU'RE RIGHT.
BUT RIGHT NOW, THERE ARE MILLIONS OF SOULS AT STAKE. THERE'S A GHOST RIDER RUNNING AROUND OUT OF HIS MIND.
AND A WAR IS COMING THAT COULD END EVERYTHING.
IF I HAVE TO PUT OUR LIVES ON THE LINE TO PREVENT THAT, THEN SO BE IT. IT'S A SMALL PRICE TO PAY.
YOU'VE BEEN A GHOST RIDER LONG ENOUGH TO KNOW THE STAKES.
WASN'T YOUR LIFE YOU PUT ON THE LINE, CARETAKER. IT WAS MINE.
NOW SOBER UP...
SMASH

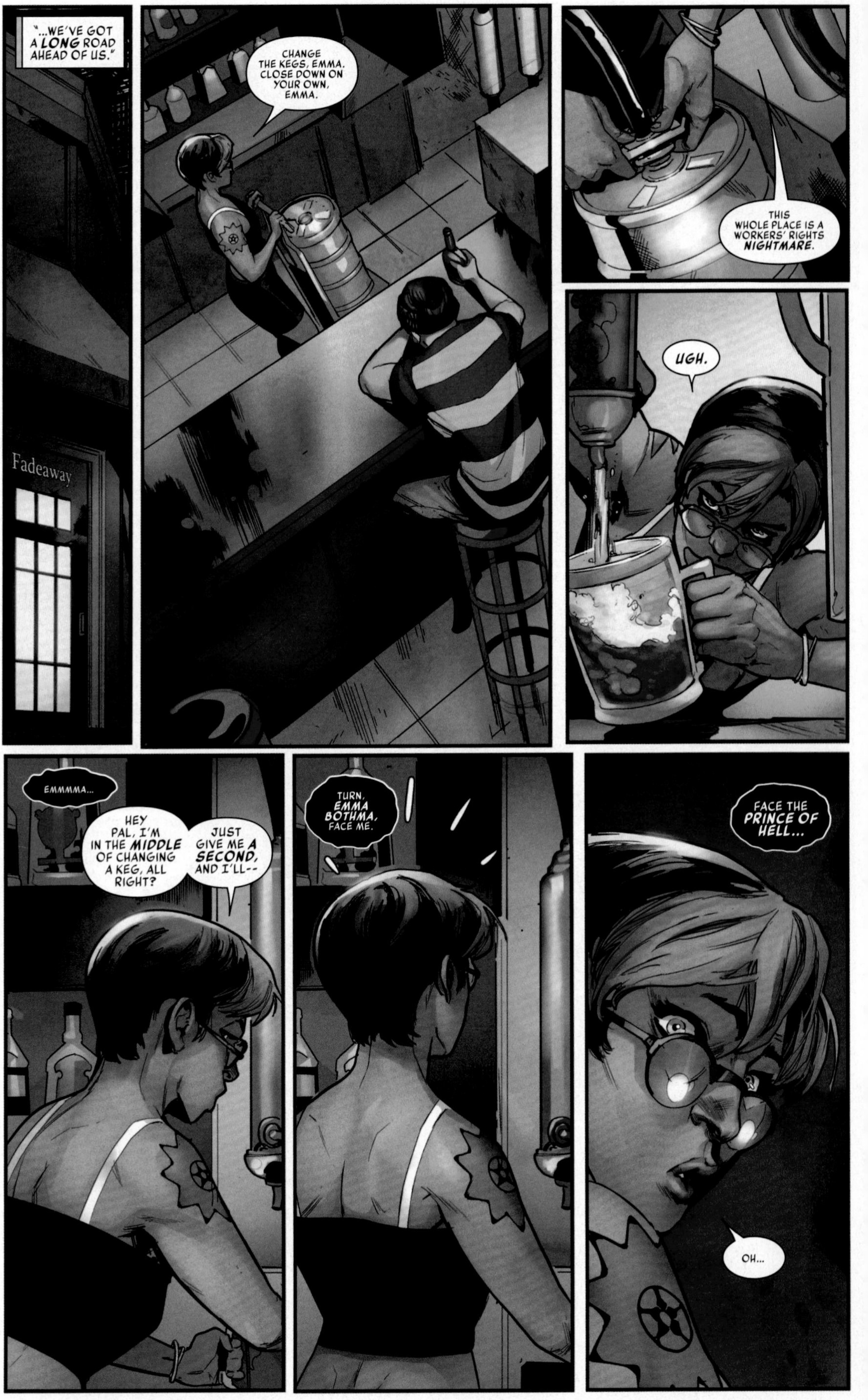
"...WE'VE GOT A LONG ROAD AHEAD OF US."
Fadeaway
CHANGE THE KEGS, EMMA. CLOSE DOWN ON YOUR OWN, EMMA.
THIS WHOLE PLACE IS A WORKERS' RIGHTS NIGHTMARE.
UGH.
EMMMMA...
HEY PAL, I'M IN THE MIDDLE OF CHANGING A KEG, ALL RIGHT?
JUST GIVE ME A SECOND, AND I'LL--
TURN, EMMA BOTHMA, FACE ME.
FACE THE PRINCE OF HELL...
OH...

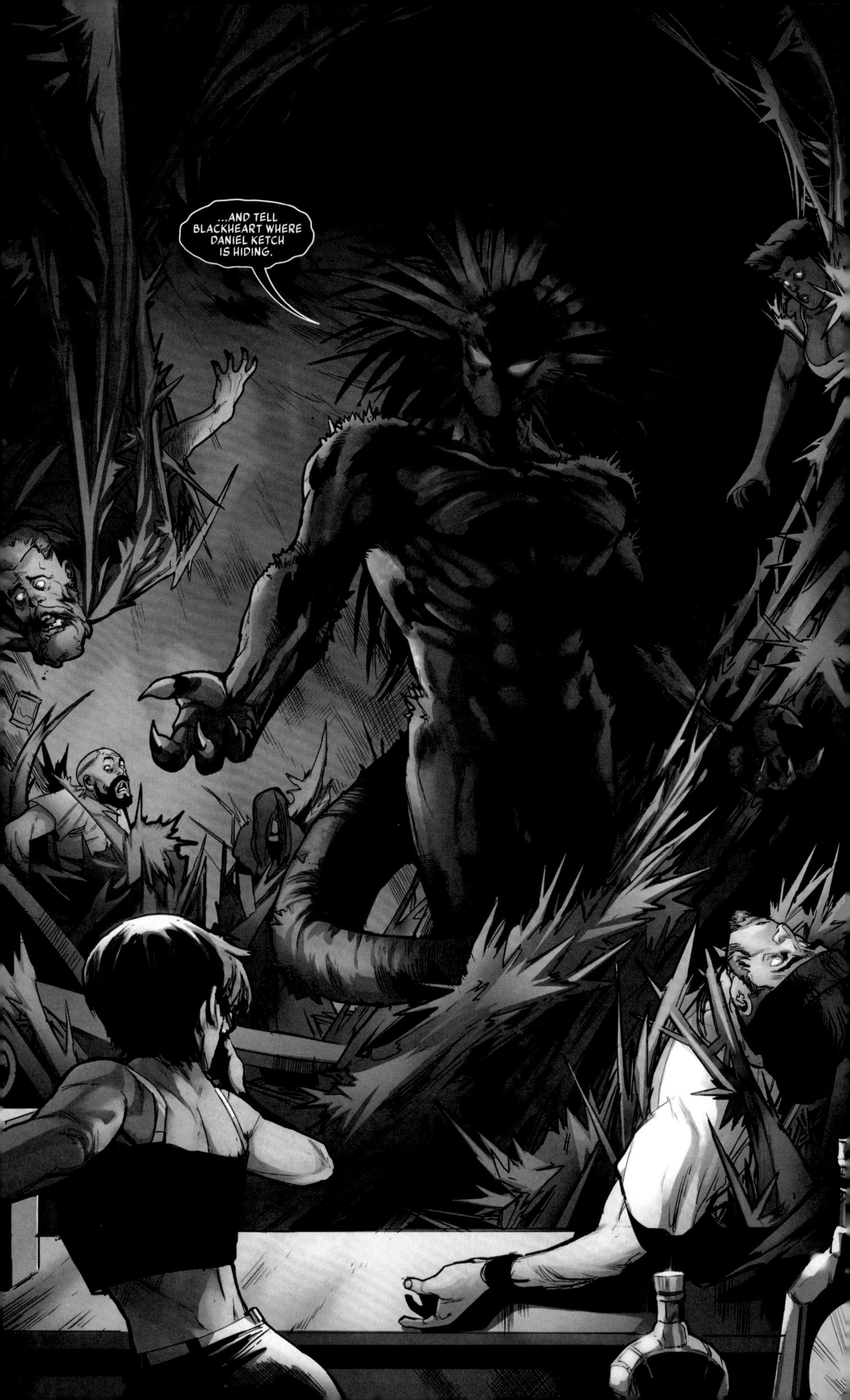
...AND TELL BLACKHEART WHERE DANIEL KETCH IS HIDING.

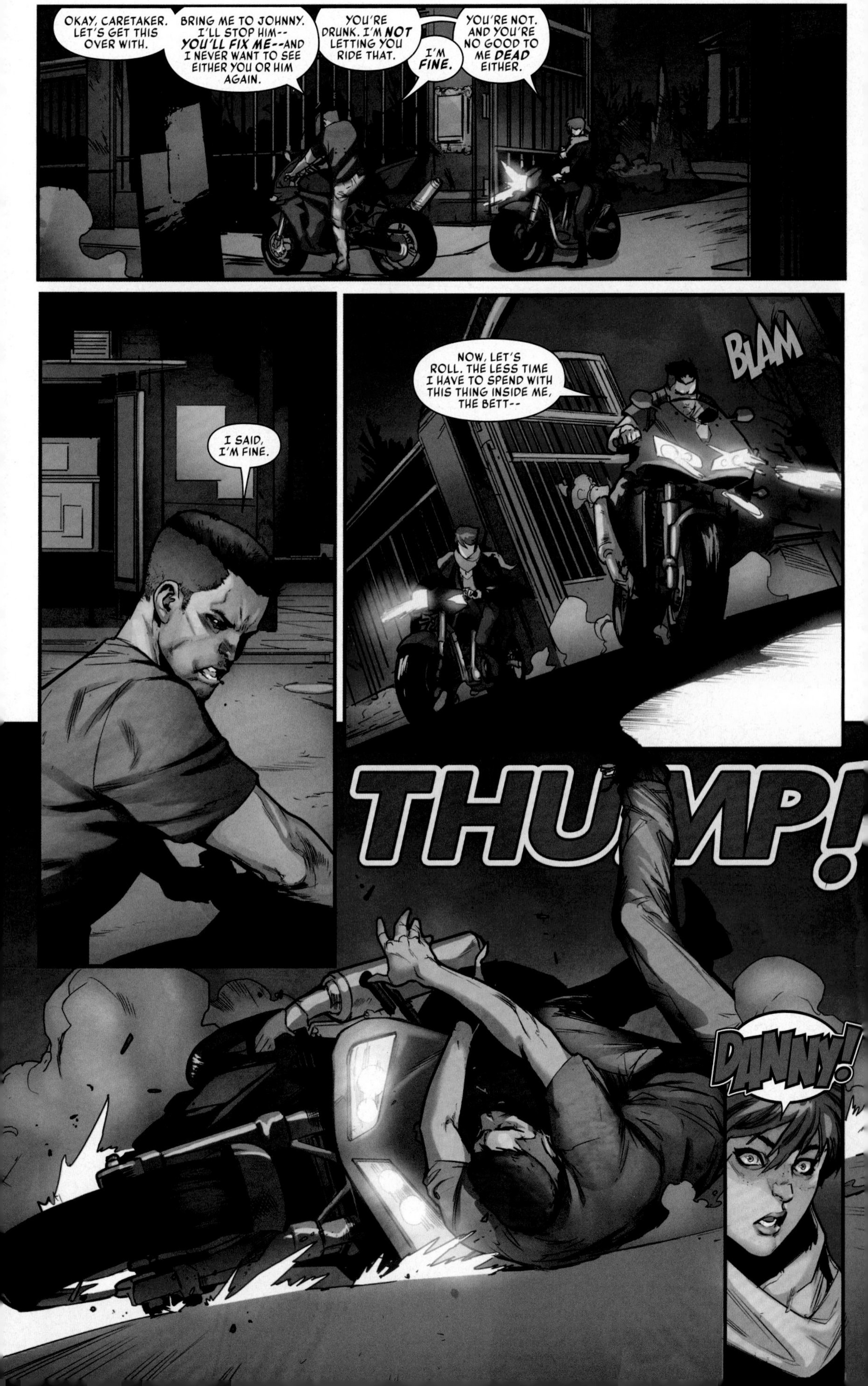
OKAY, CARETAKER. LET'S GET THIS OVER WITH.
BRING ME TO JOHNNY. I'LL STOP HIM-- YOU'LL FIX ME--AND I NEVER WANT TO SEE EITHER YOU OR HIM AGAIN.
YOU'RE DRUNK. I'M NOT LETTING YOU RIDE THAT.
I'M FINE.
YOU'RE NOT. AND YOU'RE NO GOOD TO ME DEAD EITHER.
I SAID, I'M FINE.
BLAM
NOW, LET'S ROLL. THE LESS TIME I HAVE TO SPEND WITH THIS THING INSIDE ME, THE BETT--
THUMP!
DANNY!

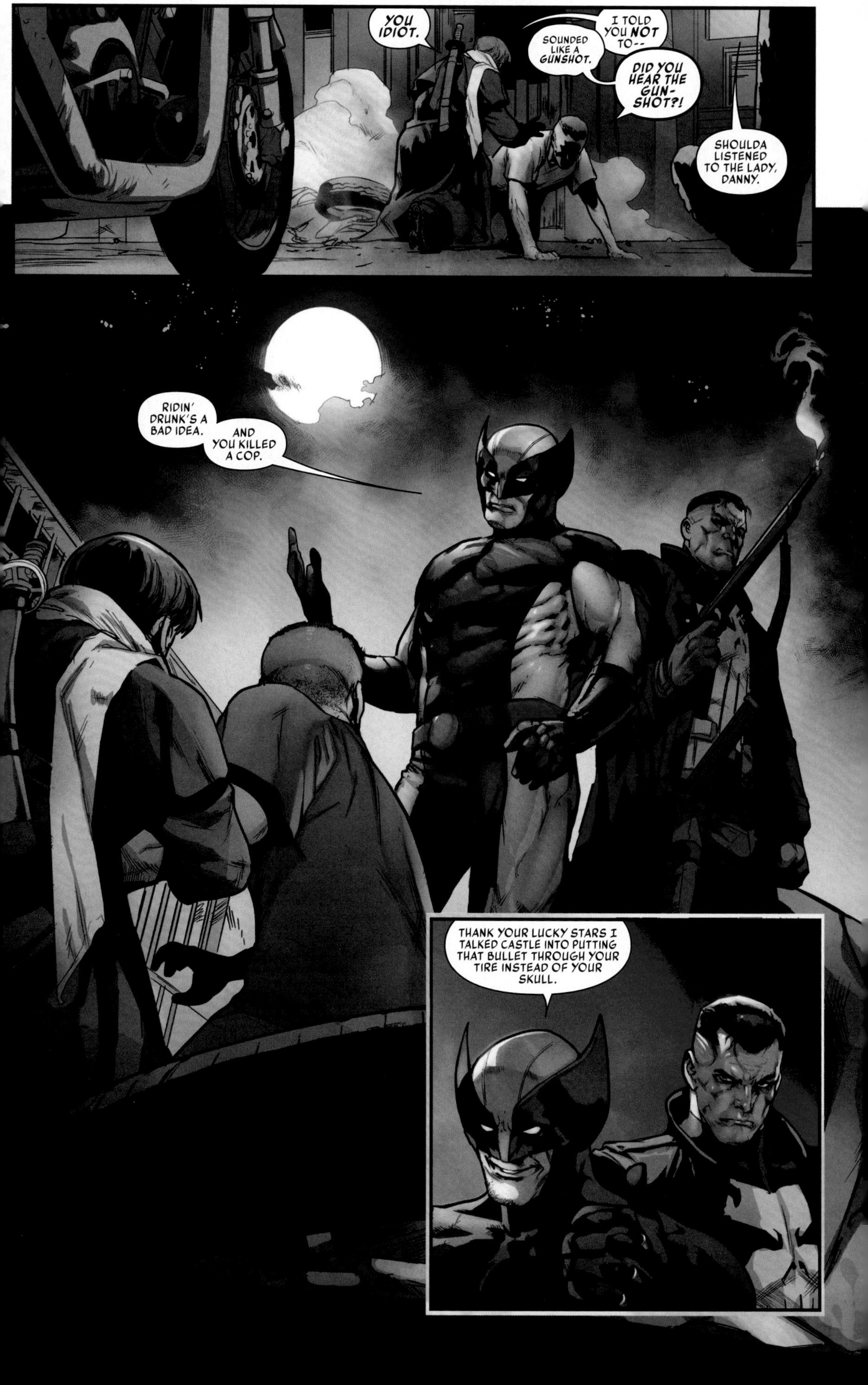
YOU IDIOT.
SOUNDED LIKE A GUNSHOT.
I TOLD YOU NOT TO--
DID YOU HEAR THE GUN-SHOT?!
SHOULDA LISTENED TO THE LADY, DANNY.
RIDIN' DRUNK'S A BAD IDEA.
AND YOU KILLED A COP.
THANK YOUR LUCKY STARS I TALKED CASTLE INTO PUTTING THAT BULLET THROUGH YOUR TIRE INSTEAD OF YOUR SKULL.

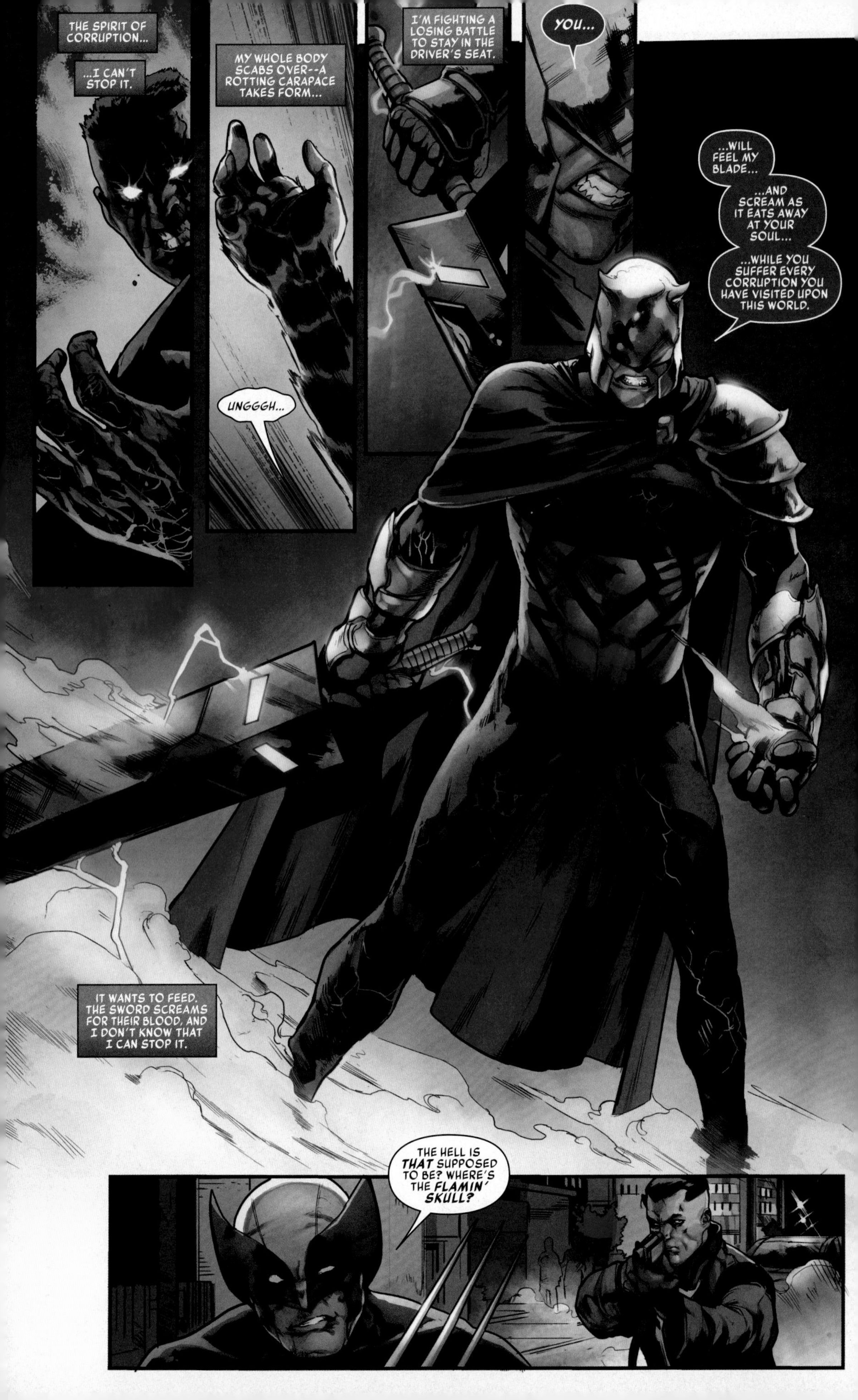
THE SPIRIT OF CORRUPTION...
...I CAN'T STOP IT.
MY WHOLE BODY SCABS OVER--A ROTTING CARAPACE TAKES FORM...
UNGGGH...
I'M FIGHTING A LOSING BATTLE TO STAY IN THE DRIVER'S SEAT.
YOU...
...WILL FEEL MY BLADE...
...AND SCREAM AS IT EATS AWAY AT YOUR SOUL...
...WHILE YOU SUFFER EVERY CORRUPTION YOU HAVE VISITED UPON THIS WORLD.
IT WANTS TO FEED. THE SWORD SCREAMS FOR THEIR BLOOD, AND I DON'T KNOW THAT I CAN STOP IT.
THE HELL IS THAT SUPPOSED TO BE? WHERE'S THE FLAMIN' SKULL?

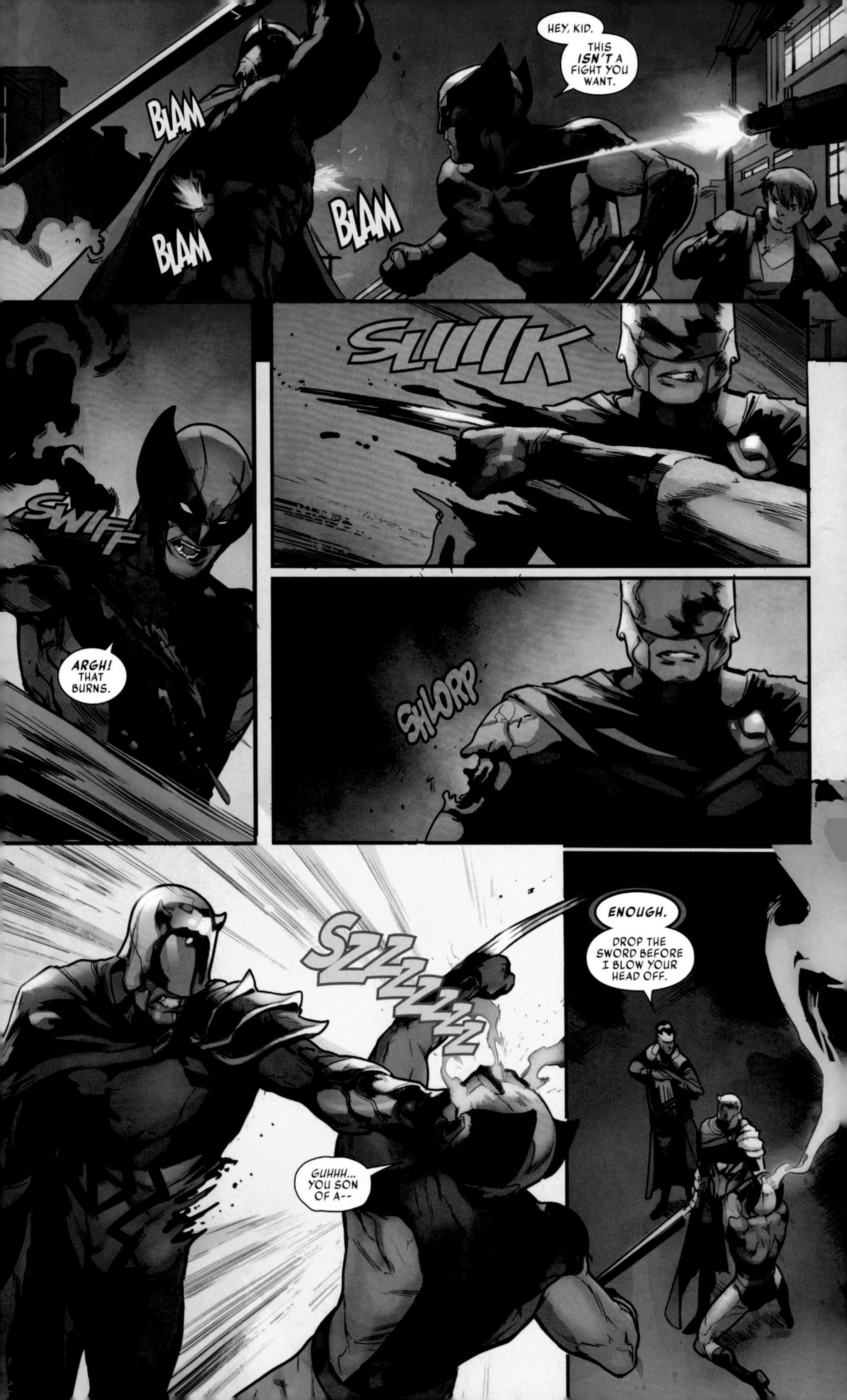
BLAM
HEY, KID.
THIS ISN'T A FIGHT YOU WANT.
BLAM
BLAM
SWIFF
ARGH! THAT BURNS.
SLIIIK
SHLORP
SZZZZZZ
GUHHH... YOU SON OF A--
ENOUGH.
DROP THE SWORD BEFORE I BLOW YOUR HEAD OFF.

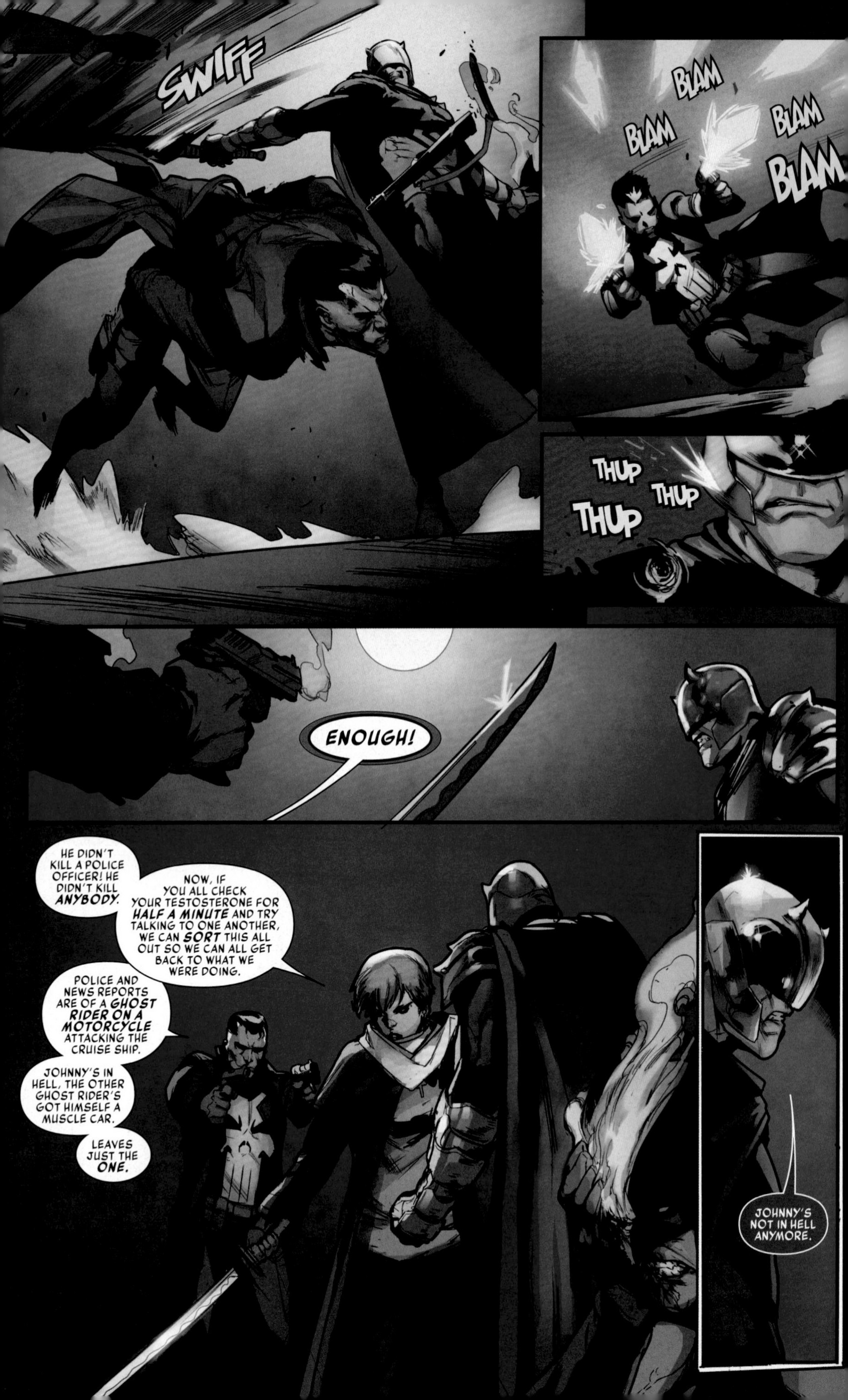
SWIFF
BLAM
BLAM
BLAM
BLAM
THUP
THUP
THUP
ENOUGH!
HE DIDN'T KILL A POLICE OFFICER! HE DIDN'T KILL ANYBODY.
NOW, IF YOU ALL CHECK YOUR TESTOSTERONE FOR HALF A MINUTE AND TRY TALKING TO ONE ANOTHER, WE CAN SORT THIS ALL OUT SO WE CAN ALL GET BACK TO WHAT WE WERE DOING.
POLICE AND NEWS REPORTS ARE OF A GHOST RIDER ON A MOTORCYCLE ATTACKING THE CRUISE SHIP.
JOHNNY'S IN HELL, THE OTHER GHOST RIDER'S GOT HIMSELF A MUSCLE CAR.
LEAVES JUST THE ONE.
JOHNNY'S NOT IN HELL ANYMORE.

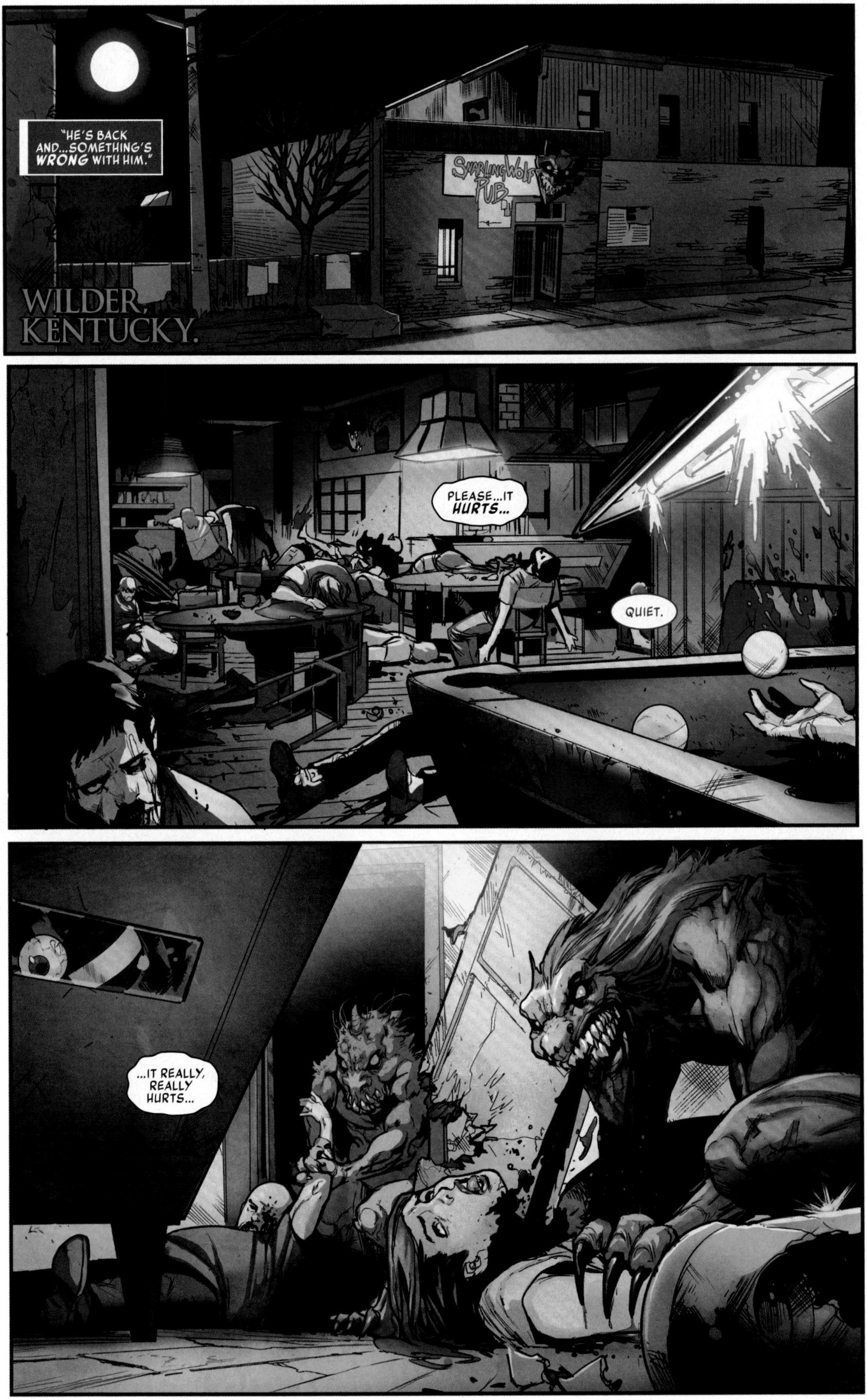
"HE'S BACK AND...SOMETHING'S *WRONG* WITH HIM."
SNARLING WOLF PUB
WILDER, KENTUCKY.
PLEASE...IT *HURTS*...
QUIET.
...IT REALLY, REALLY HURTS...

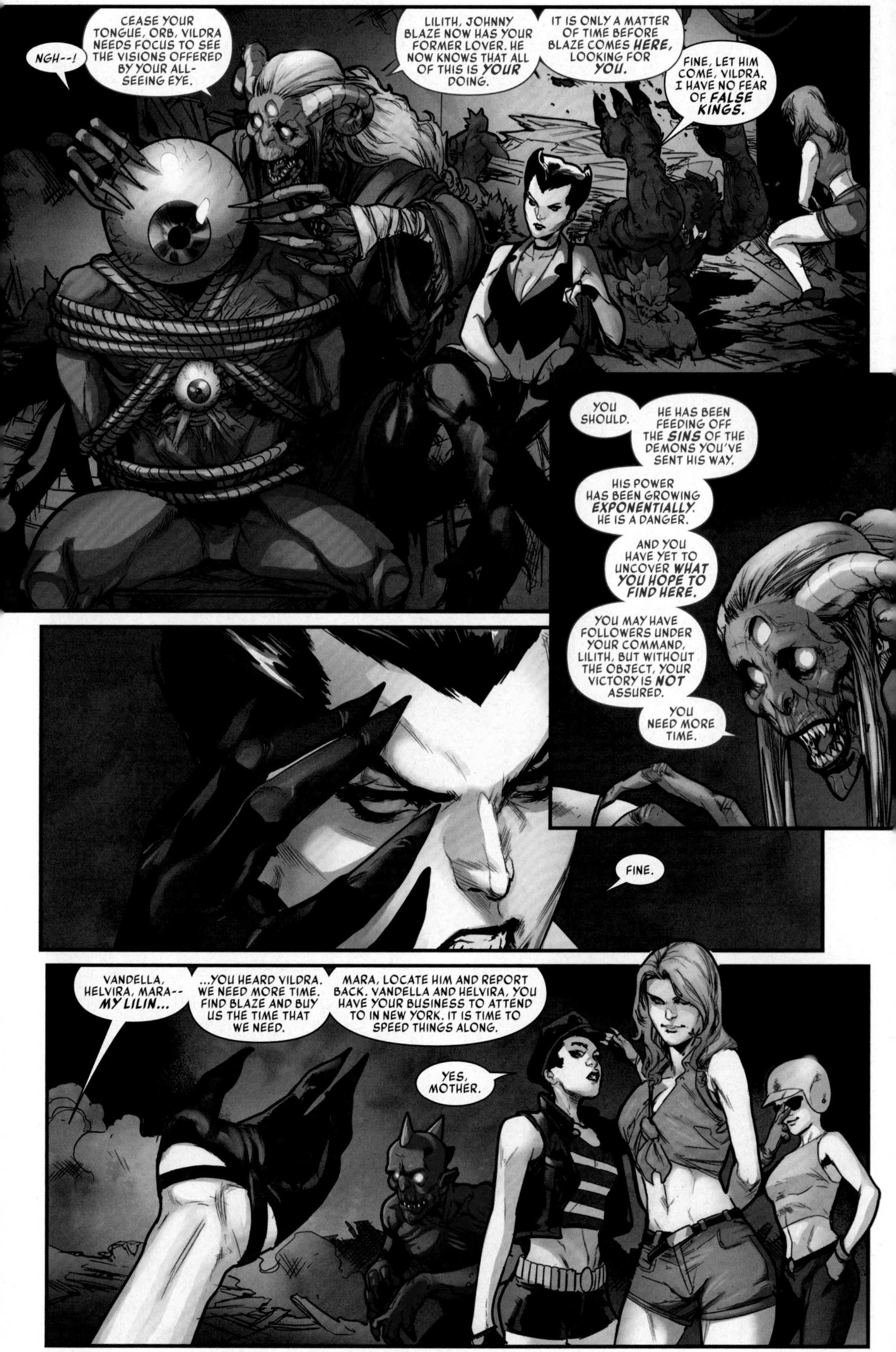
NGH--!
CEASE YOUR TONGUE, ORB. VILDRA NEEDS FOCUS TO SEE THE VISIONS OFFERED BY YOUR ALL-SEEING EYE.
LILITH, JOHNNY BLAZE NOW HAS YOUR FORMER LOVER. HE NOW KNOWS THAT ALL OF THIS IS YOUR DOING.
IT IS ONLY A MATTER OF TIME BEFORE BLAZE COMES HERE, LOOKING FOR YOU.
FINE, LET HIM COME, VILDRA. I HAVE NO FEAR OF FALSE KINGS.
YOU SHOULD.
HE HAS BEEN FEEDING OFF THE SINS OF THE DEMONS YOU'VE SENT HIS WAY.
HIS POWER HAS BEEN GROWING EXPONENTIALLY. HE IS A DANGER.
AND YOU HAVE YET TO UNCOVER WHAT YOU HOPE TO FIND HERE.
YOU MAY HAVE FOLLOWERS UNDER YOUR COMMAND, LILITH, BUT WITHOUT THE OBJECT, YOUR VICTORY IS NOT ASSURED.
YOU NEED MORE TIME.
FINE.
VANDELLA, HELVIRA, MARA-- MY LILIN...
...YOU HEARD VILDRA. WE NEED MORE TIME. FIND BLAZE AND BUY US THE TIME THAT WE NEED.
MARA, LOCATE HIM AND REPORT BACK. VANDELLA AND HELVIRA, YOU HAVE YOUR BUSINESS TO ATTEND TO IN NEW YORK. IT IS TIME TO SPEED THINGS ALONG.
YES, MOTHER.

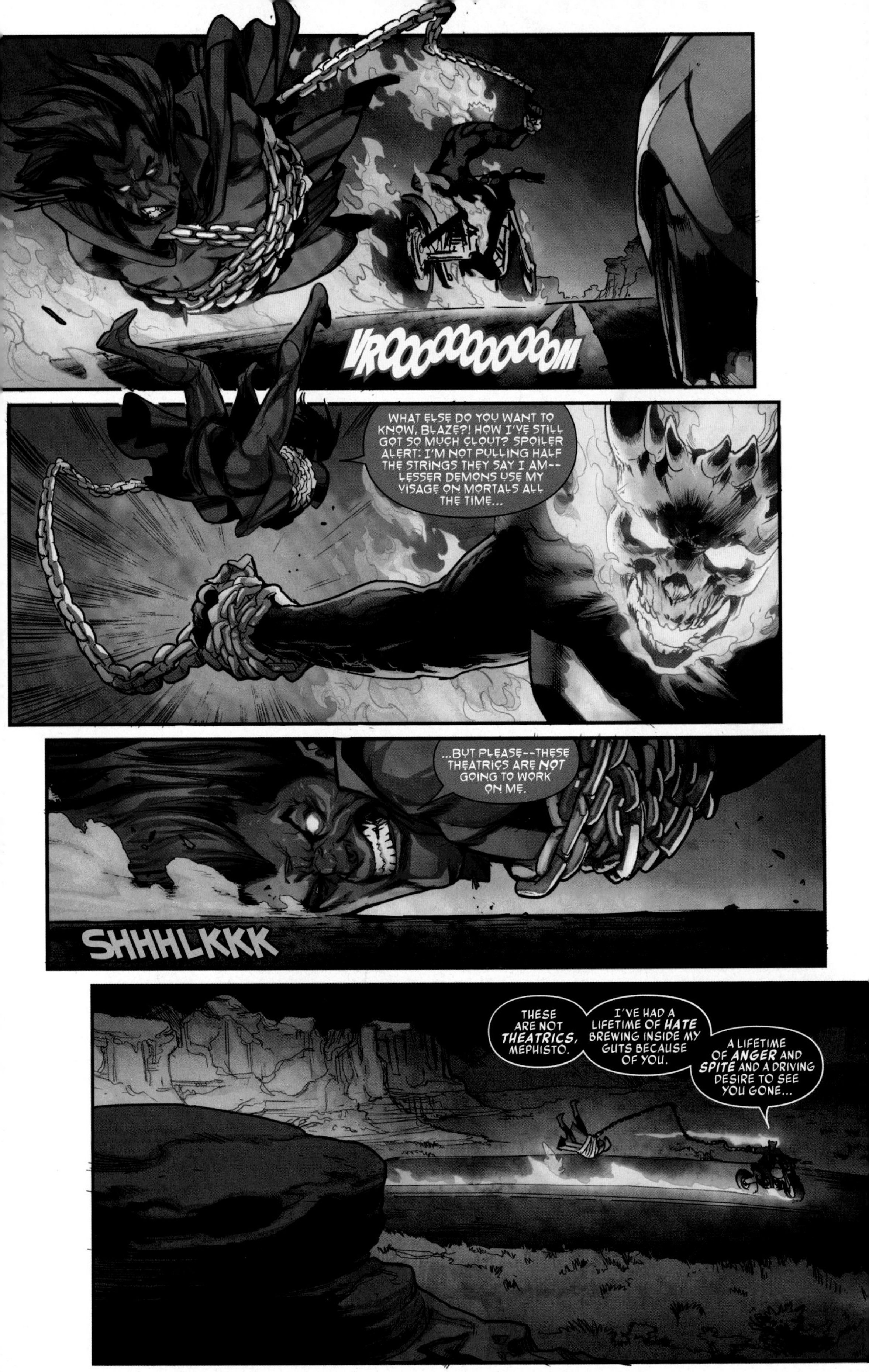

VROOOOOOOOOOOM
WHAT ELSE DO YOU WANT TO KNOW, BLAZE?! HOW I'VE STILL GOT SO MUCH CLOUT? SPOILER ALERT: I'M NOT PULLING HALF THE STRINGS THEY SAY I AM-- LESSER DEMONS USE MY VISAGE ON MORTALS ALL THE TIME...
...BUT PLEASE--THESE THEATRICS ARE NOT GOING TO WORK ON ME.
SHHHLKKK
THESE ARE NOT THEATRICS, MEPHISTO.
I'VE HAD A LIFETIME OF HATE BREWING INSIDE MY GUTS BECAUSE OF YOU.
A LIFETIME OF ANGER AND SPITE AND A DRIVING DESIRE TO SEE YOU GONE...

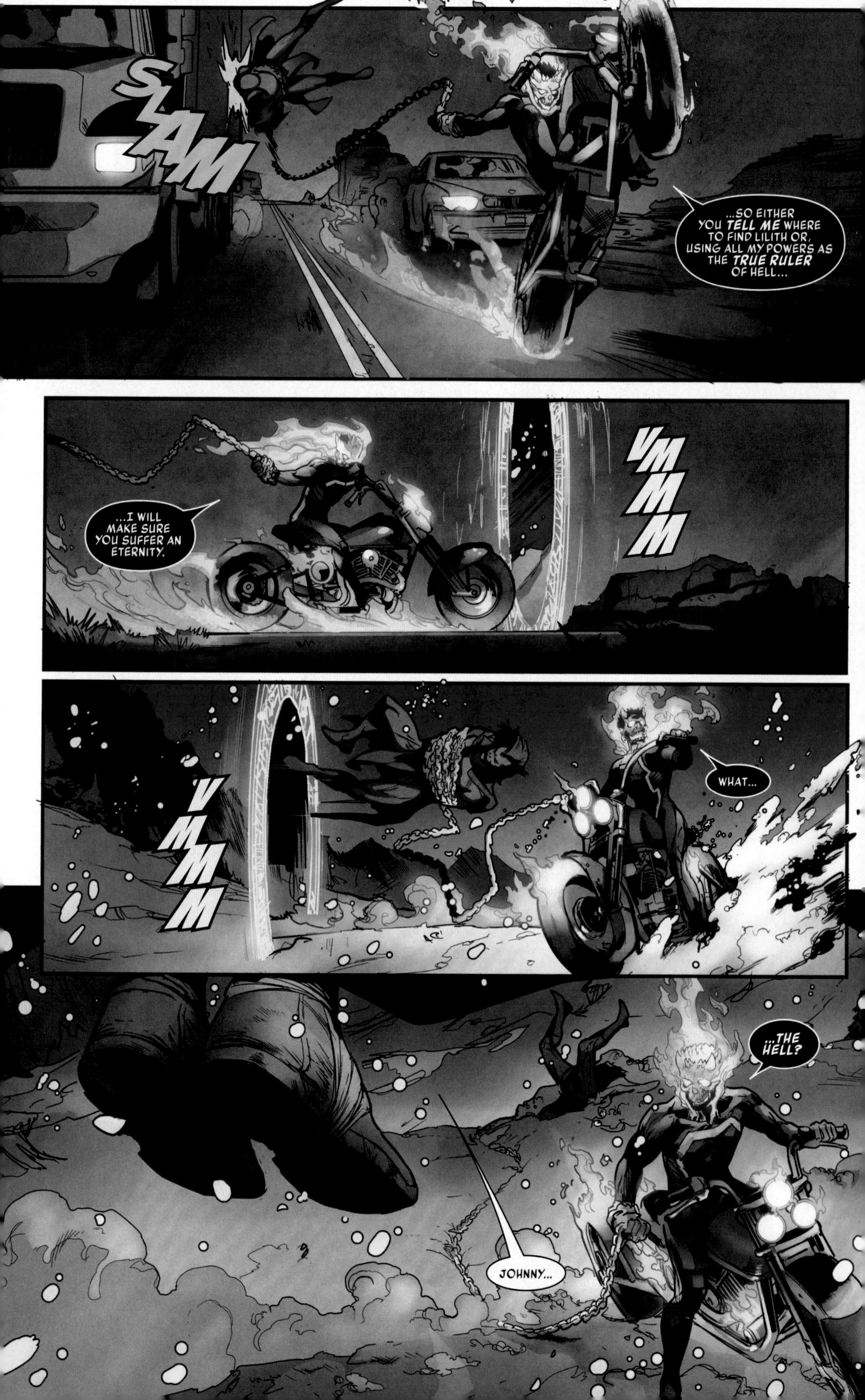
SLAM
...SO EITHER YOU TELL ME WHERE TO FIND LILITH OR, USING ALL MY POWERS AS THE TRUE RULER OF HELL...
...I WILL MAKE SURE YOU SUFFER AN ETERNITY.
VMMM
VMMM
WHAT...
...THE HELL?
JOHNNY...

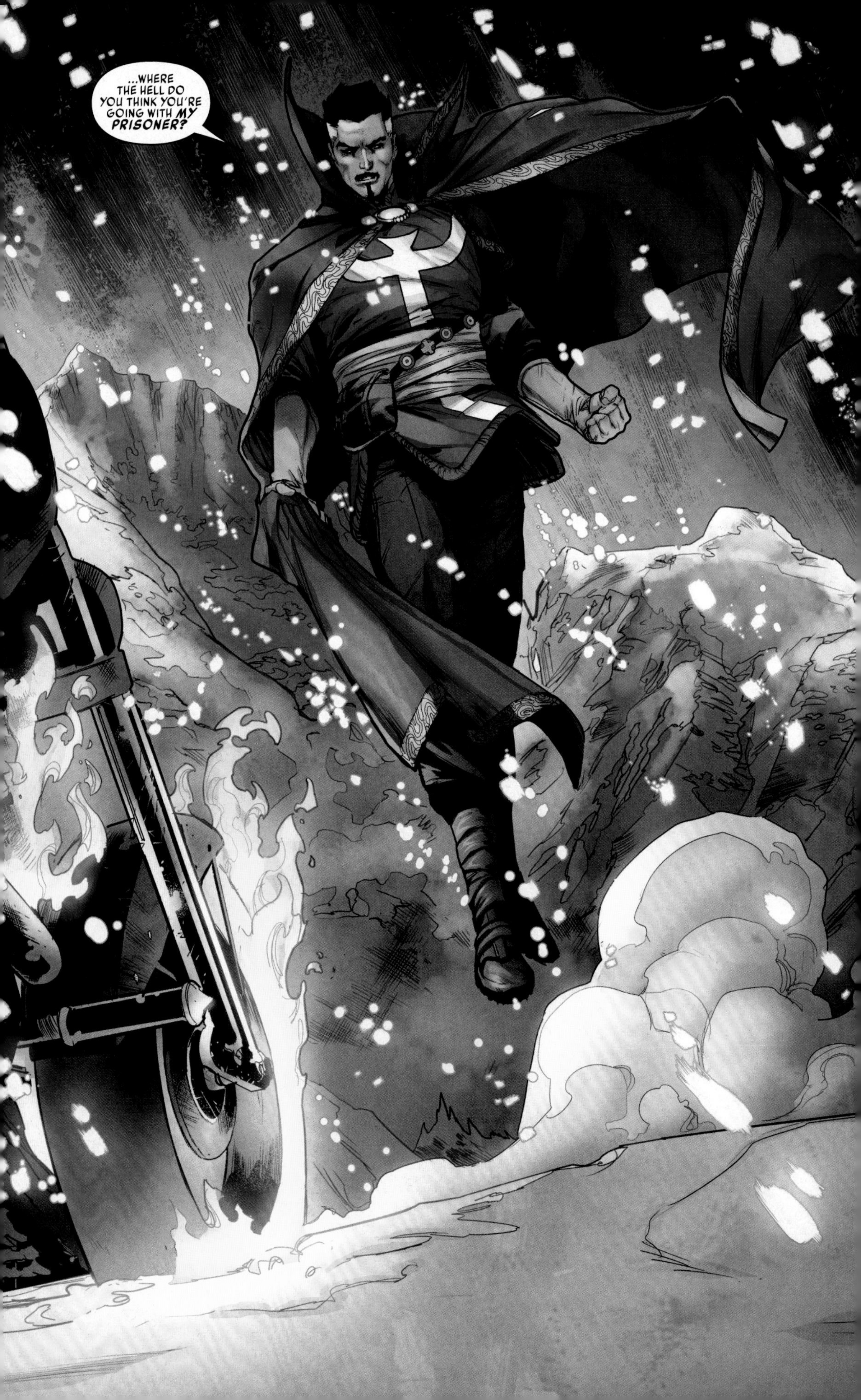
...WHERE THE HELL DO YOU THINK YOU'RE GOING WITH MY PRISONER?

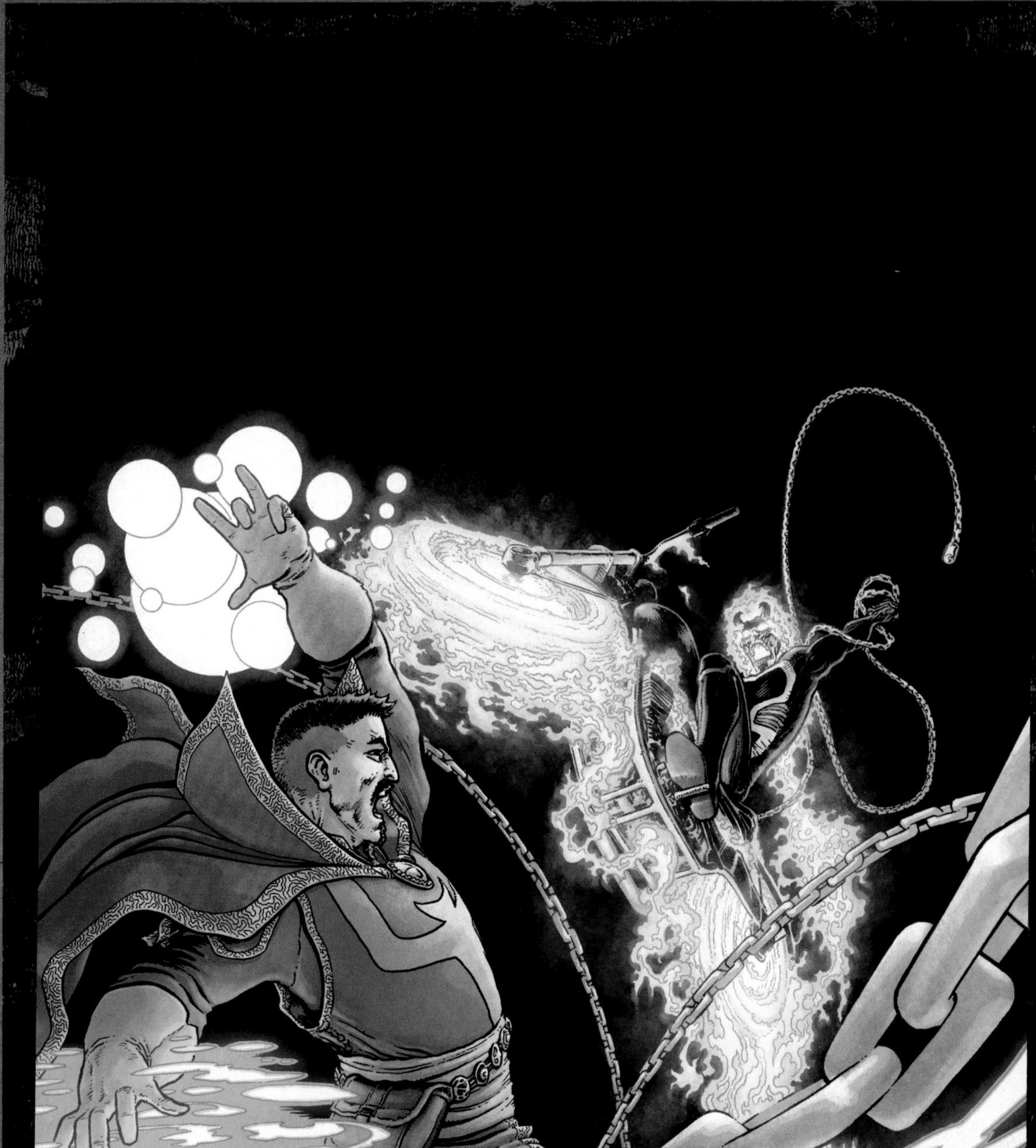

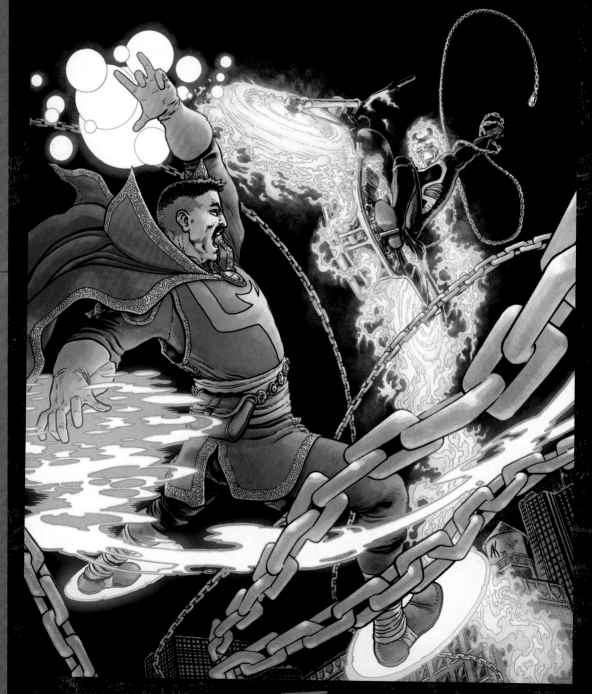

6

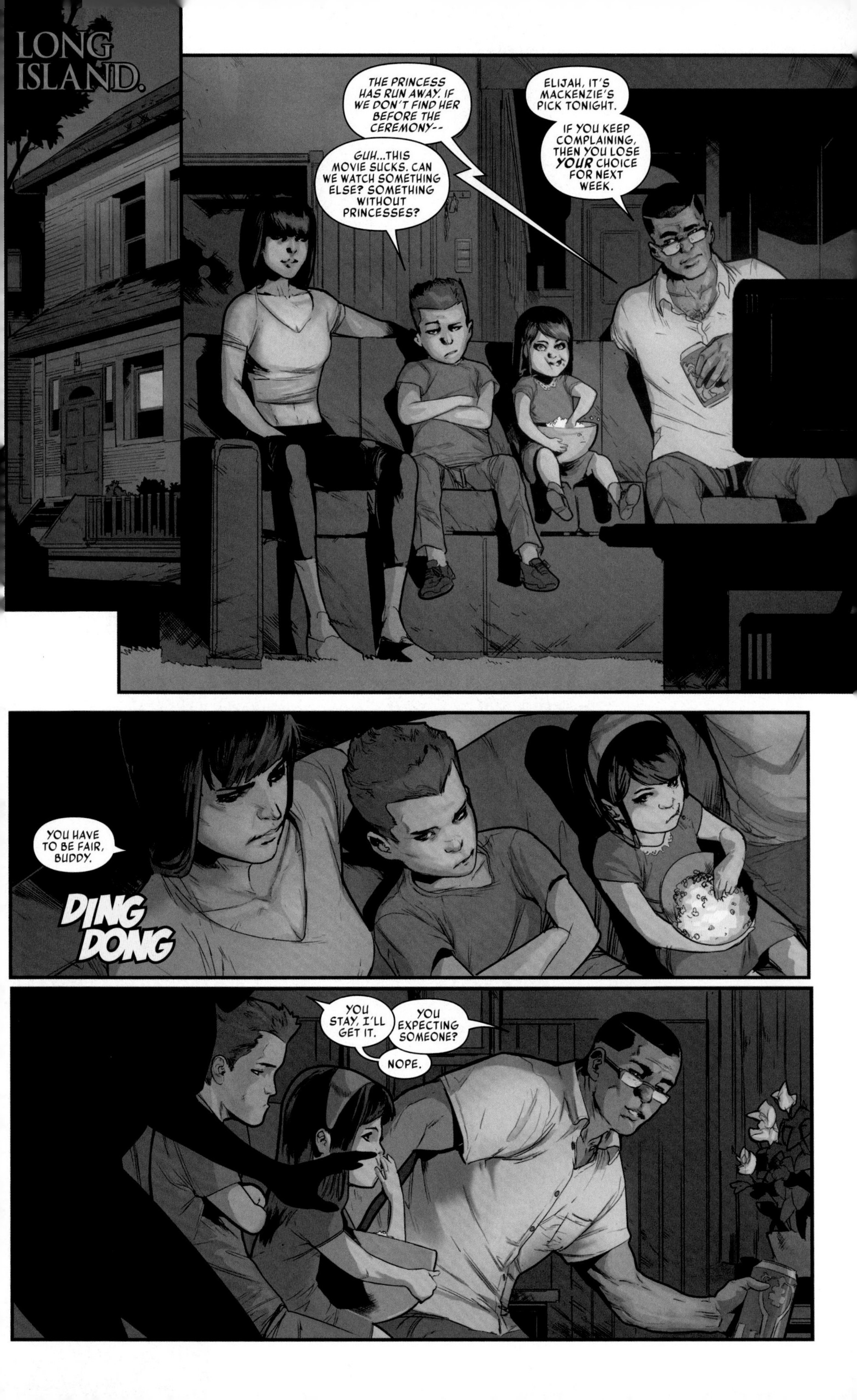
LONG ISLAND.
THE PRINCESS HAS RUN AWAY. IF WE DON'T FIND HER BEFORE THE CEREMONY--
GUH...THIS MOVIE SUCKS. CAN WE WATCH SOMETHING ELSE? SOMETHING WITHOUT PRINCESSES?
ELIJAH, IT'S MACKENZIE'S PICK TONIGHT.
IF YOU KEEP COMPLAINING, THEN YOU LOSE YOUR CHOICE FOR NEXT WEEK.
YOU HAVE TO BE FAIR, BUDDY.
DING DONG
YOU STAY, I'LL GET IT.
YOU EXPECTING SOMEONE?
NOPE.

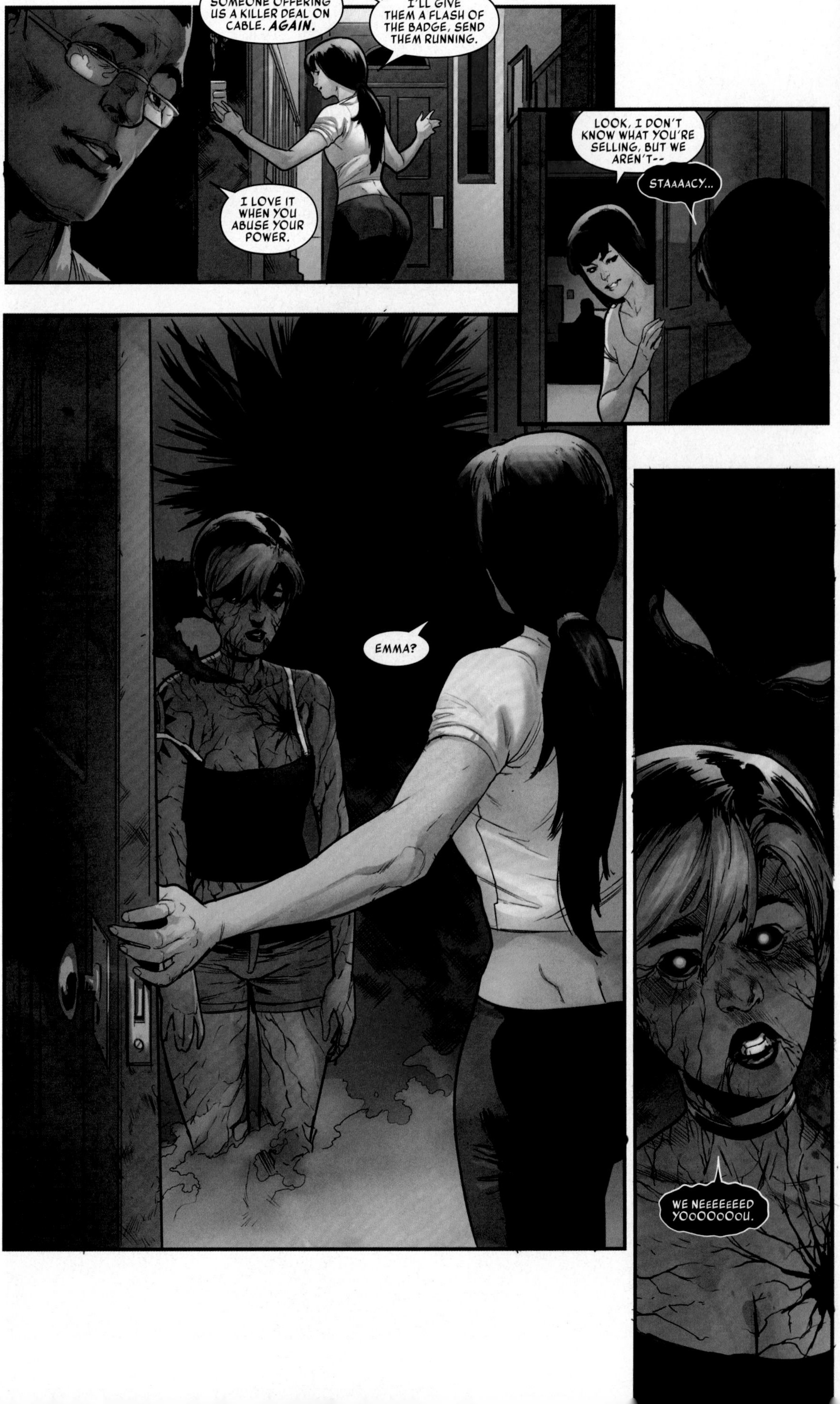
PROBABLY SOMEONE OFFERING US A KILLER DEAL ON CABLE. AGAIN.
I'LL GIVE THEM A FLASH OF THE BADGE, SEND THEM RUNNING.
I LOVE IT WHEN YOU ABUSE YOUR POWER.
LOOK, I DON'T KNOW WHAT YOU'RE SELLING, BUT WE AREN'T--
STAAAACY...
EMMA?
WE NEEEEEEED YOOOOOOOU.

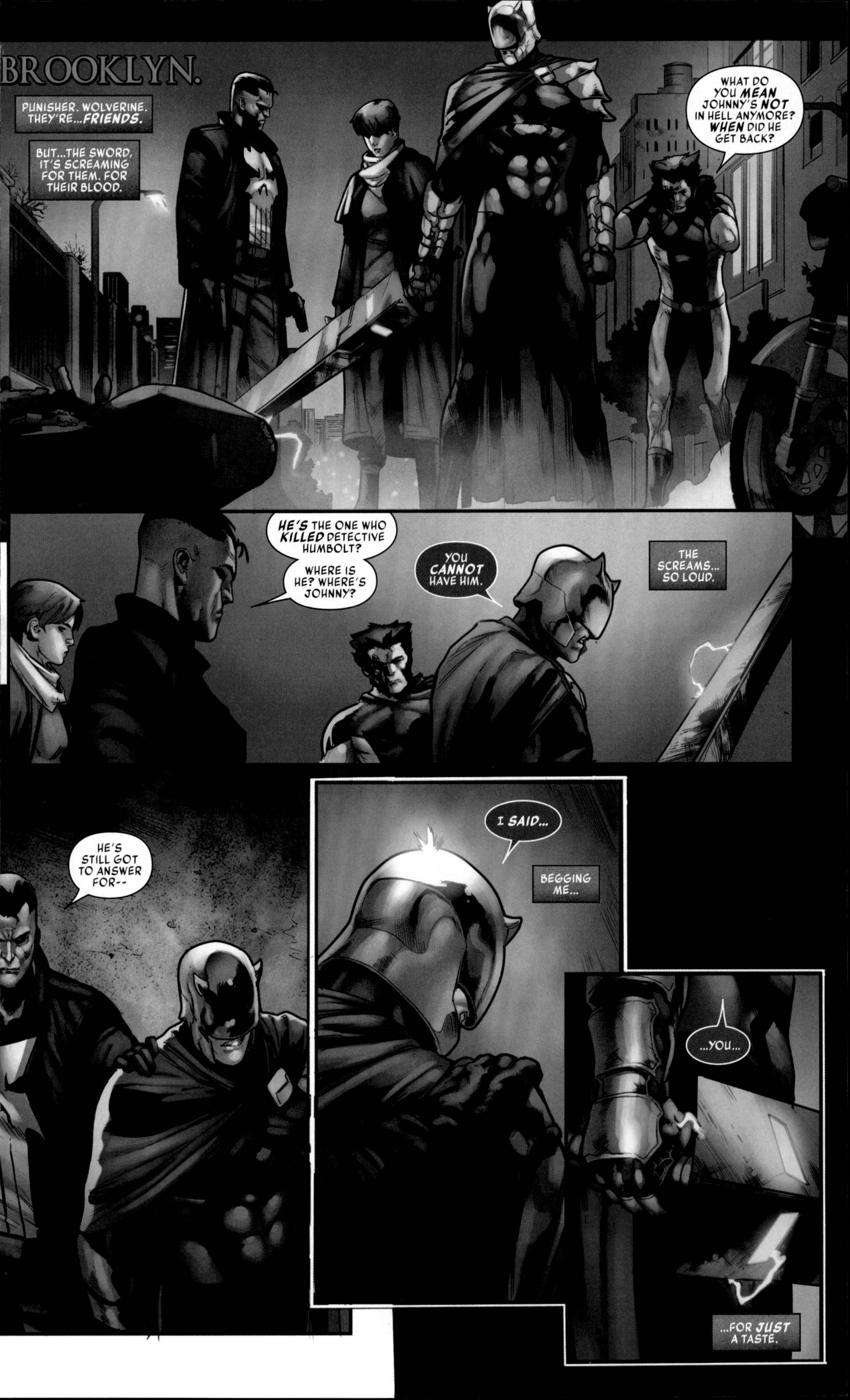
BROOKLYN.
PUNISHER. WOLVERINE. THEY'RE...FRIENDS.
BUT...THE SWORD, IT'S SCREAMING FOR THEM. FOR THEIR BLOOD.
WHAT DO YOU MEAN JOHNNY'S NOT IN HELL ANYMORE? WHEN DID HE GET BACK?
HE'S THE ONE WHO KILLED DETECTIVE HUMBOLT?
WHERE IS HE? WHERE'S JOHNNY?
YOU CANNOT HAVE HIM.
THE SCREAMS... SO LOUD.
HE'S STILL GOT TO ANSWER FOR--
I SAID...
BEGGING ME...
...YOU...
...FOR JUST A TASTE.

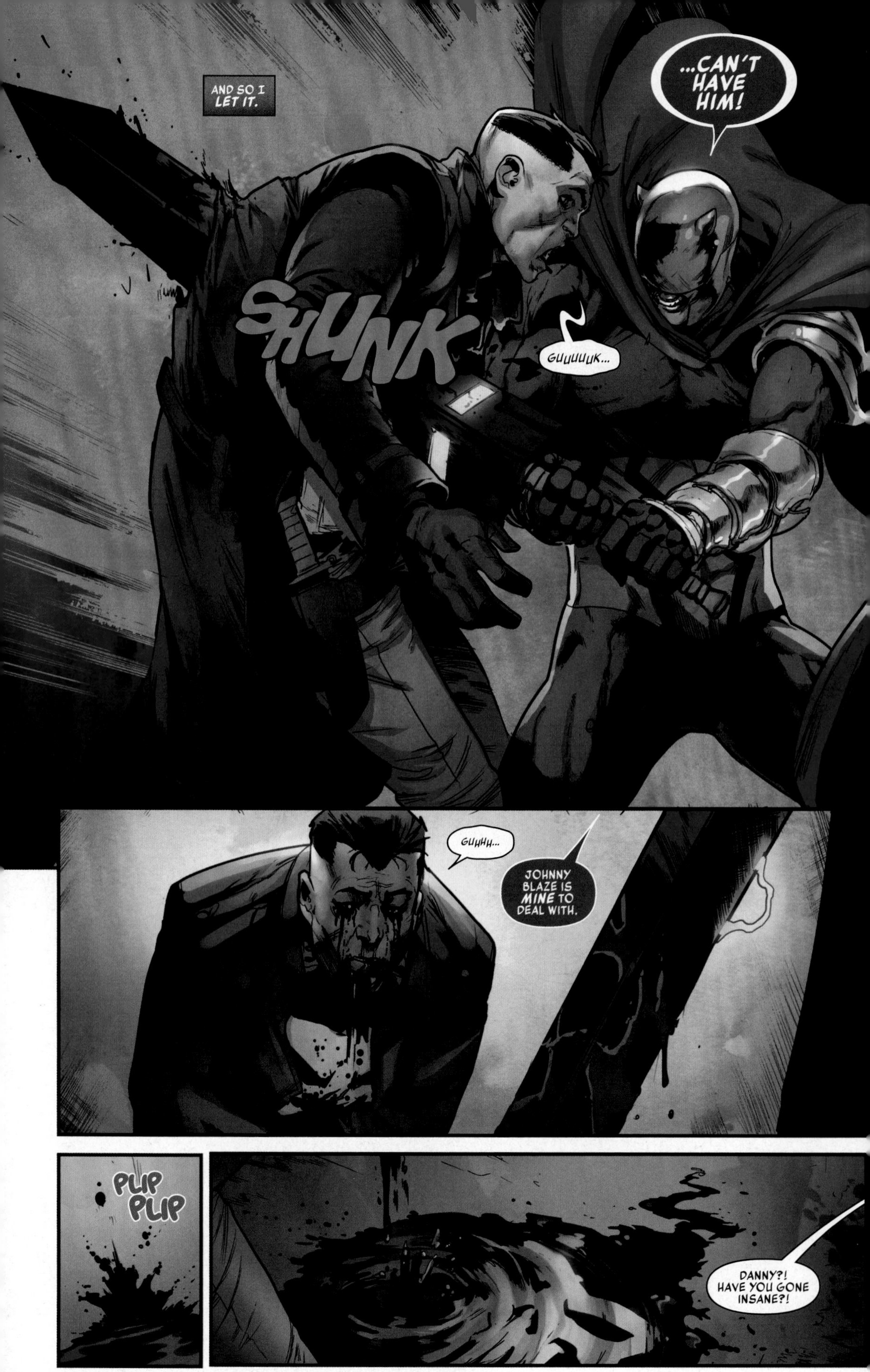
AND SO I LET IT.
...CAN'T HAVE HIM!
SHUNK
GUUUUUK...
GUHHH...
JOHNNY BLAZE IS MINE TO DEAL WITH.
PLIP PLIP
DANNY?! HAVE YOU GONE INSANE?!

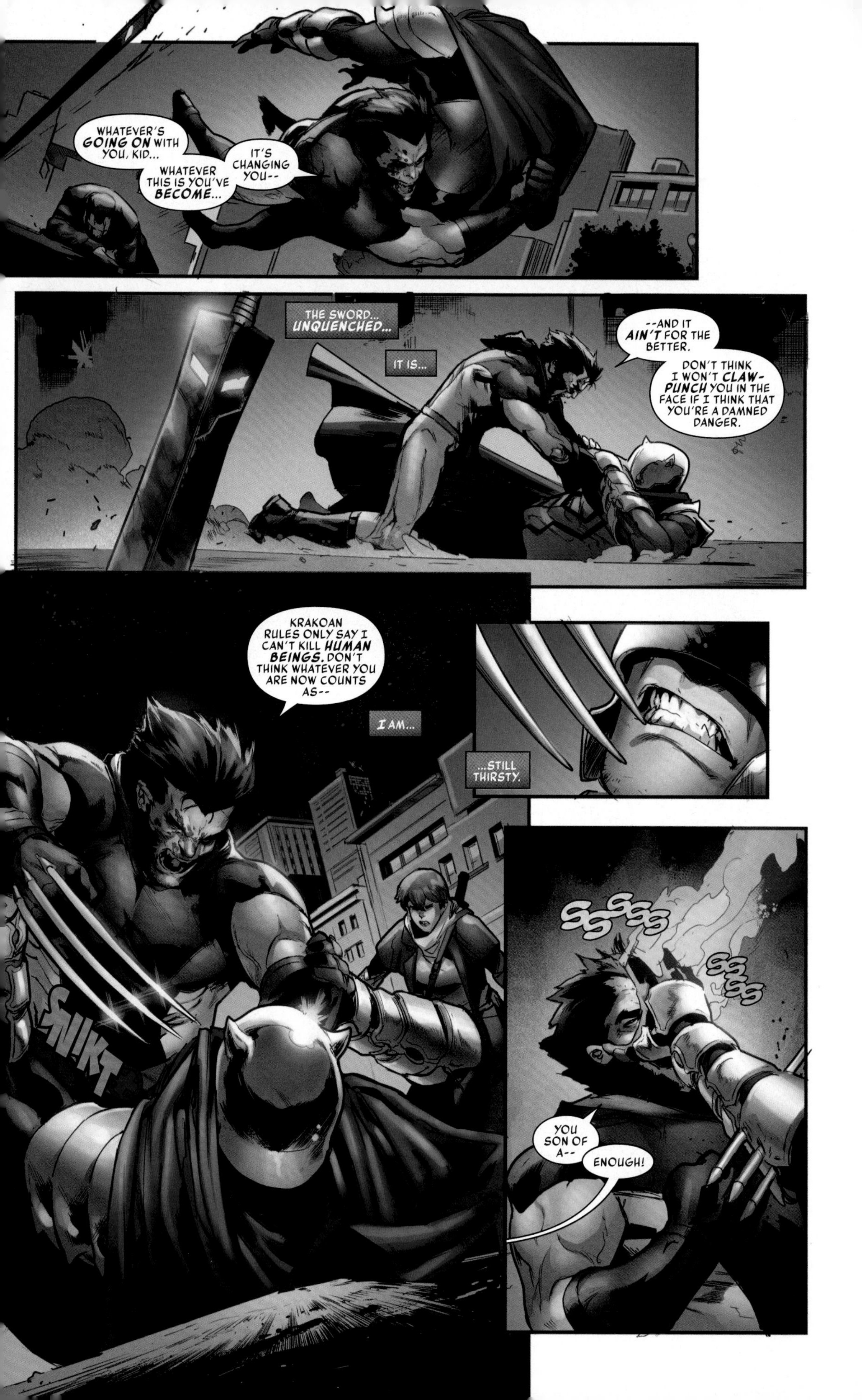

WHATEVER'S GOING ON WITH YOU, KID...
WHATEVER THIS IS YOU'VE BECOME...
IT'S CHANGING YOU--
THE SWORD... UNQUENCHED...
IT IS...
--AND IT AIN'T FOR THE BETTER.
DON'T THINK I WON'T CLAW-PUNCH YOU IN THE FACE IF I THINK THAT YOU'RE A DAMNED DANGER.
KRAKOAN RULES ONLY SAY I CAN'T KILL HUMAN BEINGS. DON'T THINK WHATEVER YOU ARE NOW COUNTS AS--
I AM...
...STILL THIRSTY.
SNIKT
SSSSS
SSSS
YOU SON OF A--
ENOUGH!

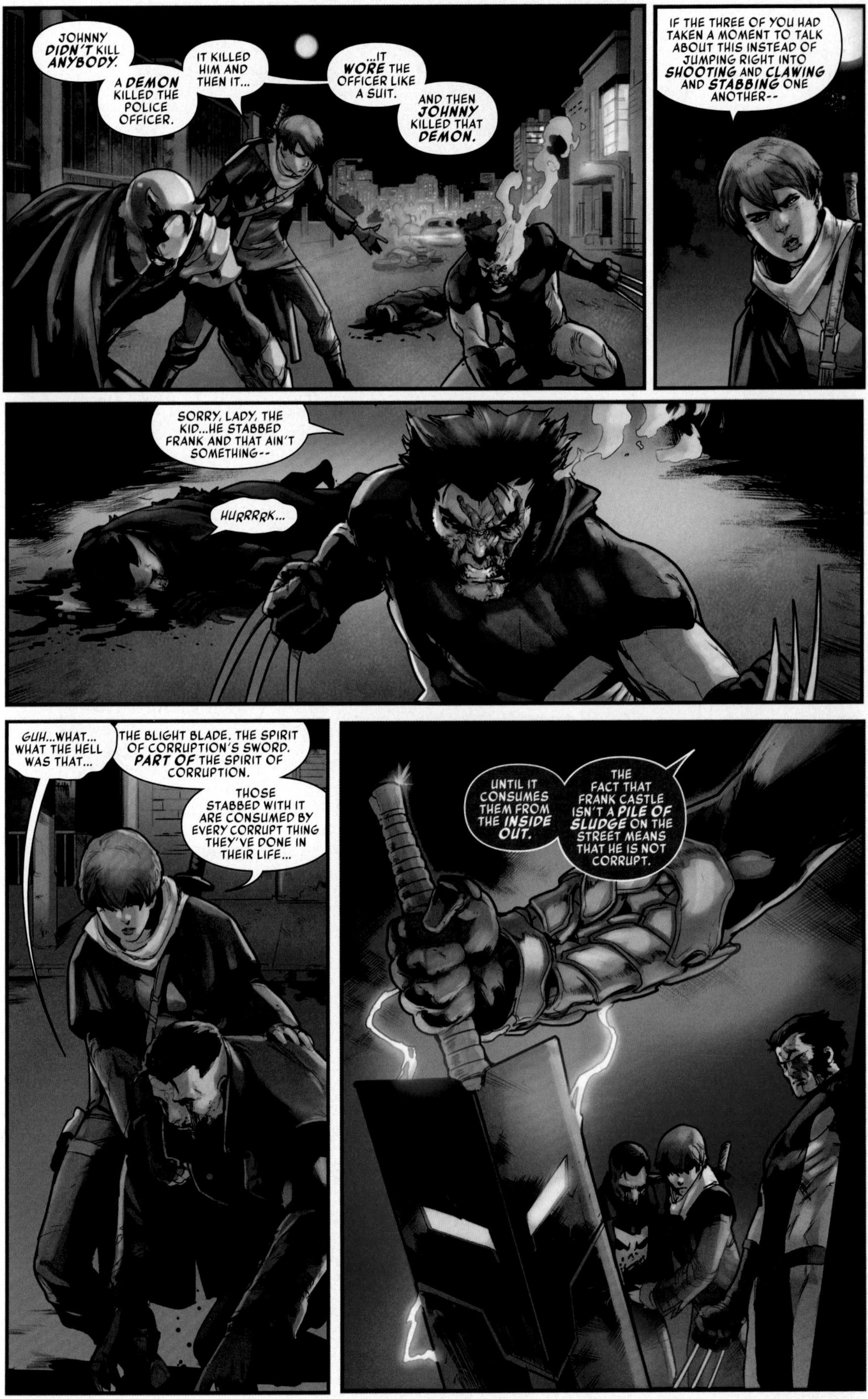
JOHNNY DIDN'T KILL ANYBODY.
A DEMON KILLED THE POLICE OFFICER.
IT KILLED HIM AND THEN IT...
...IT WORE THE OFFICER LIKE A SUIT.
AND THEN JOHNNY KILLED THAT DEMON.
IF THE THREE OF YOU HAD TAKEN A MOMENT TO TALK ABOUT THIS INSTEAD OF JUMPING RIGHT INTO SHOOTING AND CLAWING AND STABBING ONE ANOTHER--
SORRY, LADY, THE KID...HE STABBED FRANK AND THAT AIN'T SOMETHING--
HURRRRK...
GUH...WHAT... WHAT THE HELL WAS THAT...
THE BLIGHT BLADE. THE SPIRIT OF CORRUPTION'S SWORD. PART OF THE SPIRIT OF CORRUPTION.
THOSE STABBED WITH IT ARE CONSUMED BY EVERY CORRUPT THING THEY'VE DONE IN THEIR LIFE...
UNTIL IT CONSUMES THEM FROM THE INSIDE OUT.
THE FACT THAT FRANK CASTLE ISN'T A PILE OF SLUDGE ON THE STREET MEANS THAT HE IS NOT CORRUPT.

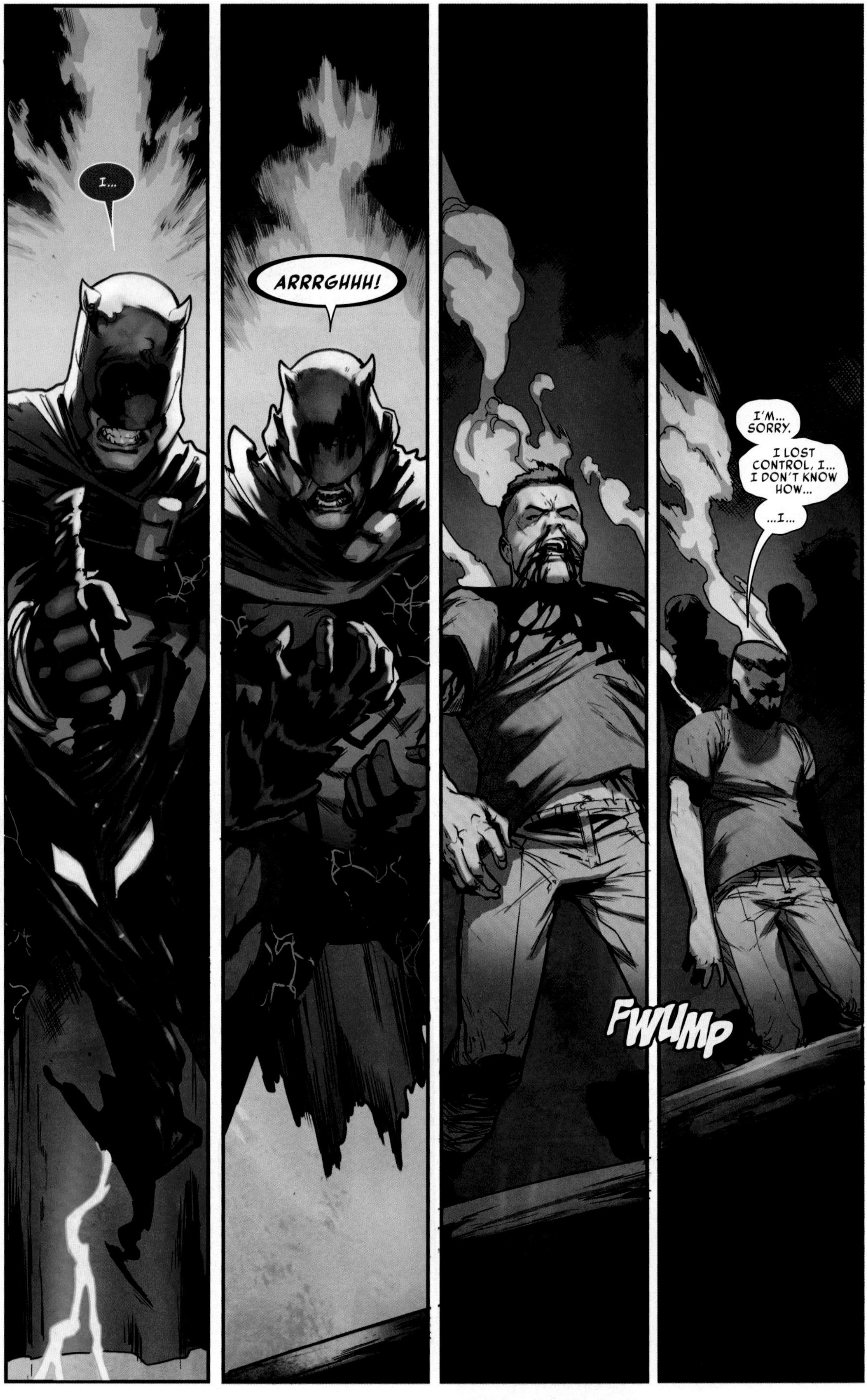
I...
ARRRGHHH!
FWUMP
I'M... SORRY.
I LOST CONTROL, I... I DON'T KNOW HOW...
...I...

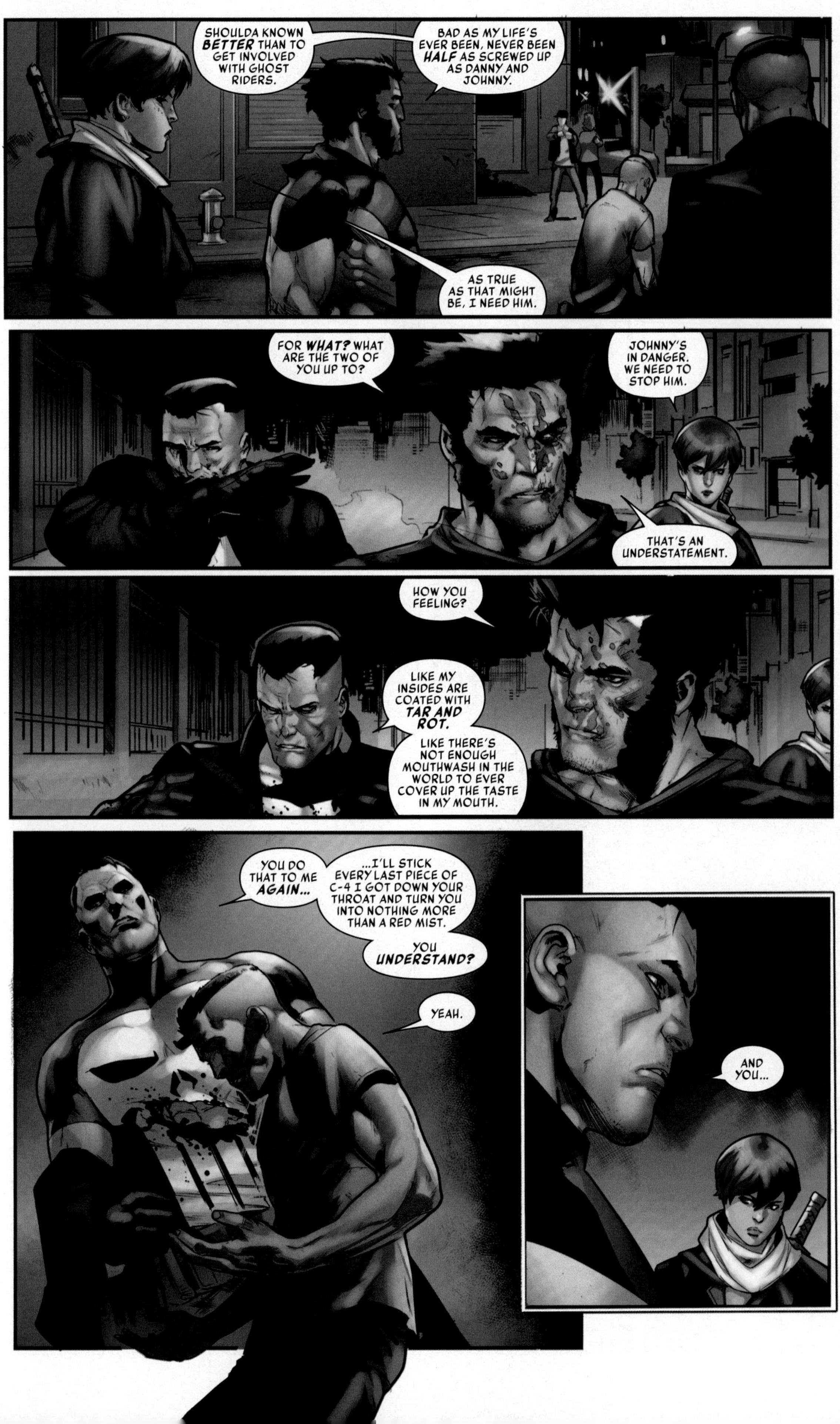
SHOULDA KNOWN BETTER THAN TO GET INVOLVED WITH GHOST RIDERS.
BAD AS MY LIFE'S EVER BEEN, NEVER BEEN HALF AS SCREWED UP AS DANNY AND JOHNNY.
AS TRUE AS THAT MIGHT BE, I NEED HIM.
FOR WHAT? WHAT ARE THE TWO OF YOU UP TO?
JOHNNY'S IN DANGER. WE NEED TO STOP HIM.
THAT'S AN UNDERSTATEMENT.
HOW YOU FEELING?
LIKE MY INSIDES ARE COATED WITH TAR AND ROT.
LIKE THERE'S NOT ENOUGH MOUTHWASH IN THE WORLD TO EVER COVER UP THE TASTE IN MY MOUTH.
YOU DO THAT TO ME AGAIN...
...I'LL STICK EVERY LAST PIECE OF C-4 I GOT DOWN YOUR THROAT AND TURN YOU INTO NOTHING MORE THAN A RED MIST.
YOU UNDERSTAND?
YEAH.
AND YOU...

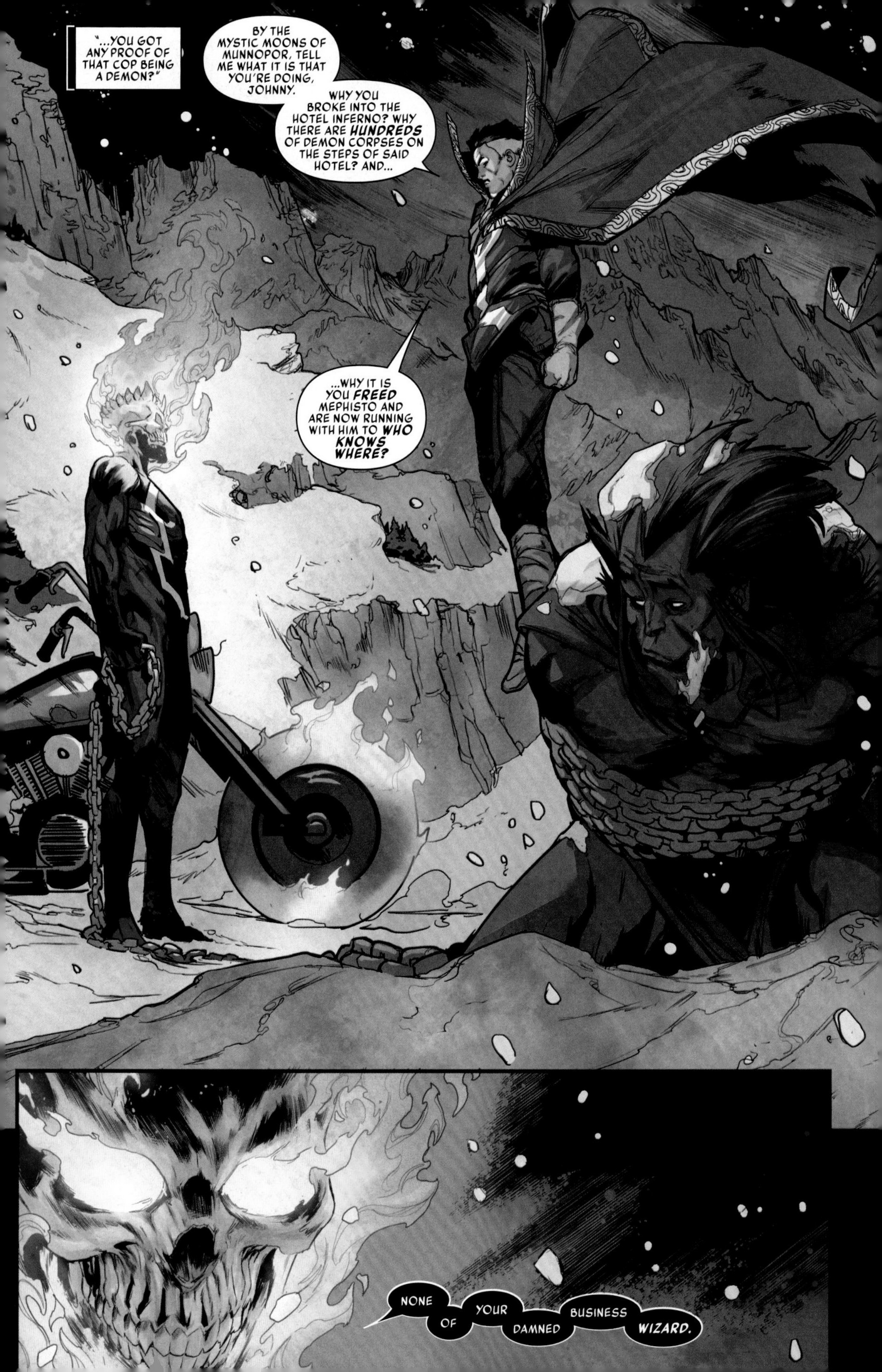
"...YOU GOT ANY PROOF OF THAT COP BEING A DEMON?"
BY THE MYSTIC MOONS OF MUNNOPOR, TELL ME WHAT IT IS THAT YOU'RE DOING, JOHNNY.
WHY YOU BROKE INTO THE HOTEL INFERNO? WHY THERE ARE HUNDREDS OF DEMON CORPSES ON THE STEPS OF SAID HOTEL? AND...
...WHY IT IS YOU FREED MEPHISTO AND ARE NOW RUNNING WITH HIM TO WHO KNOWS WHERE?
NONE OF YOUR DAMNED BUSINESS WIZARD.

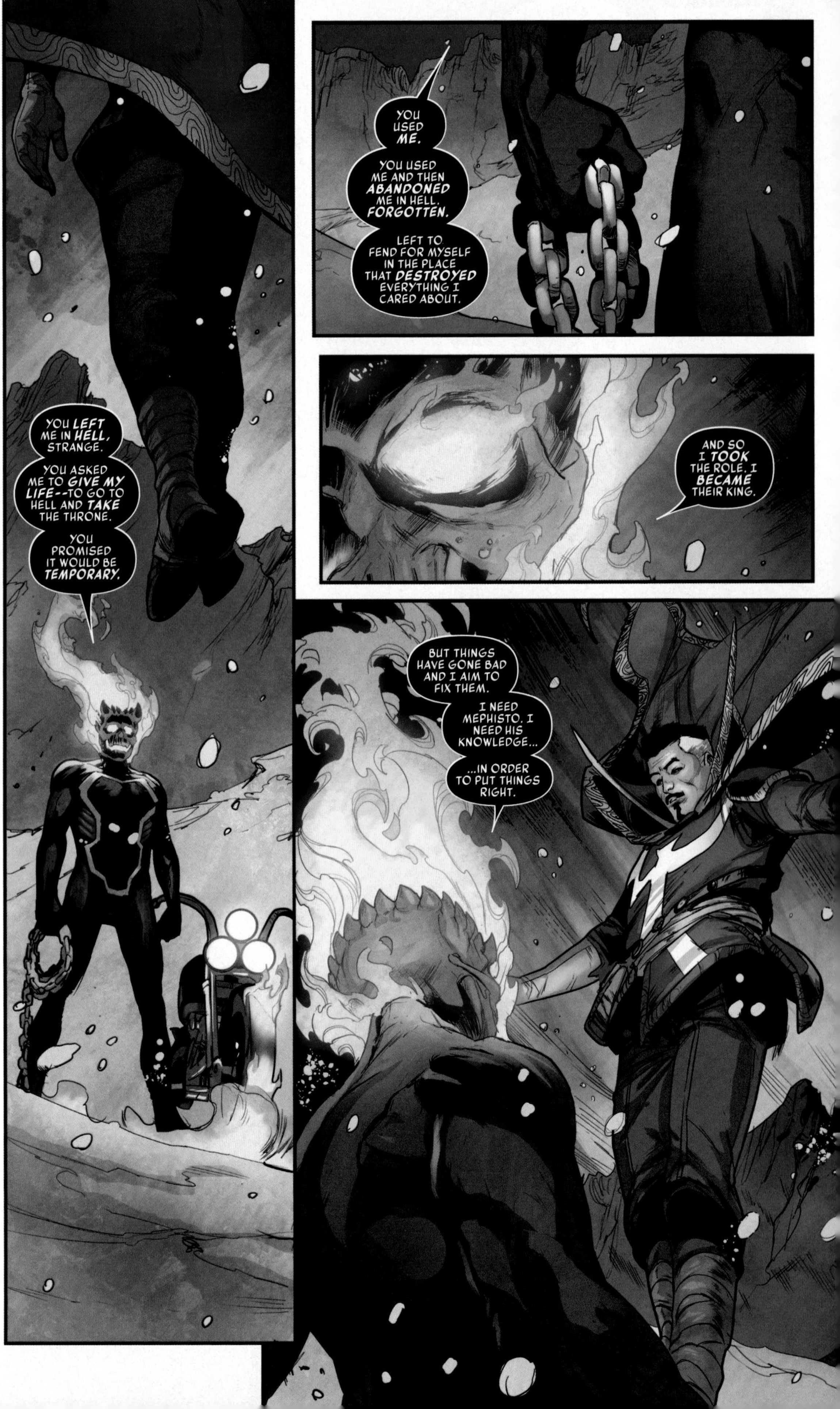
YOU LEFT ME IN HELL, STRANGE.
YOU ASKED ME TO GIVE MY LIFE--TO GO TO HELL AND TAKE THE THRONE.
YOU PROMISED IT WOULD BE TEMPORARY.
YOU USED ME.
YOU USED ME AND THEN ABANDONED ME IN HELL. FORGOTTEN.
LEFT TO FEND FOR MYSELF IN THE PLACE THAT DESTROYED EVERYTHING I CARED ABOUT.
AND SO I TOOK THE ROLE. I BECAME THEIR KING.
BUT THINGS HAVE GONE BAD AND I AIM TO FIX THEM.
I NEED MEPHISTO. I NEED HIS KNOWLEDGE...
...IN ORDER TO PUT THINGS RIGHT.

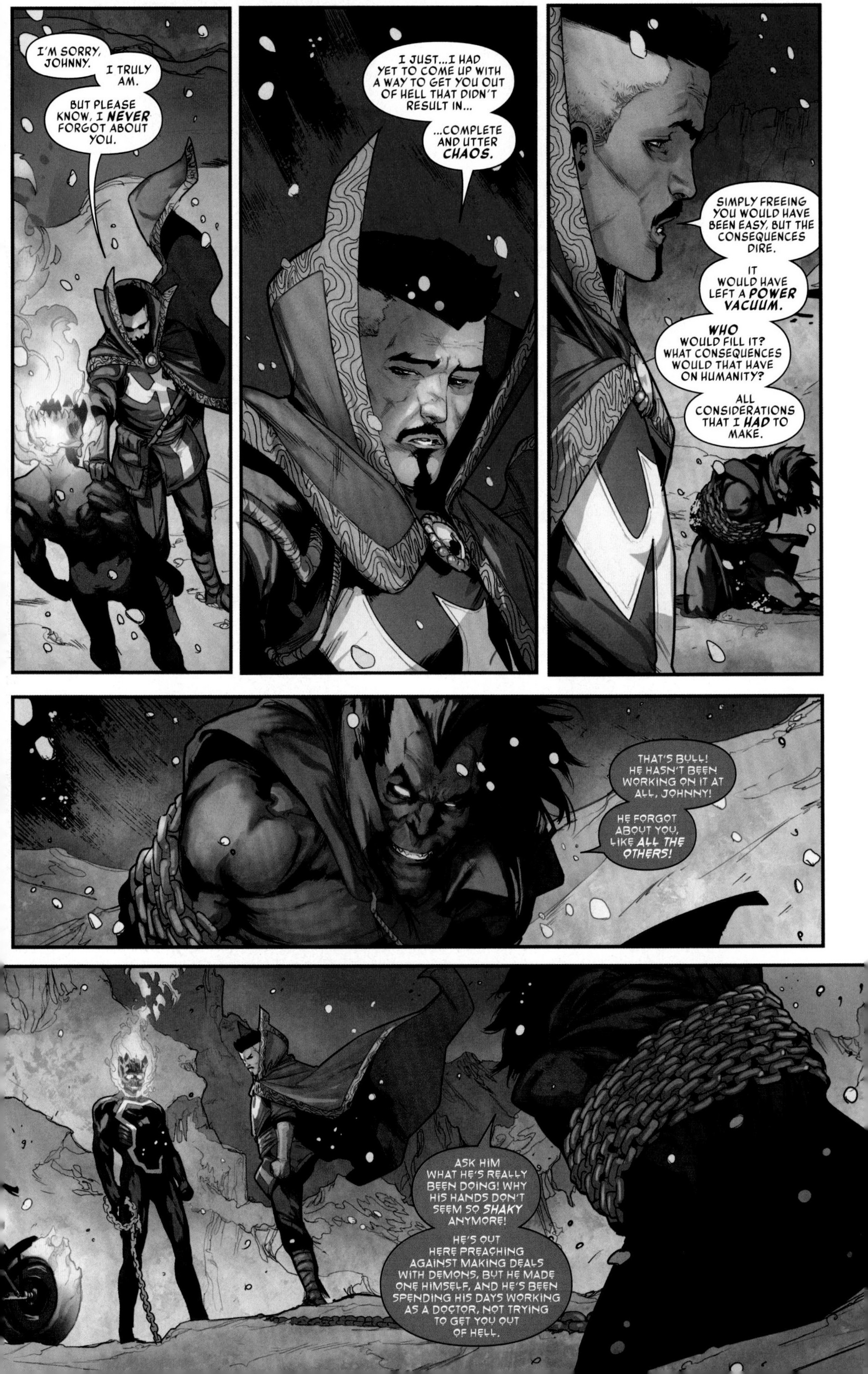

I'M SORRY, JOHNNY.
I TRULY AM.
BUT PLEASE KNOW, I NEVER FORGOT ABOUT YOU.
I JUST...I HAD YET TO COME UP WITH A WAY TO GET YOU OUT OF HELL THAT DIDN'T RESULT IN...
...COMPLETE AND UTTER CHAOS.
SIMPLY FREEING YOU WOULD HAVE BEEN EASY, BUT THE CONSEQUENCES DIRE.
IT WOULD HAVE LEFT A POWER VACUUM.
WHO WOULD FILL IT? WHAT CONSEQUENCES WOULD THAT HAVE ON HUMANITY?
ALL CONSIDERATIONS THAT I HAD TO MAKE.
THAT'S BULL! HE HASN'T BEEN WORKING ON IT AT ALL, JOHNNY!
HE FORGOT ABOUT YOU, LIKE ALL THE OTHERS!
ASK HIM WHAT HE'S REALLY BEEN DOING! WHY HIS HANDS DON'T SEEM SO SHAKY ANYMORE!
HE'S OUT HERE PREACHING AGAINST MAKING DEALS WITH DEMONS, BUT HE MADE ONE HIMSELF, AND HE'S BEEN SPENDING HIS DAYS WORKING AS A DOCTOR, NOT TRYING TO GET YOU OUT OF HELL.

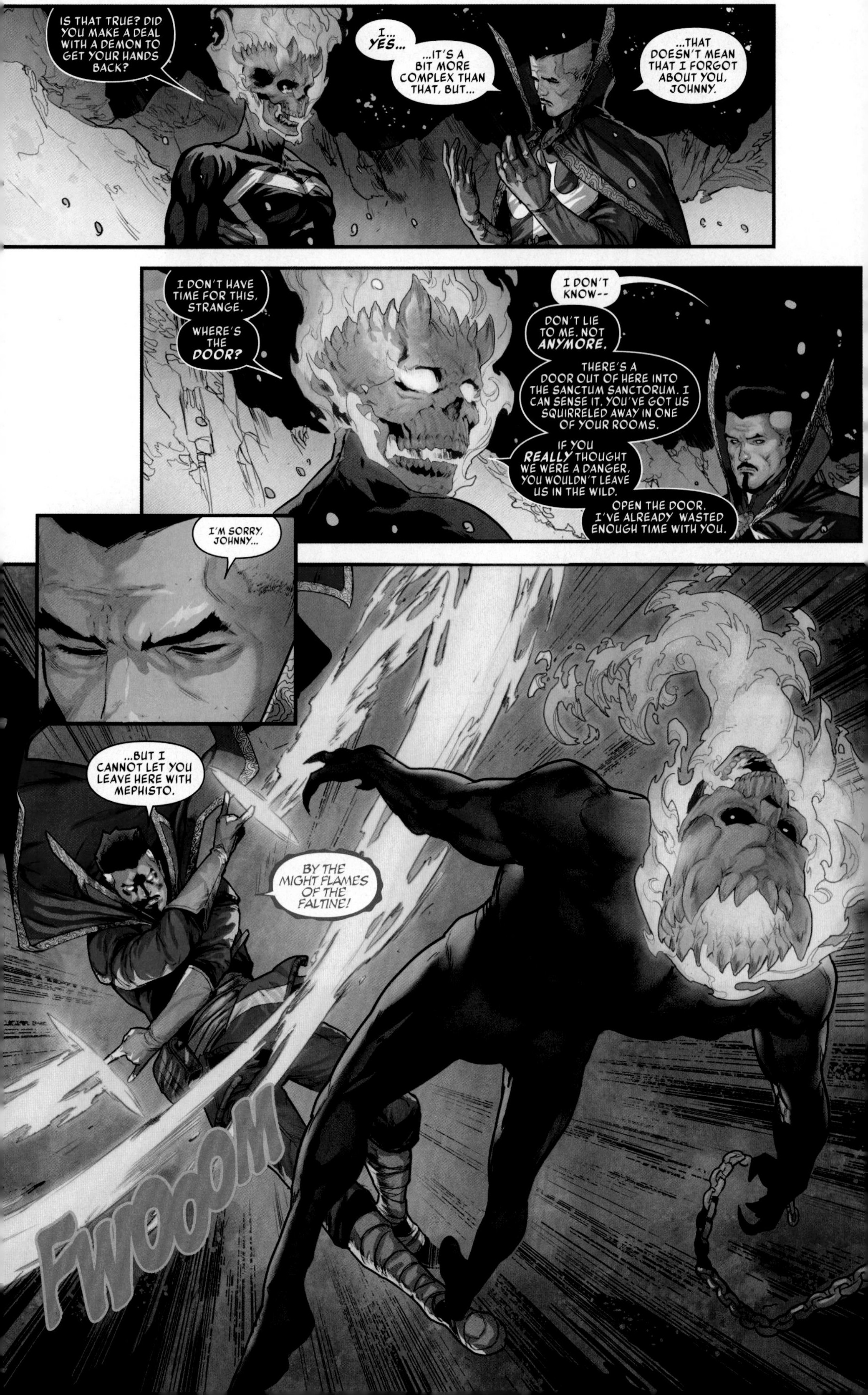
IS THAT TRUE? DID YOU MAKE A DEAL WITH A DEMON TO GET YOUR HANDS BACK?
I... YES...
...IT'S A BIT MORE COMPLEX THAN THAT, BUT...
...THAT DOESN'T MEAN THAT I FORGOT ABOUT YOU, JOHNNY.
I DON'T HAVE TIME FOR THIS, STRANGE.
WHERE'S THE DOOR?
I DON'T KNOW--
DON'T LIE TO ME. NOT ANYMORE.
THERE'S A DOOR OUT OF HERE INTO THE SANCTUM SANCTORUM. I CAN SENSE IT. YOU'VE GOT US SQUIRRELED AWAY IN ONE OF YOUR ROOMS.
IF YOU REALLY THOUGHT WE WERE A DANGER, YOU WOULDN'T LEAVE US IN THE WILD.
OPEN THE DOOR. I'VE ALREADY WASTED ENOUGH TIME WITH YOU.
I'M SORRY, JOHNNY...
...BUT I CANNOT LET YOU LEAVE HERE WITH MEPHISTO.
BY THE MIGHT FLAMES OF THE FALTINE!
FWOOOM

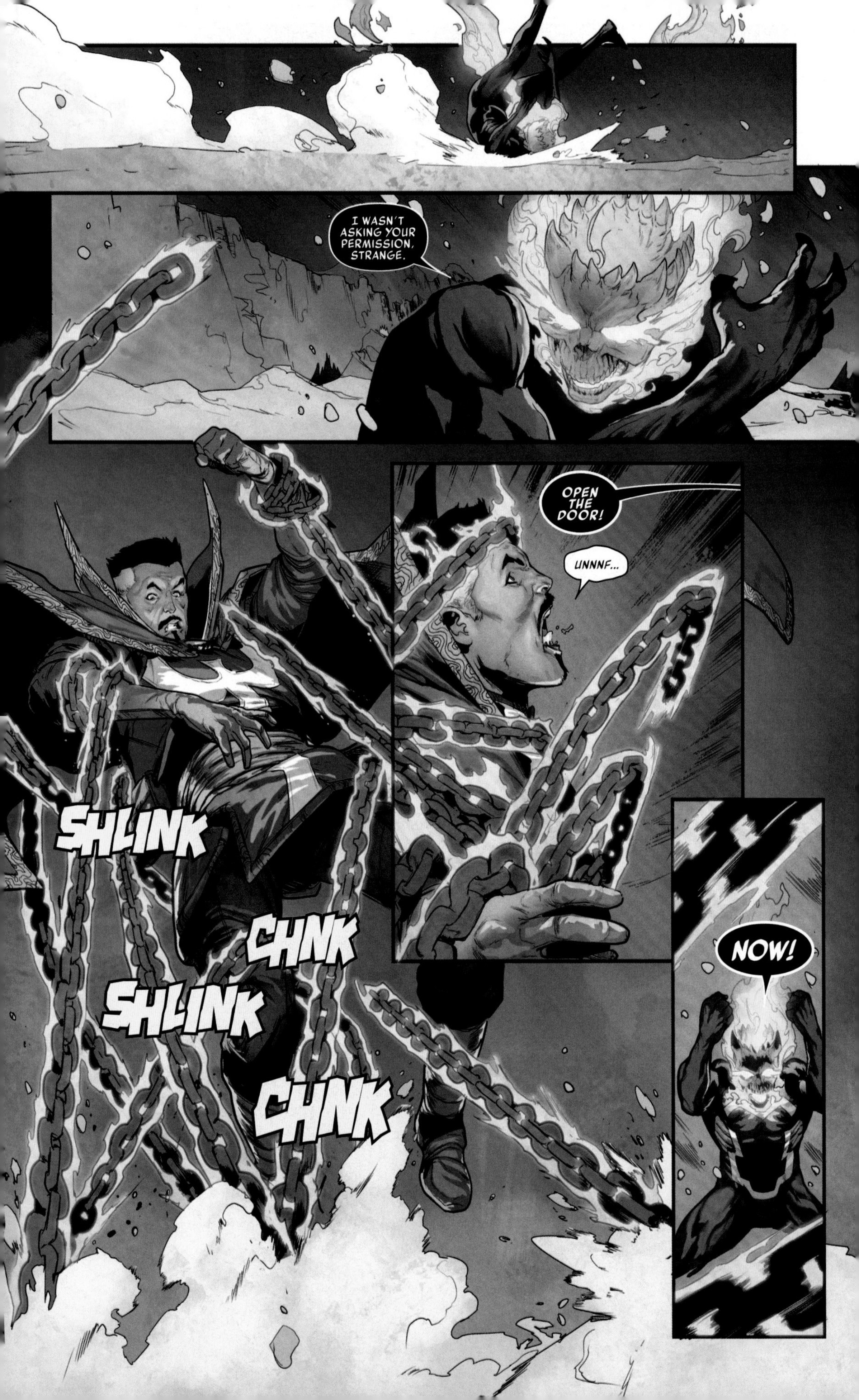
I WASN'T ASKING YOUR PERMISSION, STRANGE.
OPEN THE DOOR!
UNNNF...
SHLINK
CHNK
SHLINK
CHNK
NOW!

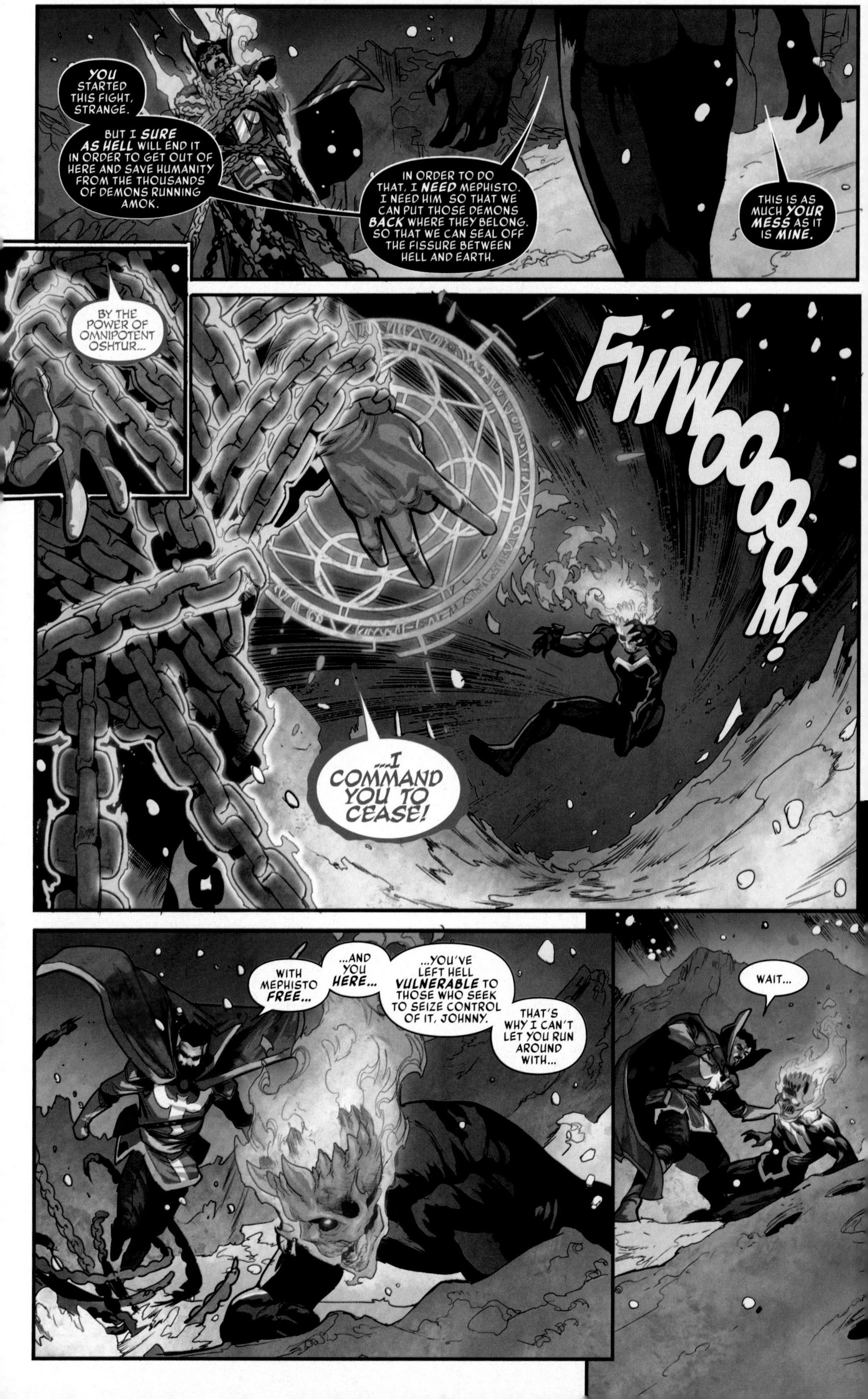

YOU STARTED THIS FIGHT, STRANGE.
BUT I SURE AS HELL WILL END IT IN ORDER TO GET OUT OF HERE AND SAVE HUMANITY FROM THE THOUSANDS OF DEMONS RUNNING AMOK.
IN ORDER TO DO THAT, I NEED MEPHISTO. I NEED HIM SO THAT WE CAN PUT THOSE DEMONS BACK WHERE THEY BELONG. SO THAT WE CAN SEAL OFF THE FISSURE BETWEEN HELL AND EARTH.
THIS IS AS MUCH YOUR MESS AS IT IS MINE.
BY THE POWER OF OMNIPOTENT OSHTUR...
FWWOOOOOM!
...I COMMAND YOU TO CEASE!
WITH MEPHISTO FREE...
...AND YOU HERE...
...YOU'VE LEFT HELL VULNERABLE TO THOSE WHO SEEK TO SEIZE CONTROL OF IT, JOHNNY.
THAT'S WHY I CAN'T LET YOU RUN AROUND WITH...
WAIT...

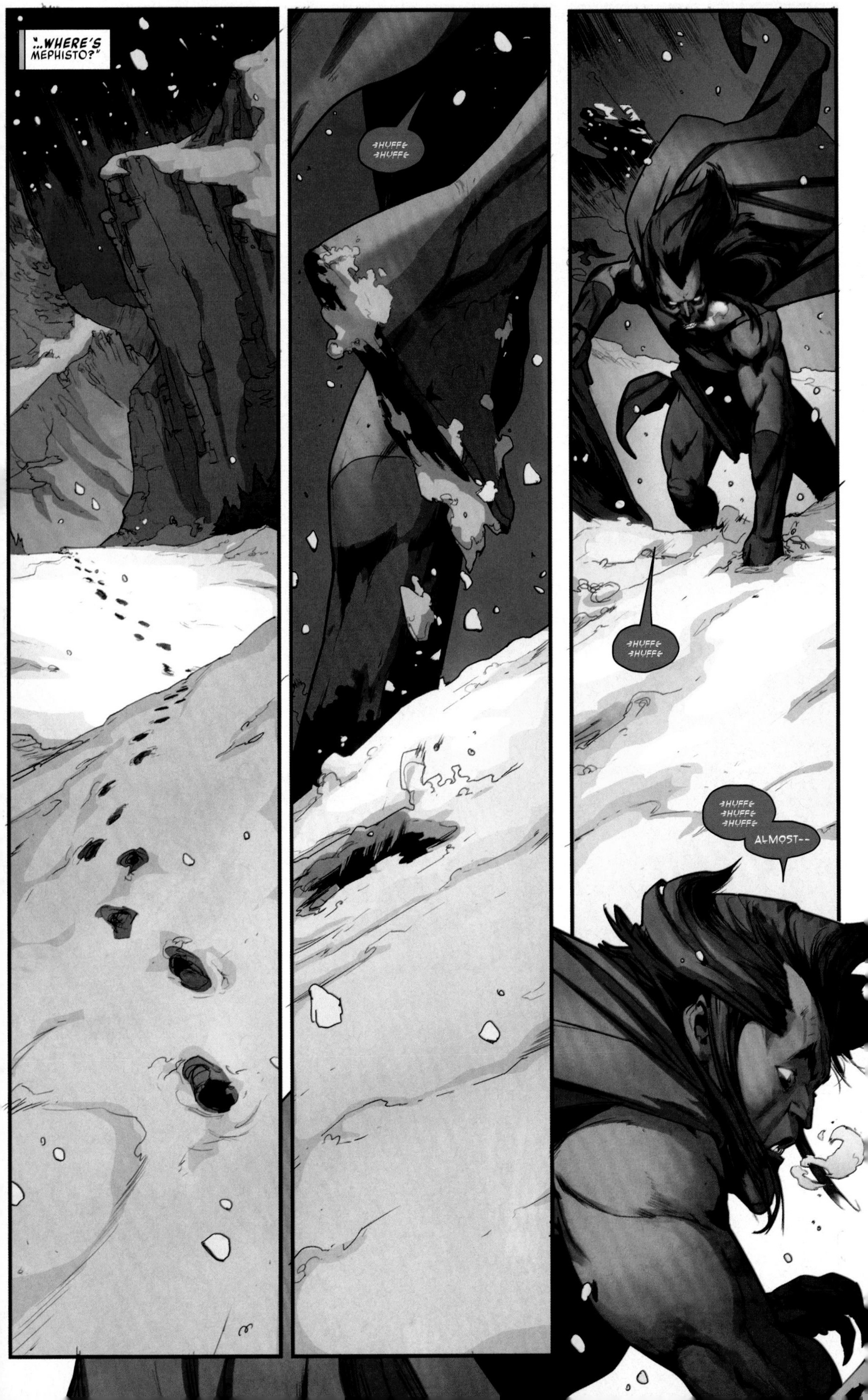
"...WHERE'S MEPHISTO?"
HUFF HUFF
HUFF HUFF
HUFF HUFF HUFF
ALMOST--

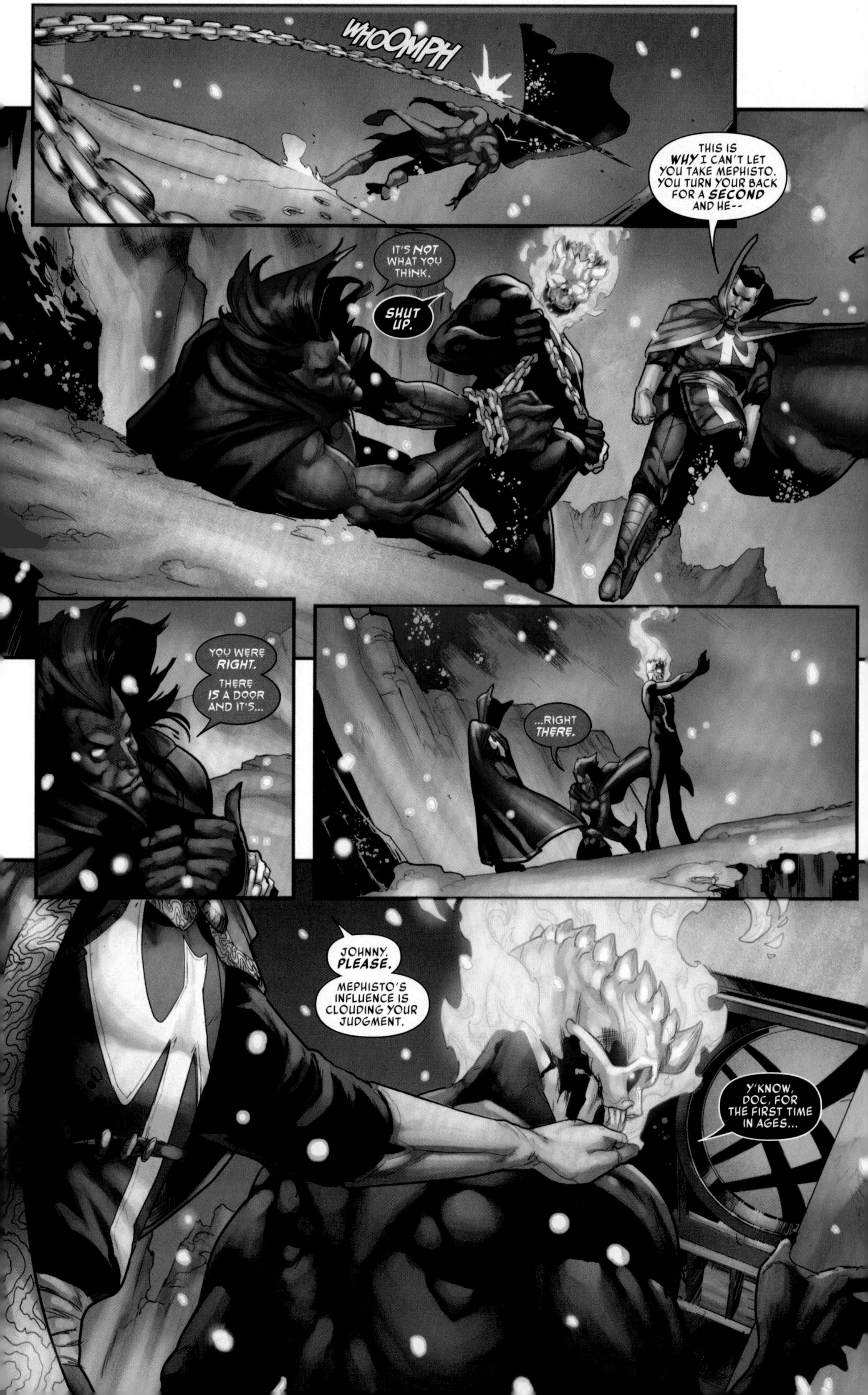
WHOOMPH
THIS IS WHY I CAN'T LET YOU TAKE MEPHISTO. YOU TURN YOUR BACK FOR A SECOND AND HE--
IT'S NOT WHAT YOU THINK.
SHUT UP.
YOU WERE RIGHT.
THERE IS A DOOR AND IT'S...
...RIGHT THERE.
JOHNNY. PLEASE.
MEPHISTO'S INFLUENCE IS CLOUDING YOUR JUDGMENT.
Y'KNOW, DOC, FOR THE FIRST TIME IN AGES...

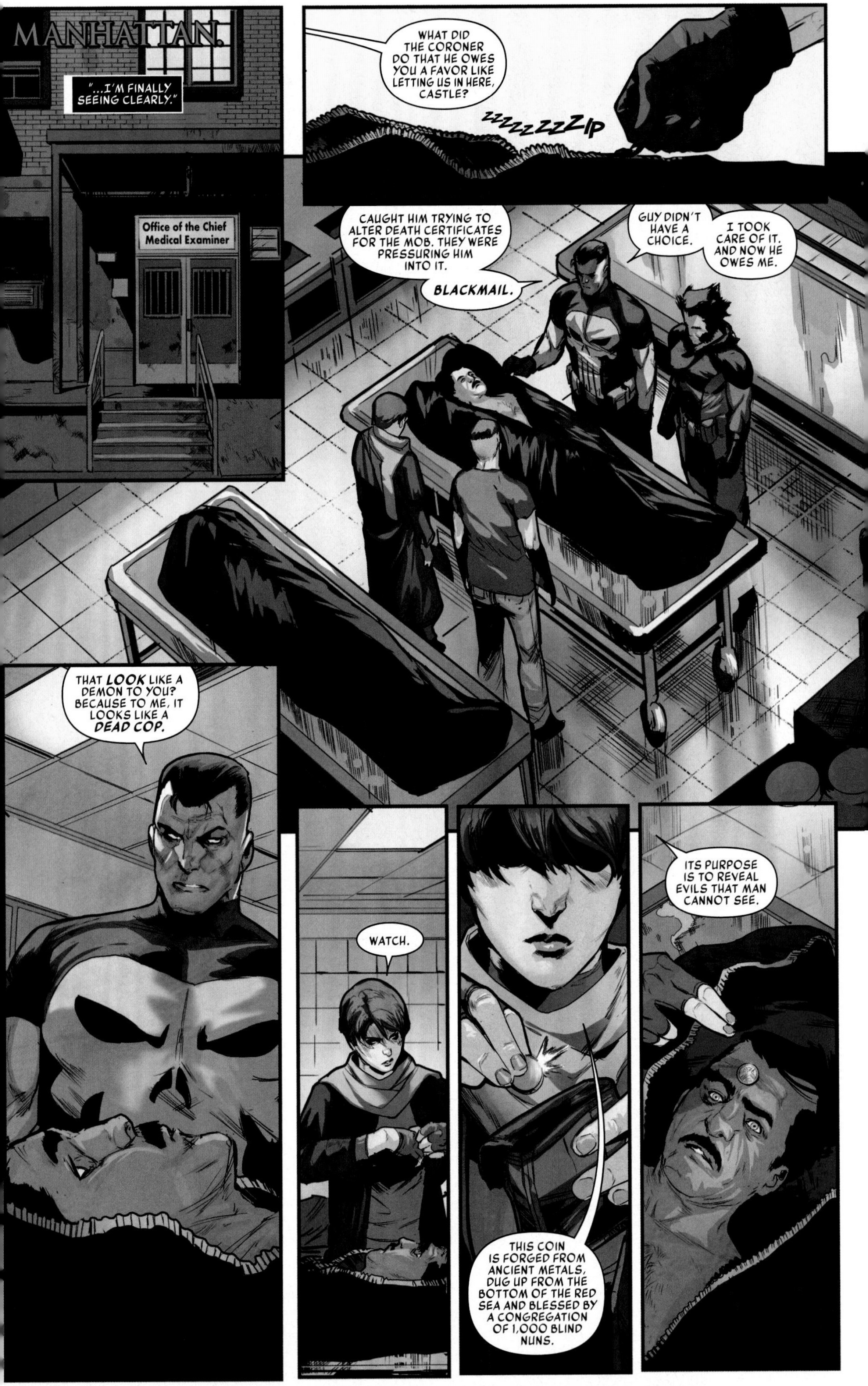
MANHATTAN.
"...I'M FINALLY SEEING CLEARLY."
Office of the Chief Medical Examiner
WHAT DID THE CORONER DO THAT HE OWES YOU A FAVOR LIKE LETTING US IN HERE, CASTLE?
ZZZZZZZZZIP
CAUGHT HIM TRYING TO ALTER DEATH CERTIFICATES FOR THE MOB. THEY WERE PRESSURING HIM INTO IT.
BLACKMAIL.
GUY DIDN'T HAVE A CHOICE.
I TOOK CARE OF IT. AND NOW HE OWES ME.
THAT LOOK LIKE A DEMON TO YOU? BECAUSE TO ME, IT LOOKS LIKE A DEAD COP.
WATCH.
THIS COIN IS FORGED FROM ANCIENT METALS, DUG UP FROM THE BOTTOM OF THE RED SEA AND BLESSED BY A CONGREGATION OF 1,000 BLIND NUNS.
ITS PURPOSE IS TO REVEAL EVILS THAT MAN CANNOT SEE.

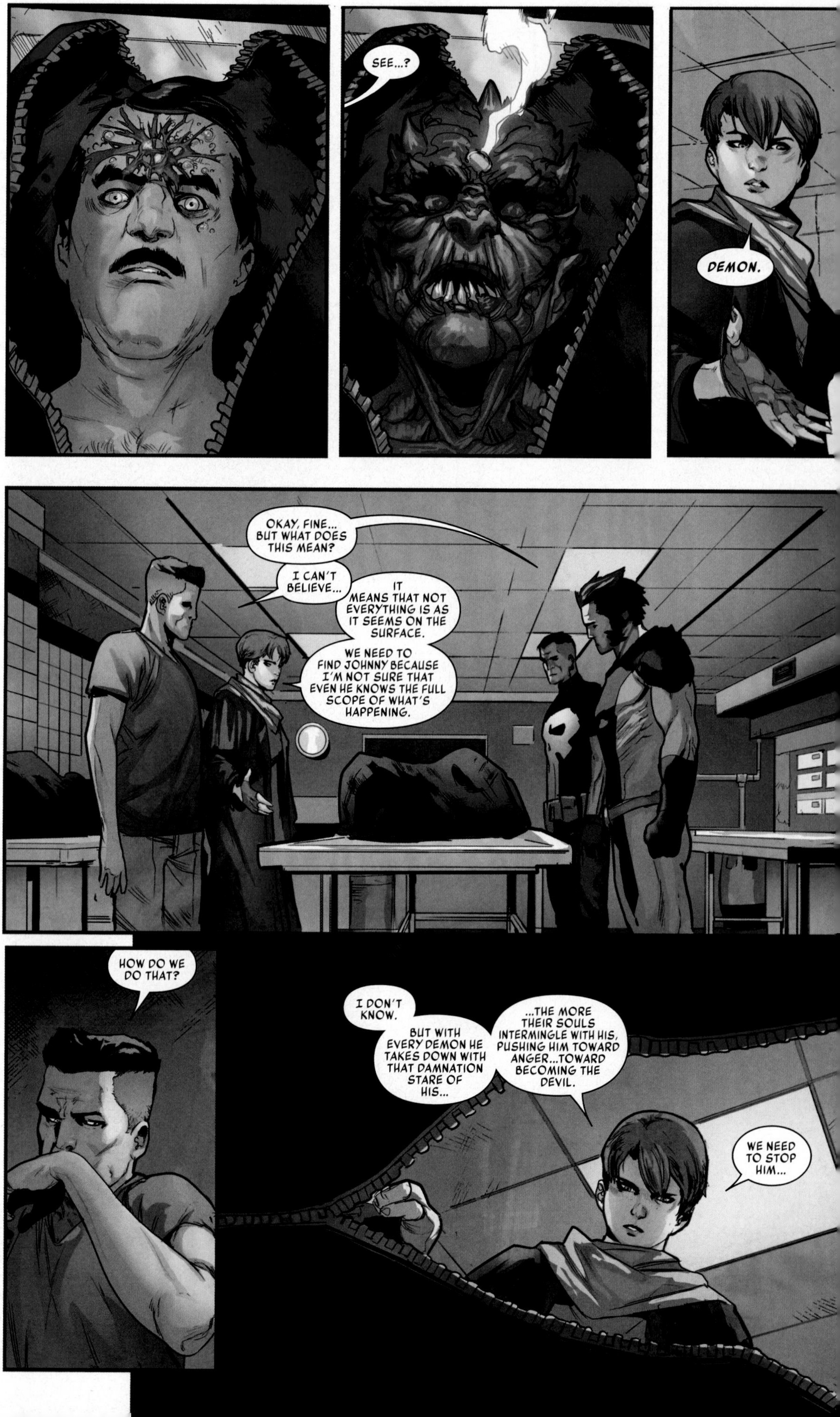
SEE...?
DEMON.
OKAY, FINE... BUT WHAT DOES THIS MEAN?
I CAN'T BELIEVE...
IT MEANS THAT NOT EVERYTHING IS AS IT SEEMS ON THE SURFACE.
WE NEED TO FIND JOHNNY BECAUSE I'M NOT SURE THAT EVEN HE KNOWS THE FULL SCOPE OF WHAT'S HAPPENING.
HOW DO WE DO THAT?
I DON'T KNOW.
BUT WITH EVERY DEMON HE TAKES DOWN WITH THAT DAMNATION STARE OF HIS...
...THE MORE THEIR SOULS INTERMINGLE WITH HIS, PUSHING HIM TOWARD ANGER...TOWARD BECOMING THE DEVIL.
WE NEED TO STOP HIM...

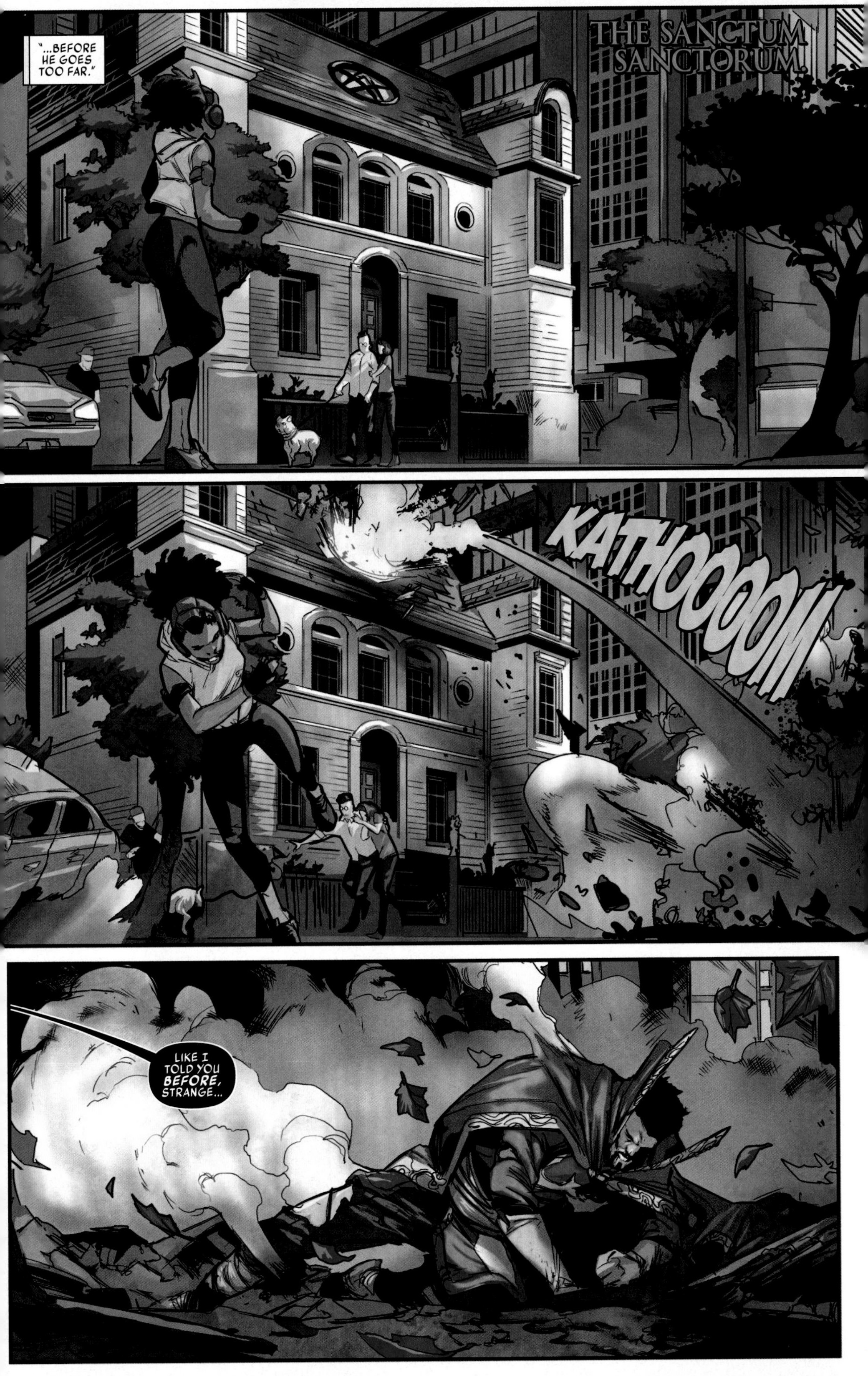
"...BEFORE HE GOES TOO FAR."
THE SANCTUM SANCTORUM.
KATHOOOOM
LIKE I TOLD YOU BEFORE, STRANGE...

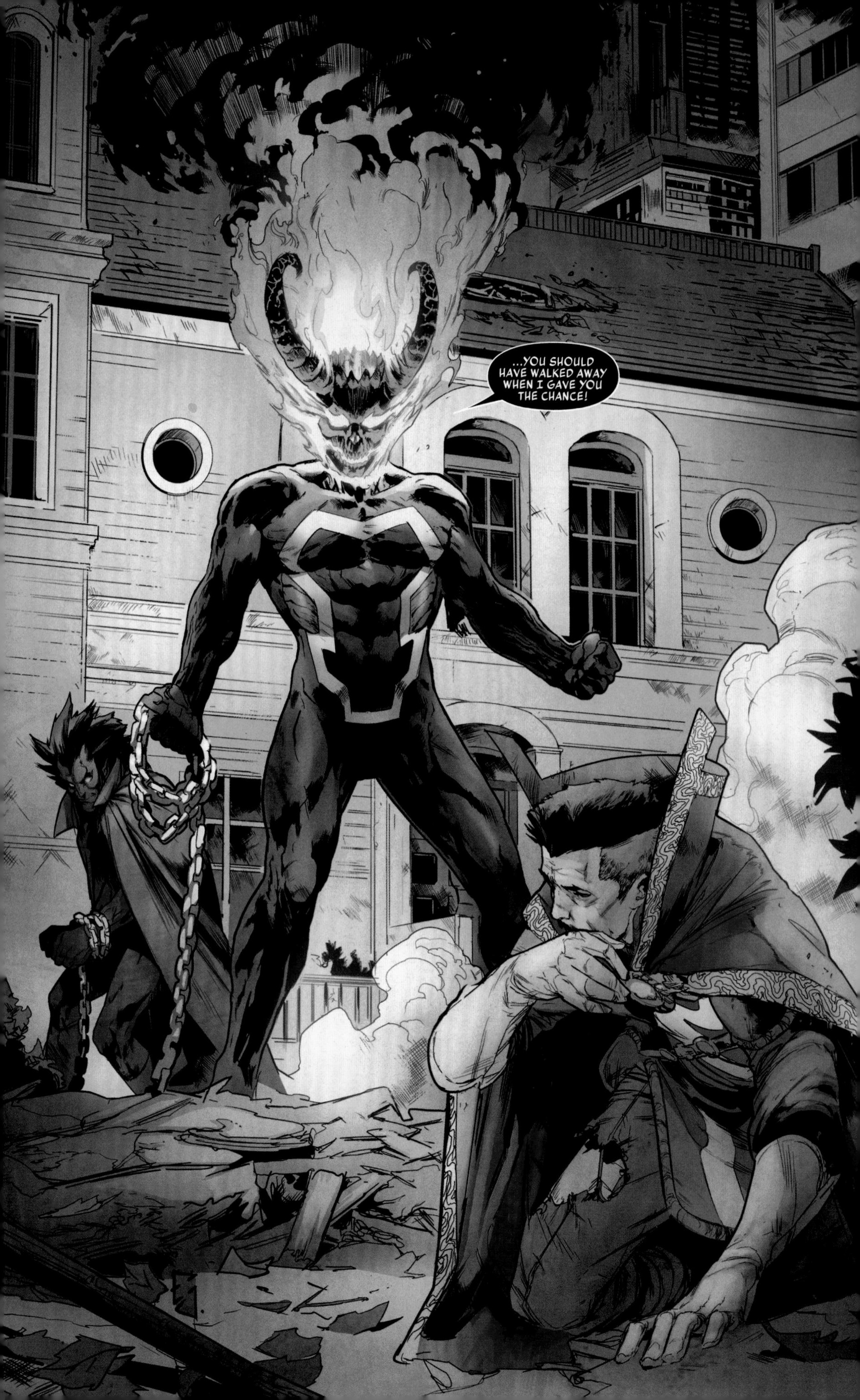
...YOU SHOULD HAVE WALKED AWAY WHEN I GAVE YOU THE CHANCE!

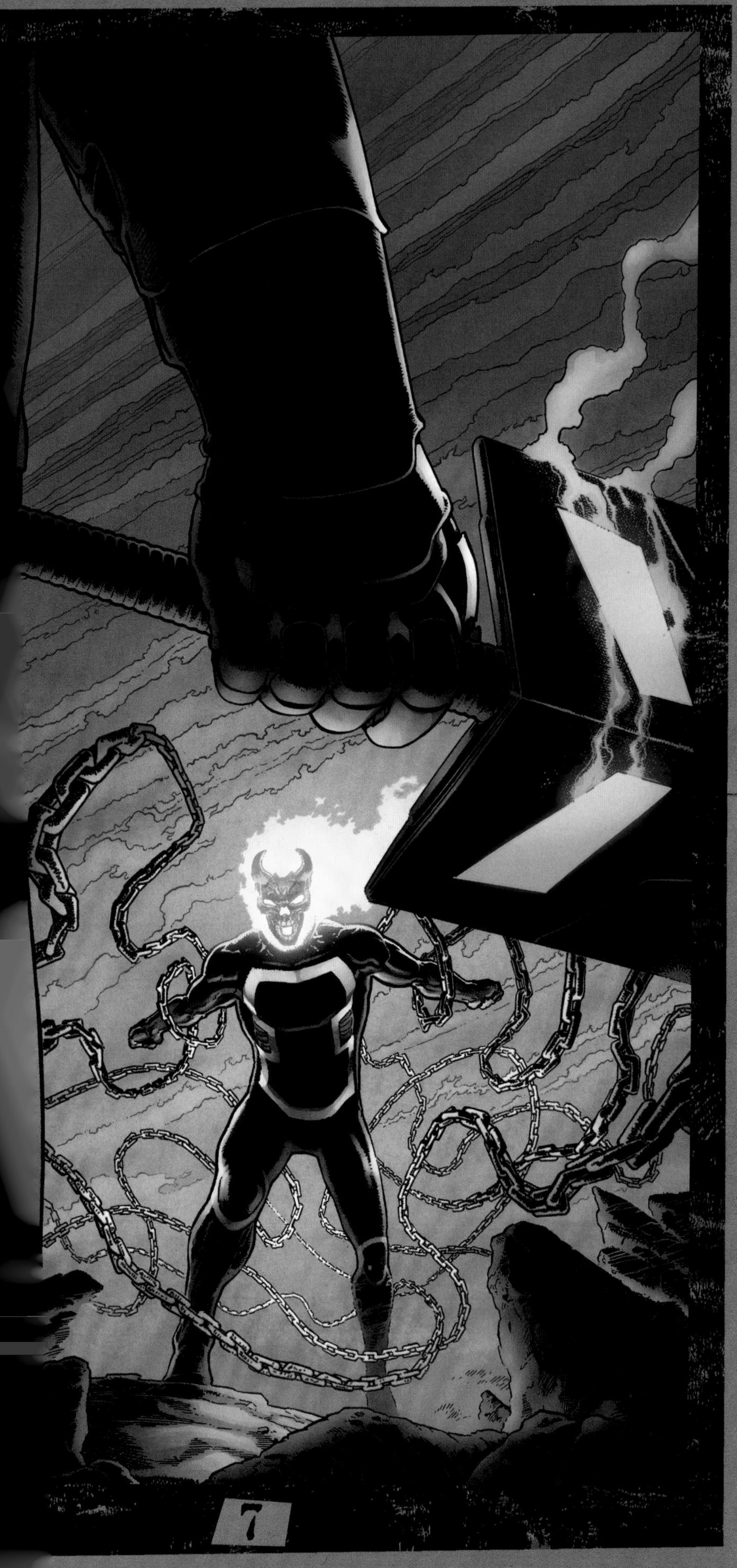
7

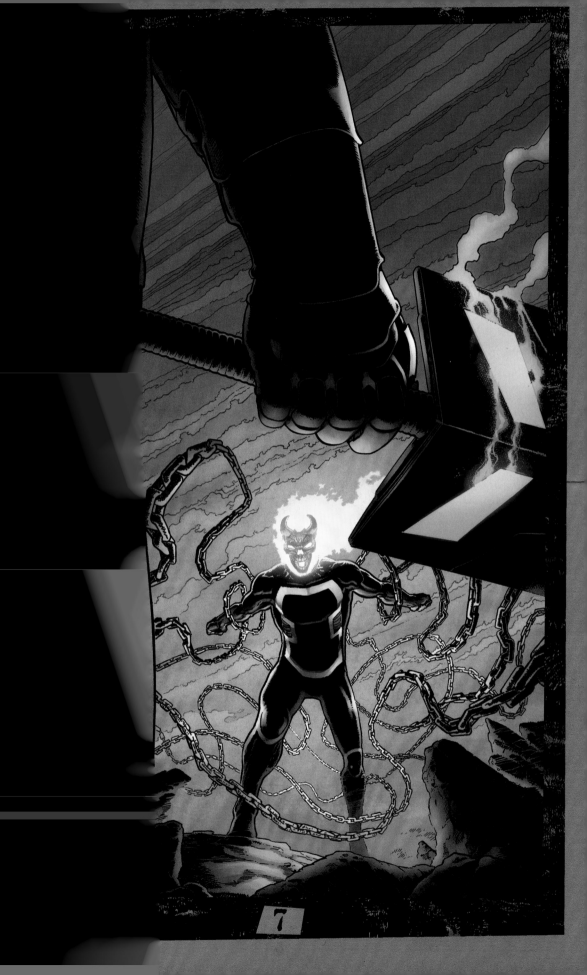

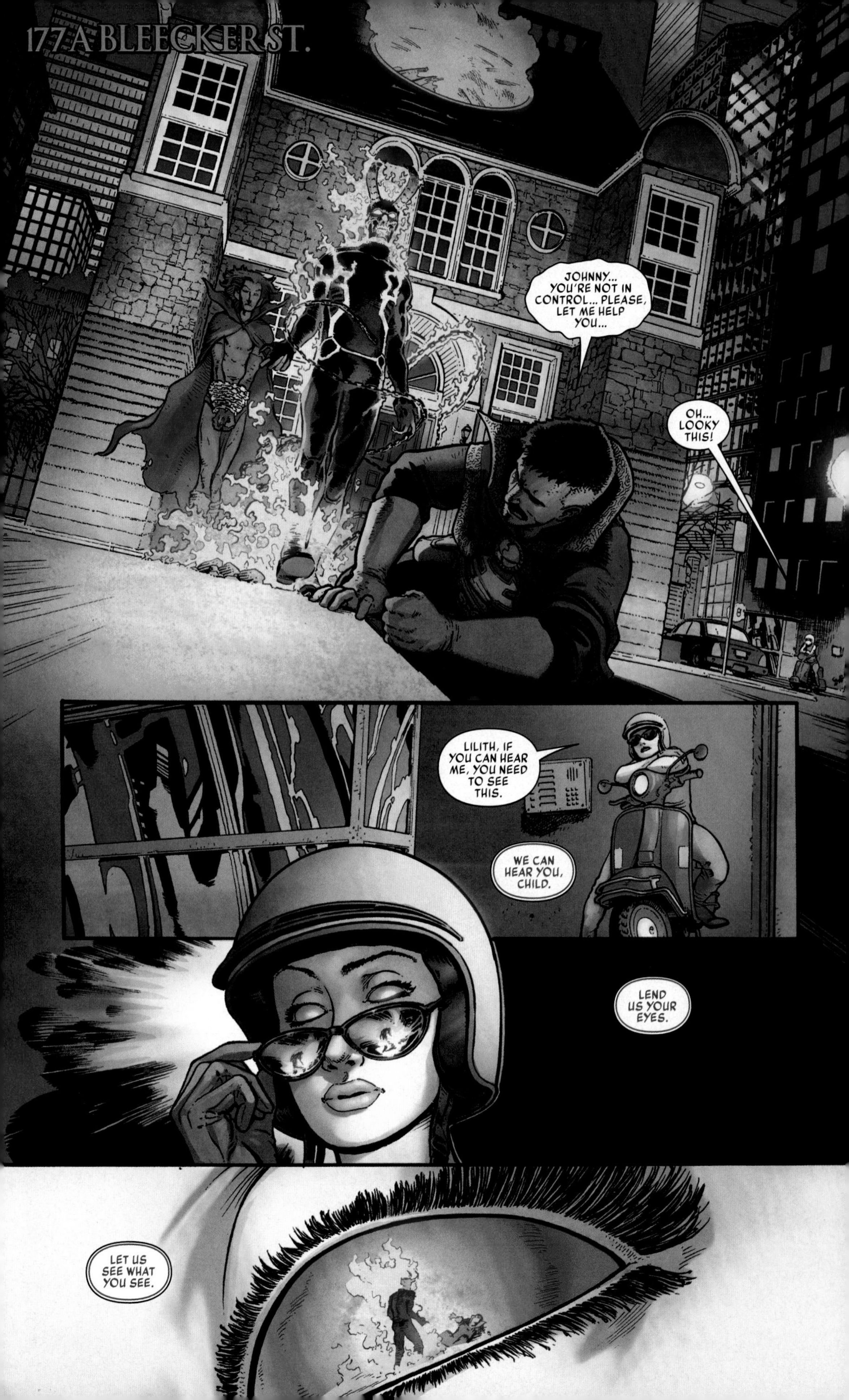
177 A BLEECKER ST.
JOHNNY... YOU'RE NOT IN CONTROL... PLEASE, LET ME HELP YOU...
OH... LOOKY THIS!
LILITH, IF YOU CAN HEAR ME, YOU NEED TO SEE THIS.
WE CAN HEAR YOU, CHILD.
LEND US YOUR EYES.
LET US SEE WHAT YOU SEE.

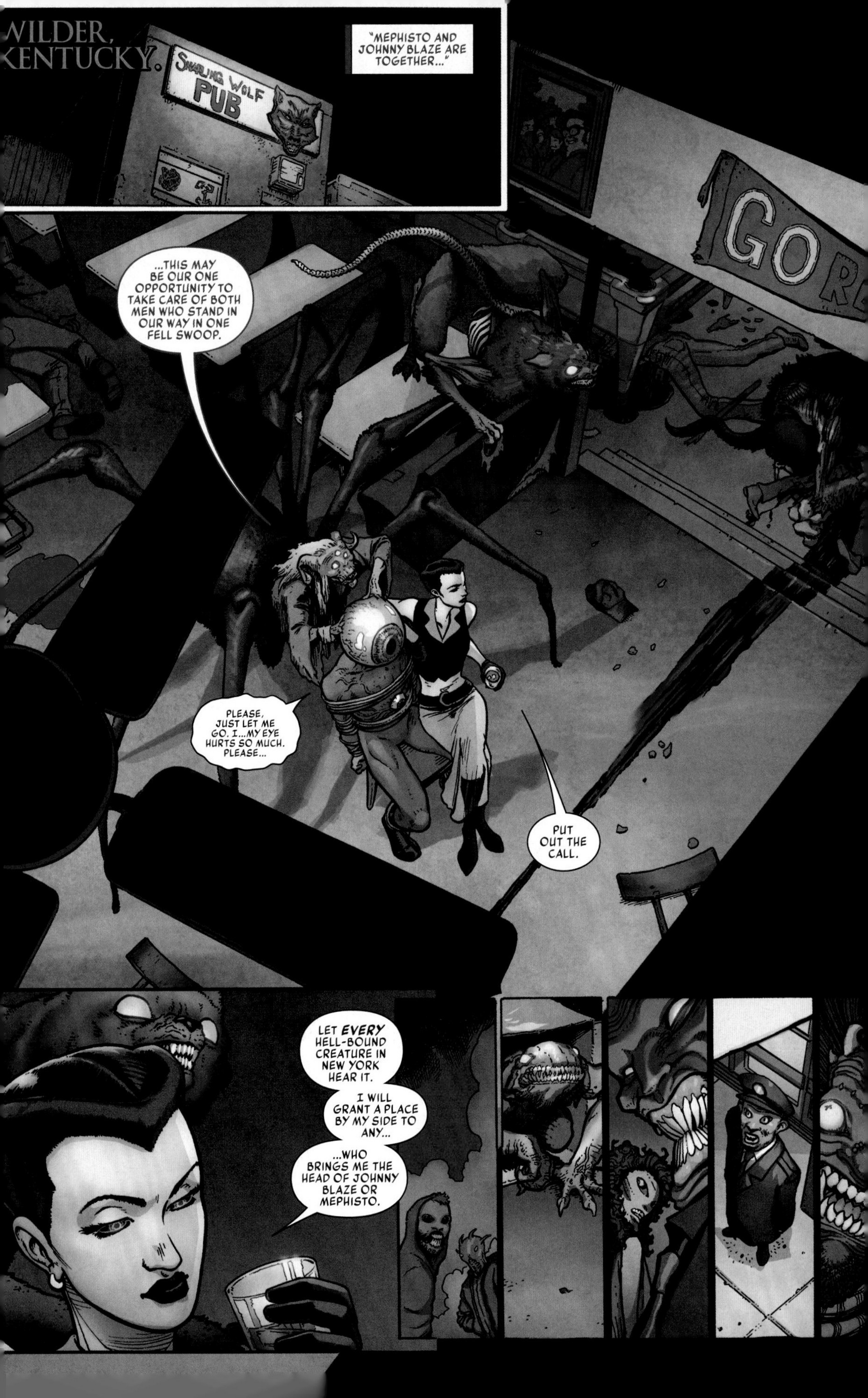
WILDER, KENTUCKY.
SNARLING WOLF PUB
"MEPHISTO AND JOHNNY BLAZE ARE TOGETHER..."
GO
...THIS MAY BE OUR ONE OPPORTUNITY TO TAKE CARE OF BOTH MEN WHO STAND IN OUR WAY IN ONE FELL SWOOP.
PLEASE, JUST LET ME GO. I...MY EYE HURTS SO MUCH. PLEASE...
PUT OUT THE CALL.
LET EVERY HELL-BOUND CREATURE IN NEW YORK HEAR IT.
I WILL GRANT A PLACE BY MY SIDE TO ANY...
...WHO BRINGS ME THE HEAD OF JOHNNY BLAZE OR MEPHISTO.

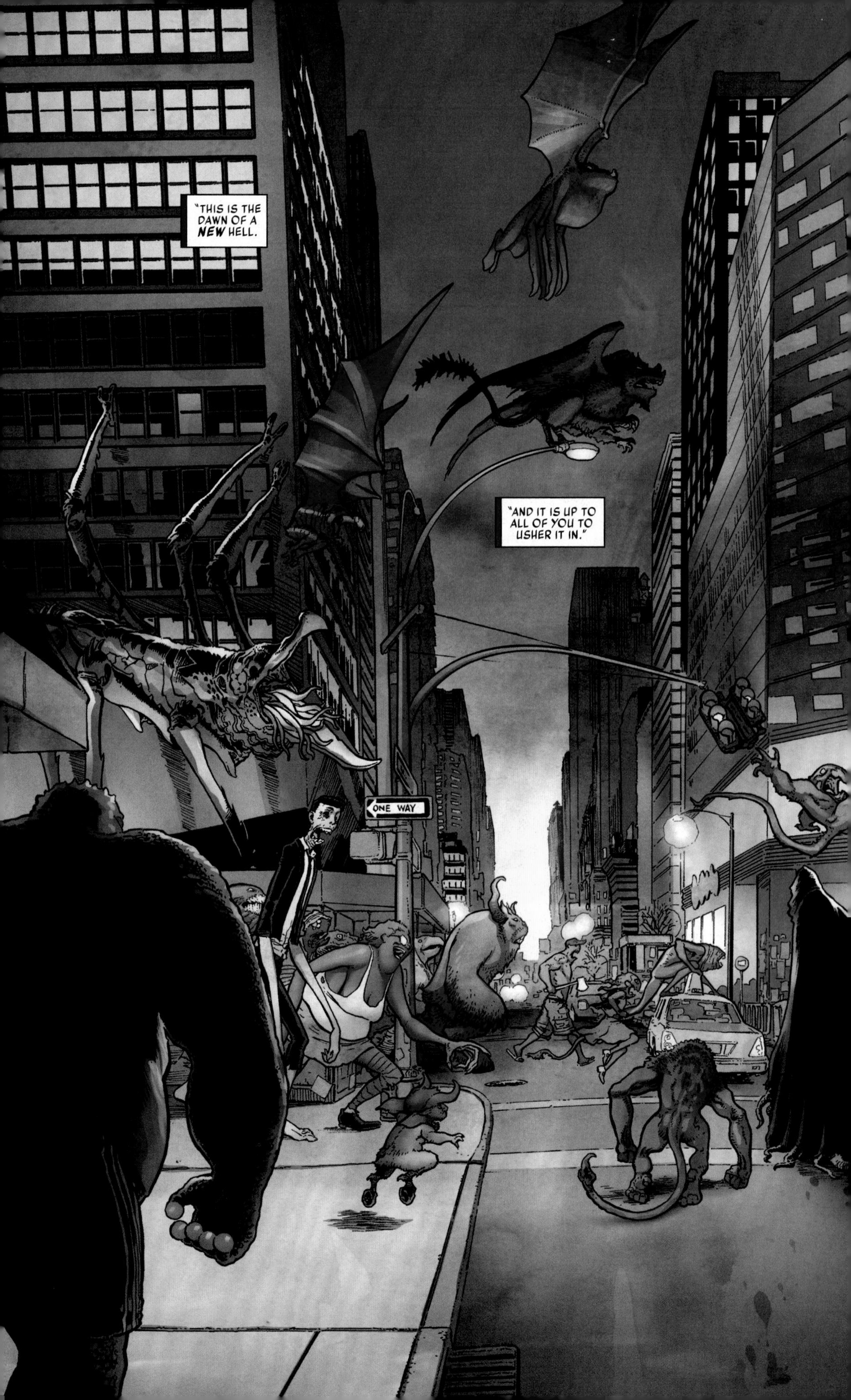

"THIS IS THE DAWN OF A NEW HELL.
"AND IT IS UP TO ALL OF YOU TO USHER IT IN."
ONE WAY

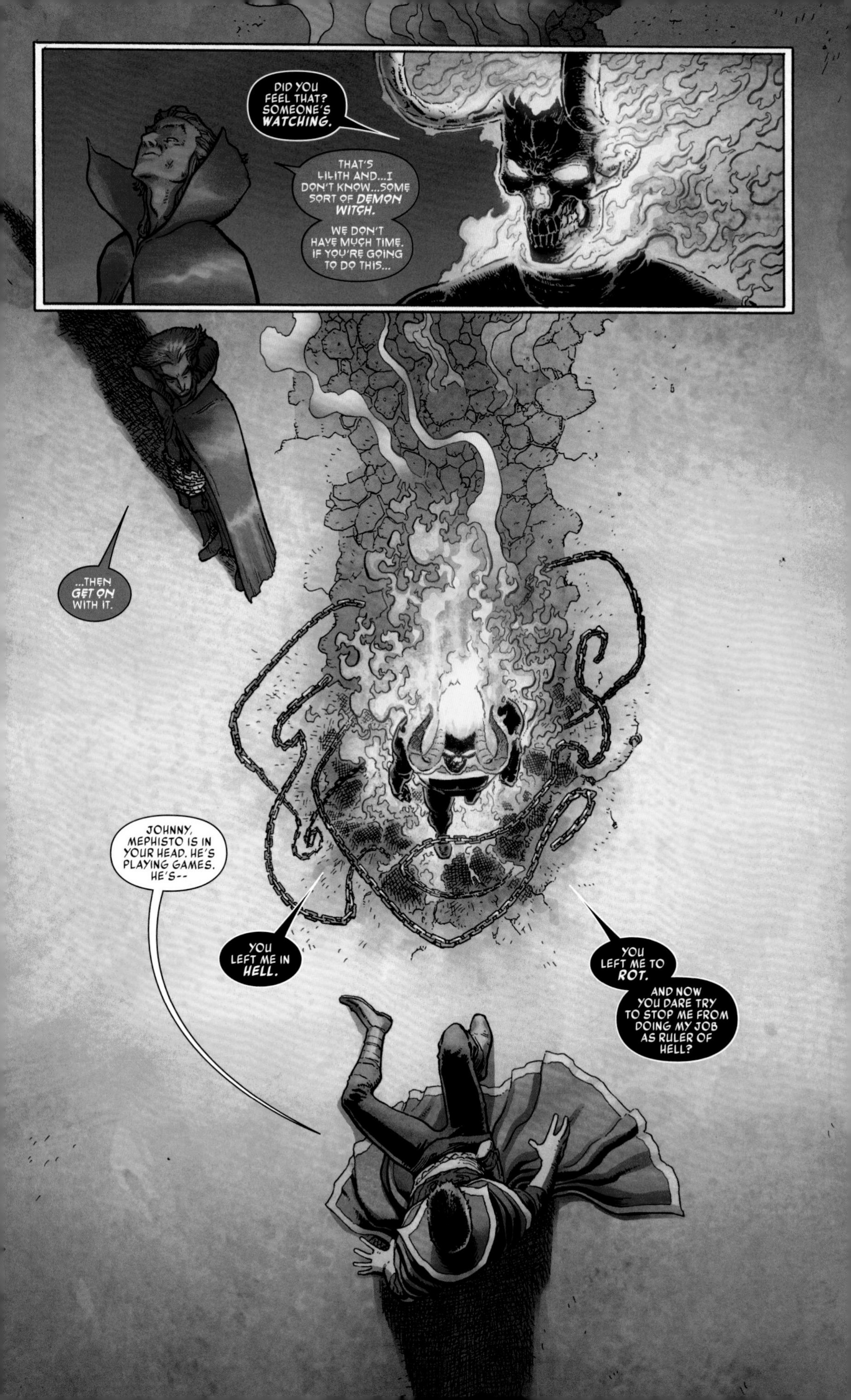
DID YOU FEEL THAT? SOMEONE'S WATCHING.
THAT'S LILITH AND...I DON'T KNOW...SOME SORT OF DEMON WITCH.
WE DON'T HAVE MUCH TIME. IF YOU'RE GOING TO DO THIS...
...THEN GET ON WITH IT.
JOHNNY, MEPHISTO IS IN YOUR HEAD. HE'S PLAYING GAMES. HE'S--
YOU LEFT ME IN HELL.
YOU LEFT ME TO ROT.
AND NOW YOU DARE TRY TO STOP ME FROM DOING MY JOB AS RULER OF HELL?

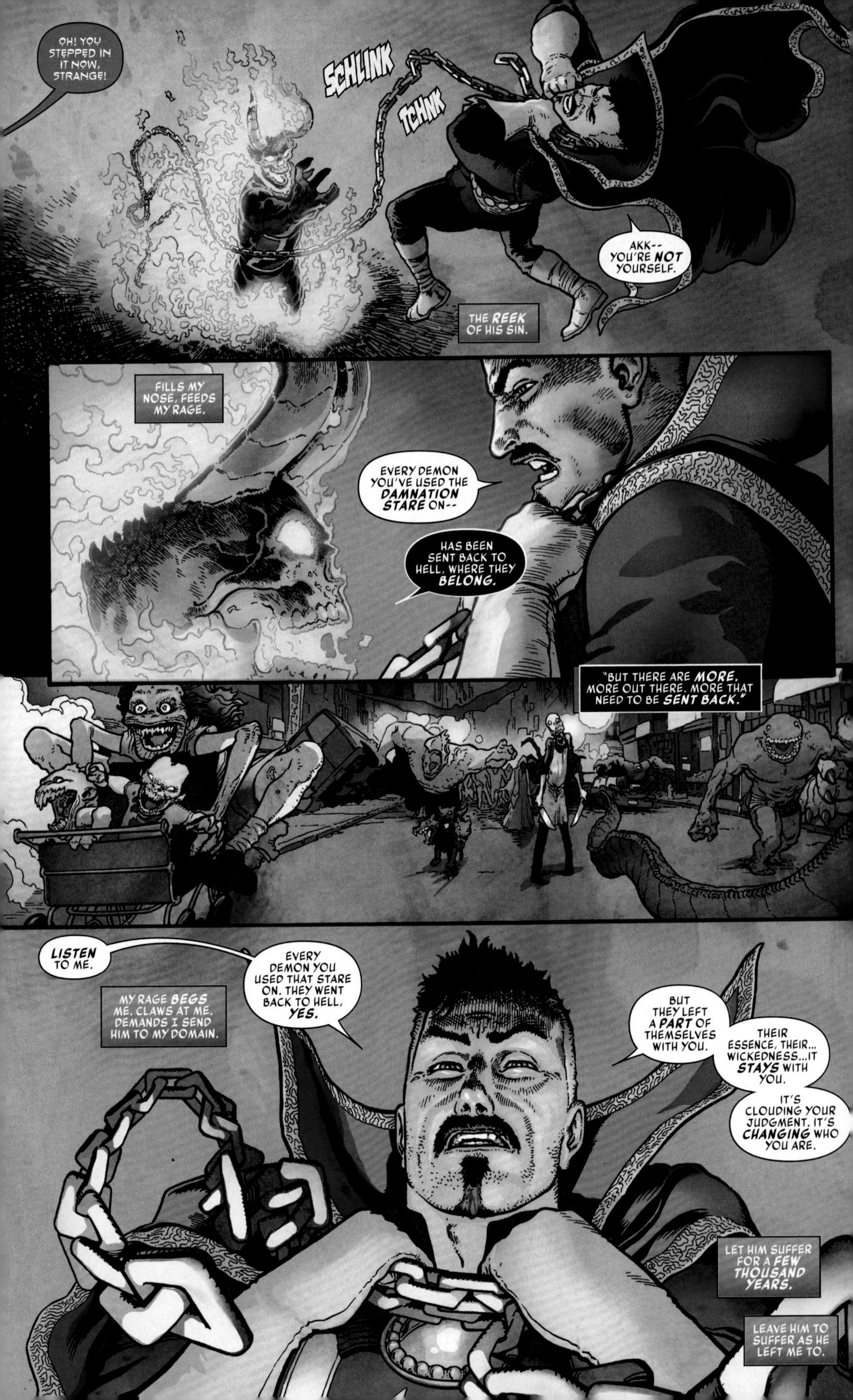
OH! YOU STEPPED IN IT NOW, STRANGE!
SCHLINK
TCHNK
AKK-- YOU'RE NOT YOURSELF.
THE REEK OF HIS SIN.
FILLS MY NOSE, FEEDS MY RAGE.
EVERY DEMON YOU'VE USED THE DAMNATION STARE ON--
HAS BEEN SENT BACK TO HELL, WHERE THEY BELONG.
"BUT THERE ARE MORE. MORE OUT THERE. MORE THAT NEED TO BE SENT BACK."
LISTEN TO ME.
EVERY DEMON YOU USED THAT STARE ON. THEY WENT BACK TO HELL, YES.
MY RAGE BEGS ME. CLAWS AT ME. DEMANDS I SEND HIM TO MY DOMAIN.
BUT THEY LEFT A PART OF THEMSELVES WITH YOU.
THEIR ESSENCE, THEIR... WICKEDNESS...IT STAYS WITH YOU.
IT'S CLOUDING YOUR JUDGMENT. IT'S CHANGING WHO YOU ARE.
LET HIM SUFFER FOR A FEW THOUSAND YEARS.
LEAVE HIM TO SUFFER AS HE LEFT ME TO.

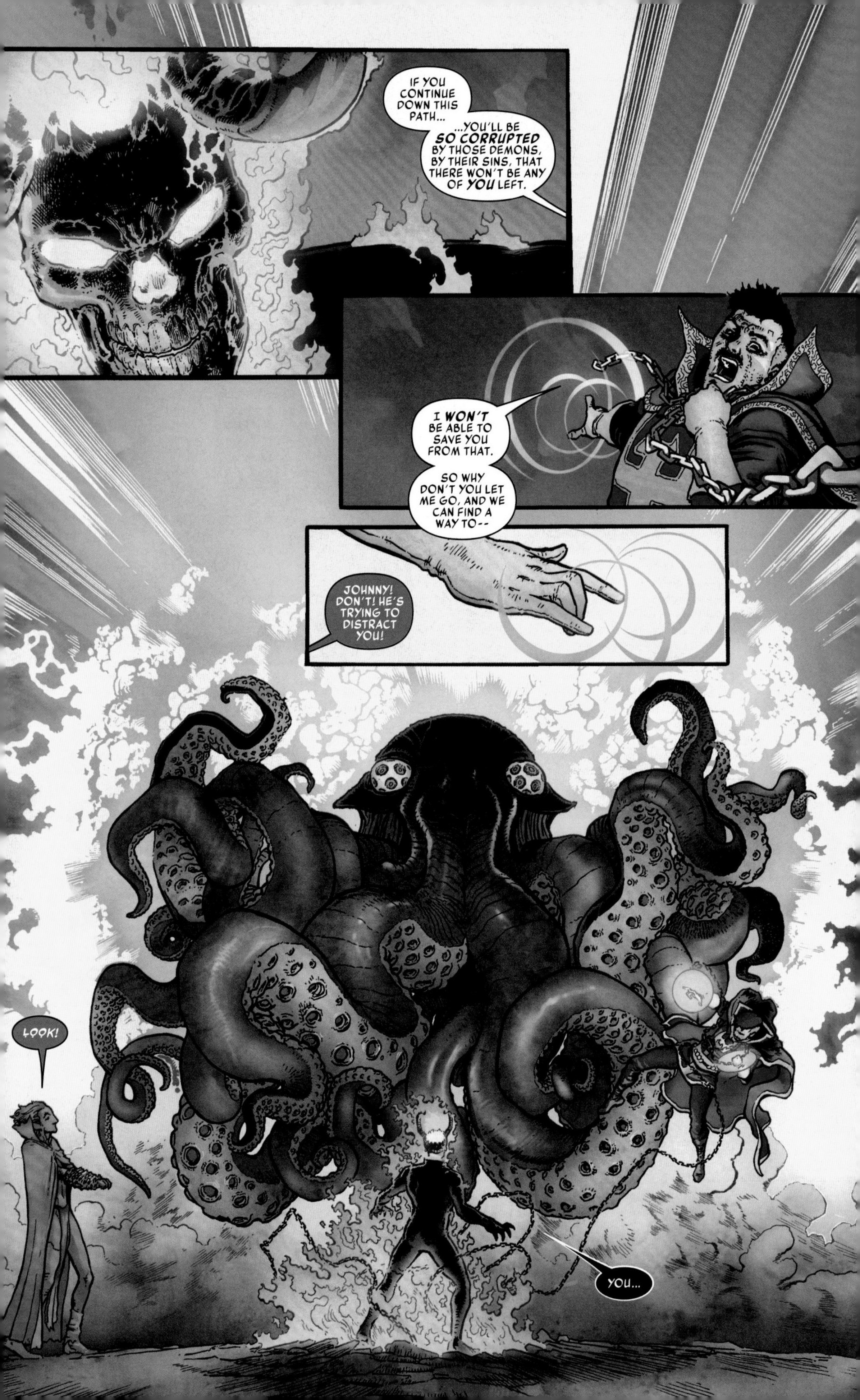
IF YOU CONTINUE DOWN THIS PATH...
...YOU'LL BE SO CORRUPTED BY THOSE DEMONS, BY THEIR SINS, THAT THERE WON'T BE ANY OF YOU LEFT.
I WON'T BE ABLE TO SAVE YOU FROM THAT.
SO WHY DON'T YOU LET ME GO, AND WE CAN FIND A WAY TO--
JOHNNY! DON'T! HE'S TRYING TO DISTRACT YOU!
LOOK!
YOU...

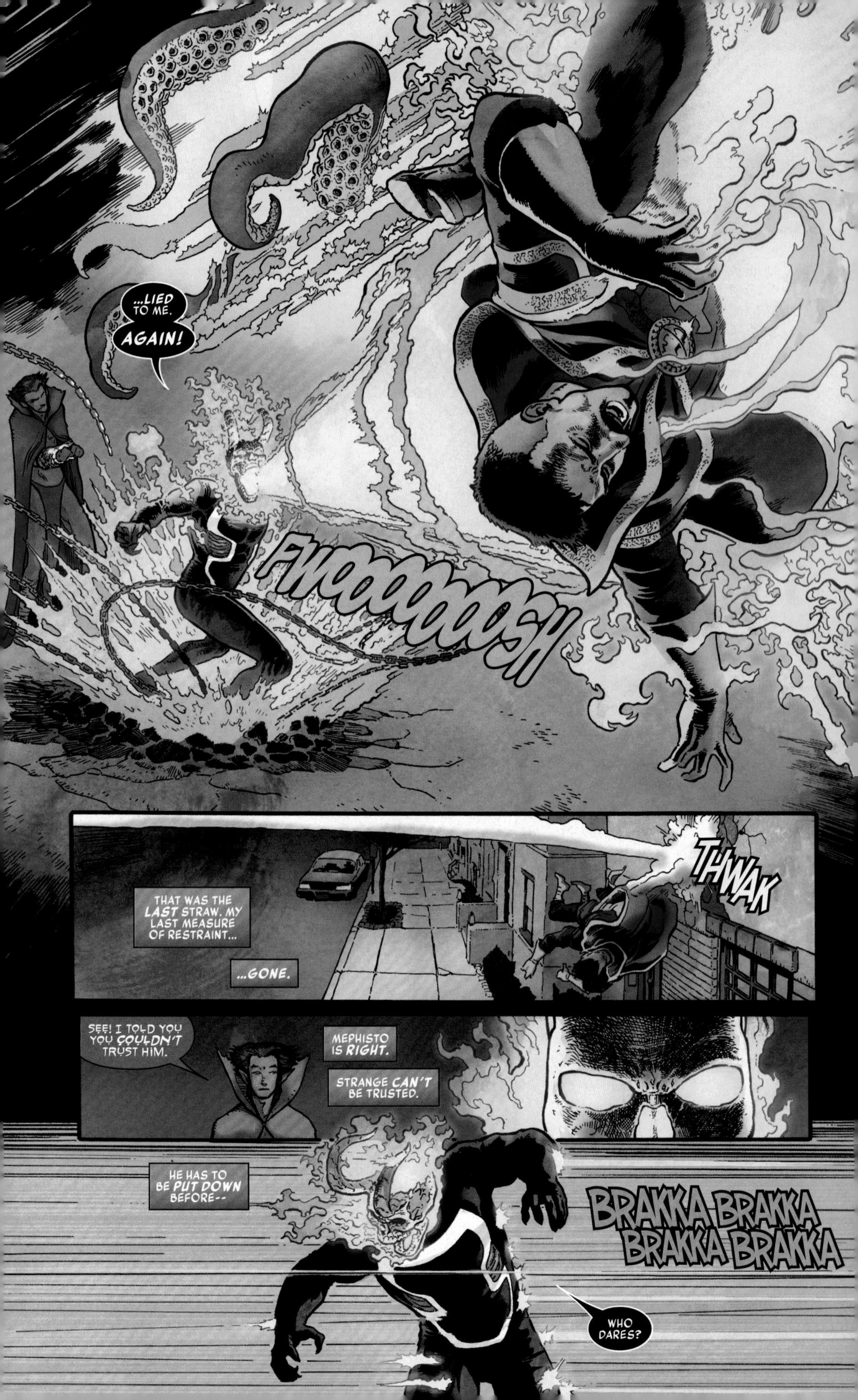
...LIED TO ME. AGAIN!
FWOOOOOOSH
THWAK
THAT WAS THE LAST STRAW. MY LAST MEASURE OF RESTRAINT...
...GONE.
SEE! I TOLD YOU YOU COULDN'T TRUST HIM.
MEPHISTO IS RIGHT.
STRANGE CAN'T BE TRUSTED.
HE HAS TO BE PUT DOWN BEFORE--
BRAKKA BRAKKA BRAKKA BRAKKA
WHO DARES?

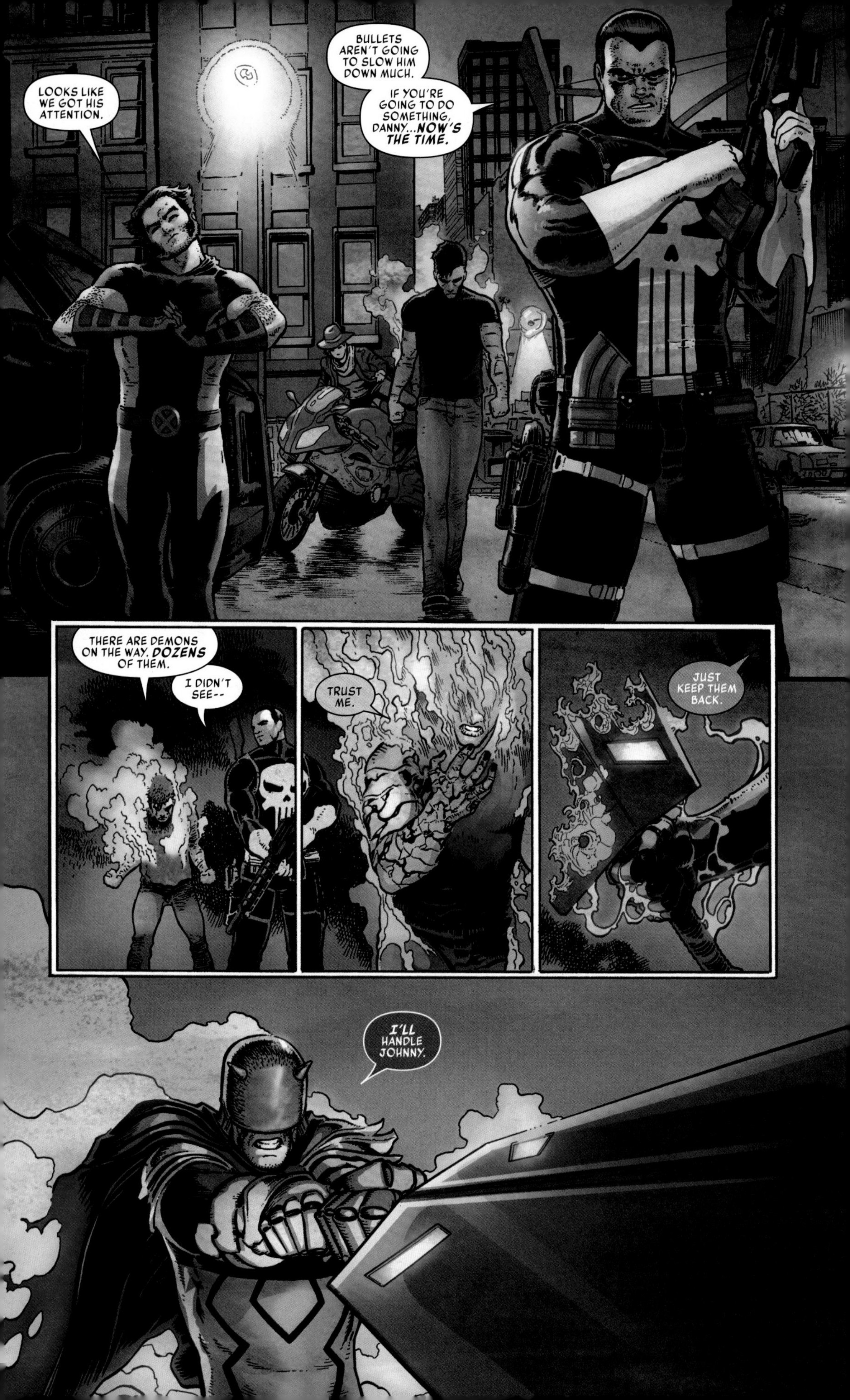

LOOKS LIKE WE GOT HIS ATTENTION.
BULLETS AREN'T GOING TO SLOW HIM DOWN MUCH.
IF YOU'RE GOING TO DO SOMETHING, DANNY...NOW'S THE TIME.
THERE ARE DEMONS ON THE WAY. DOZENS OF THEM.
I DIDN'T SEE--
TRUST ME.
JUST KEEP THEM BACK.
I'LL HANDLE JOHNNY.

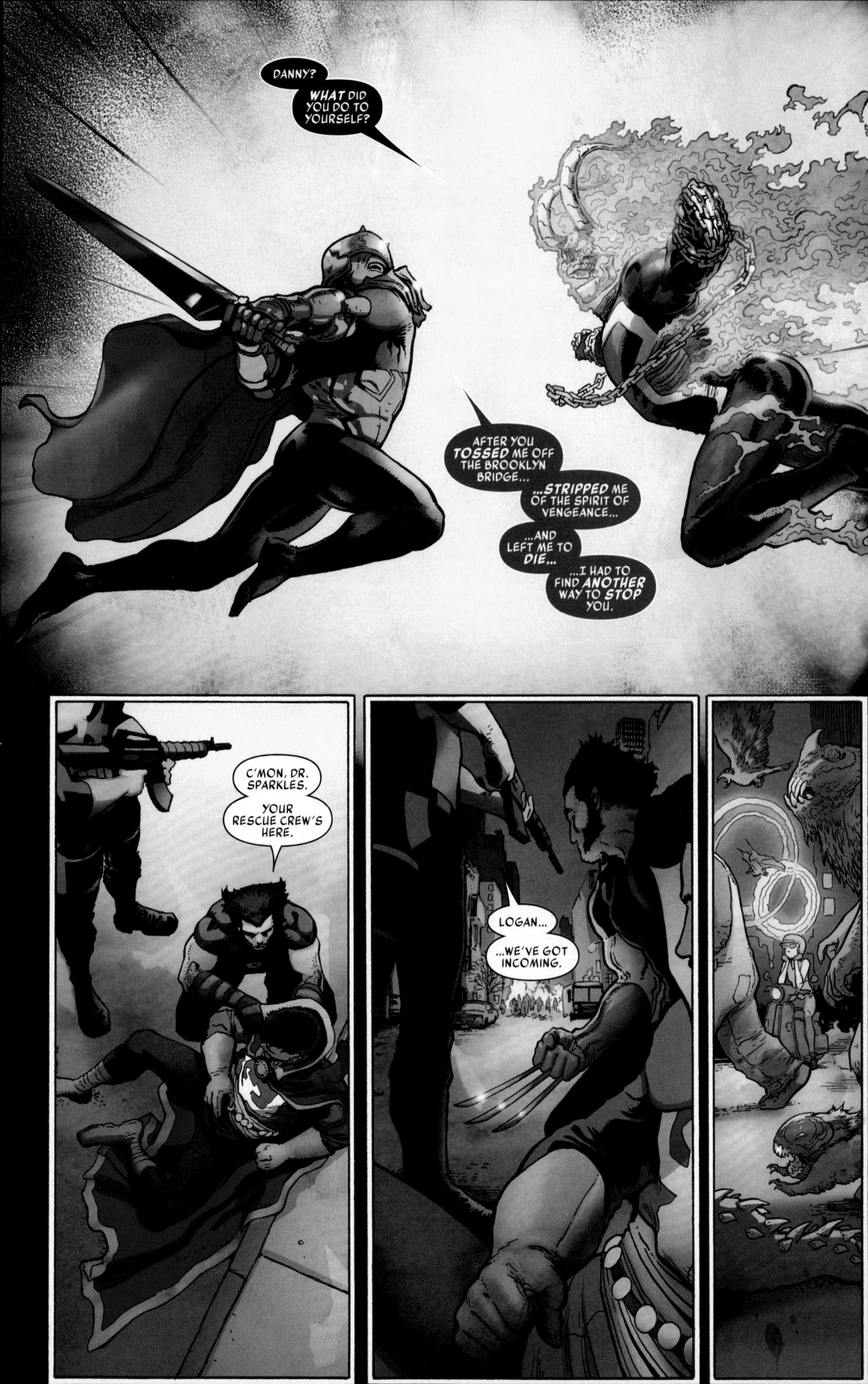
DANNY?
WHAT DID YOU DO TO YOURSELF?
AFTER YOU TOSSED ME OFF THE BROOKLYN BRIDGE...
...STRIPPED ME OF THE SPIRIT OF VENGEANCE...
...AND LEFT ME TO DIE...
...I HAD TO FIND ANOTHER WAY TO STOP YOU.
C'MON, DR. SPARKLES.
YOUR RESCUE CREW'S HERE.
LOGAN...
...WE'VE GOT INCOMING.

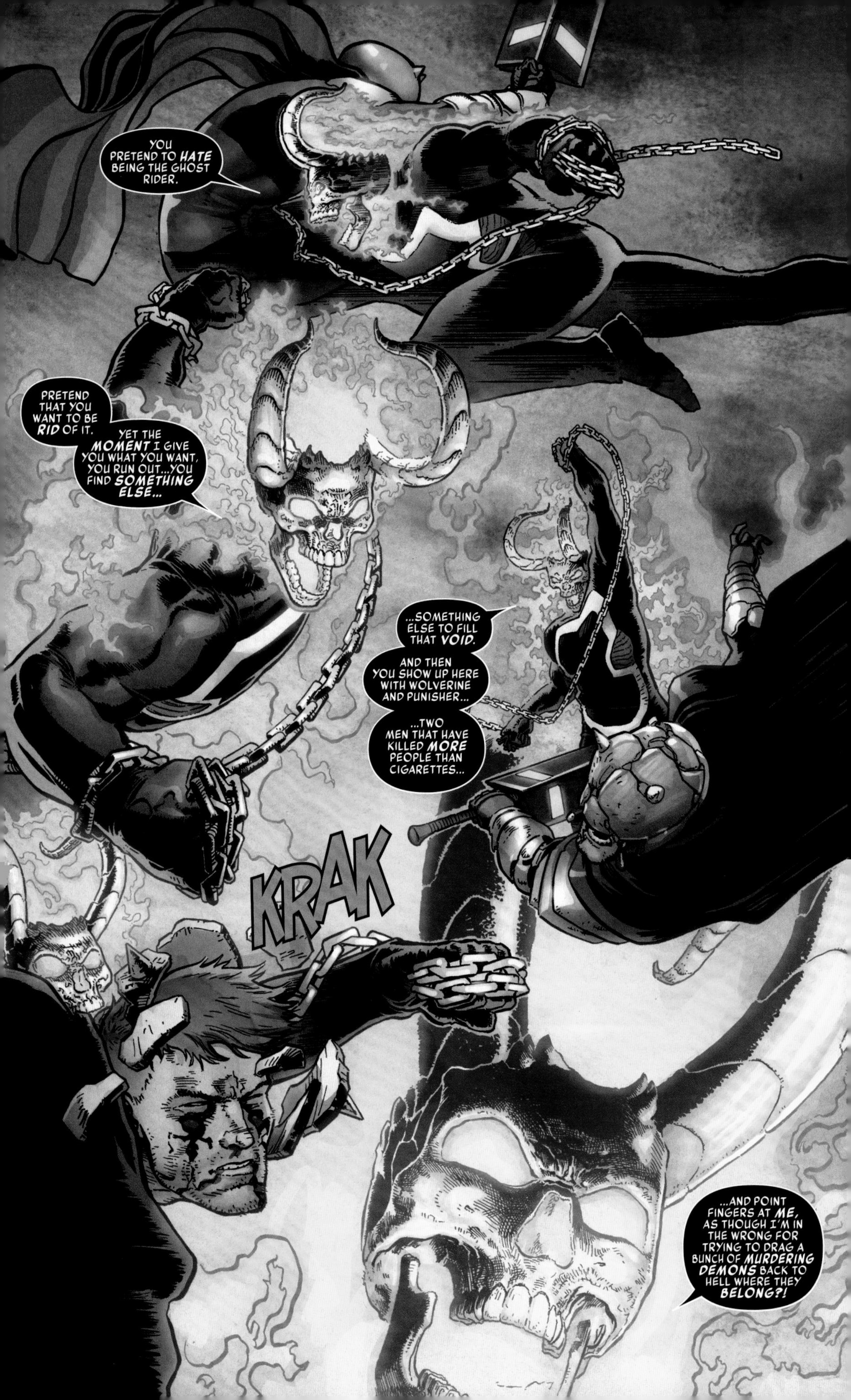
YOU PRETEND TO HATE BEING THE GHOST RIDER.
PRETEND THAT YOU WANT TO BE RID OF IT.
YET THE MOMENT I GIVE YOU WHAT YOU WANT, YOU RUN OUT...YOU FIND SOMETHING ELSE...
...SOMETHING ELSE TO FILL THAT VOID.
AND THEN YOU SHOW UP HERE WITH WOLVERINE AND PUNISHER...
...TWO MEN THAT HAVE KILLED MORE PEOPLE THAN CIGARETTES...
KRAK
...AND POINT FINGERS AT ME, AS THOUGH I'M IN THE WRONG FOR TRYING TO DRAG A BUNCH OF MURDERING DEMONS BACK TO HELL WHERE THEY BELONG?!

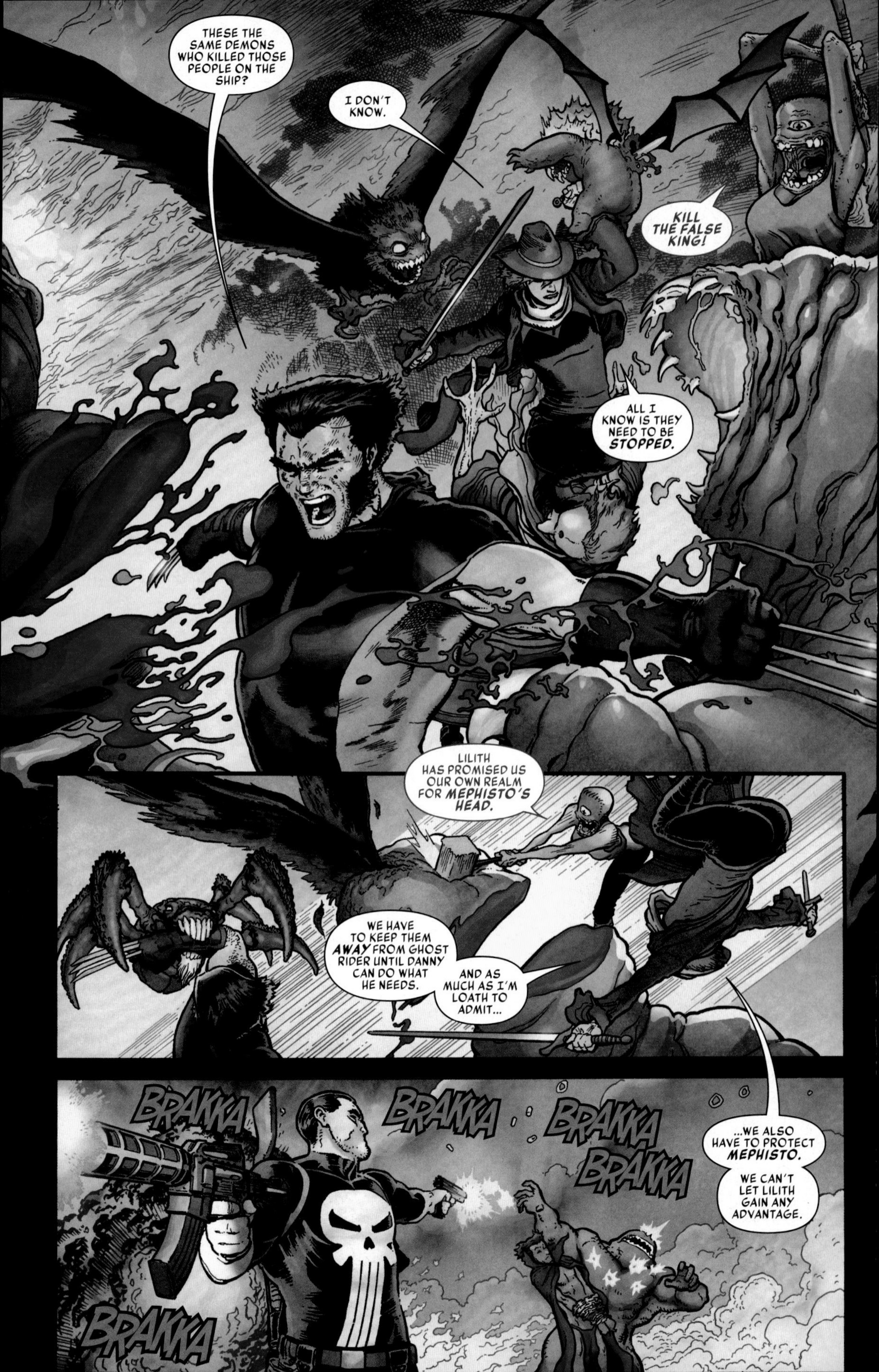
THESE THE SAME DEMONS WHO KILLED THOSE PEOPLE ON THE SHIP?
I DON'T KNOW.
KILL THE FALSE KING!
ALL I KNOW IS THEY NEED TO BE STOPPED.
LILITH HAS PROMISED US OUR OWN REALM FOR MEPHISTO'S HEAD.
WE HAVE TO KEEP THEM AWAY FROM GHOST RIDER UNTIL DANNY CAN DO WHAT HE NEEDS.
AND AS MUCH AS I'M LOATH TO ADMIT...
BRAKKA
BRAKKA
BRAKKA
BRAKKA
...WE ALSO HAVE TO PROTECT MEPHISTO.
WE CAN'T LET LILITH GAIN ANY ADVANTAGE.
BRAKKA

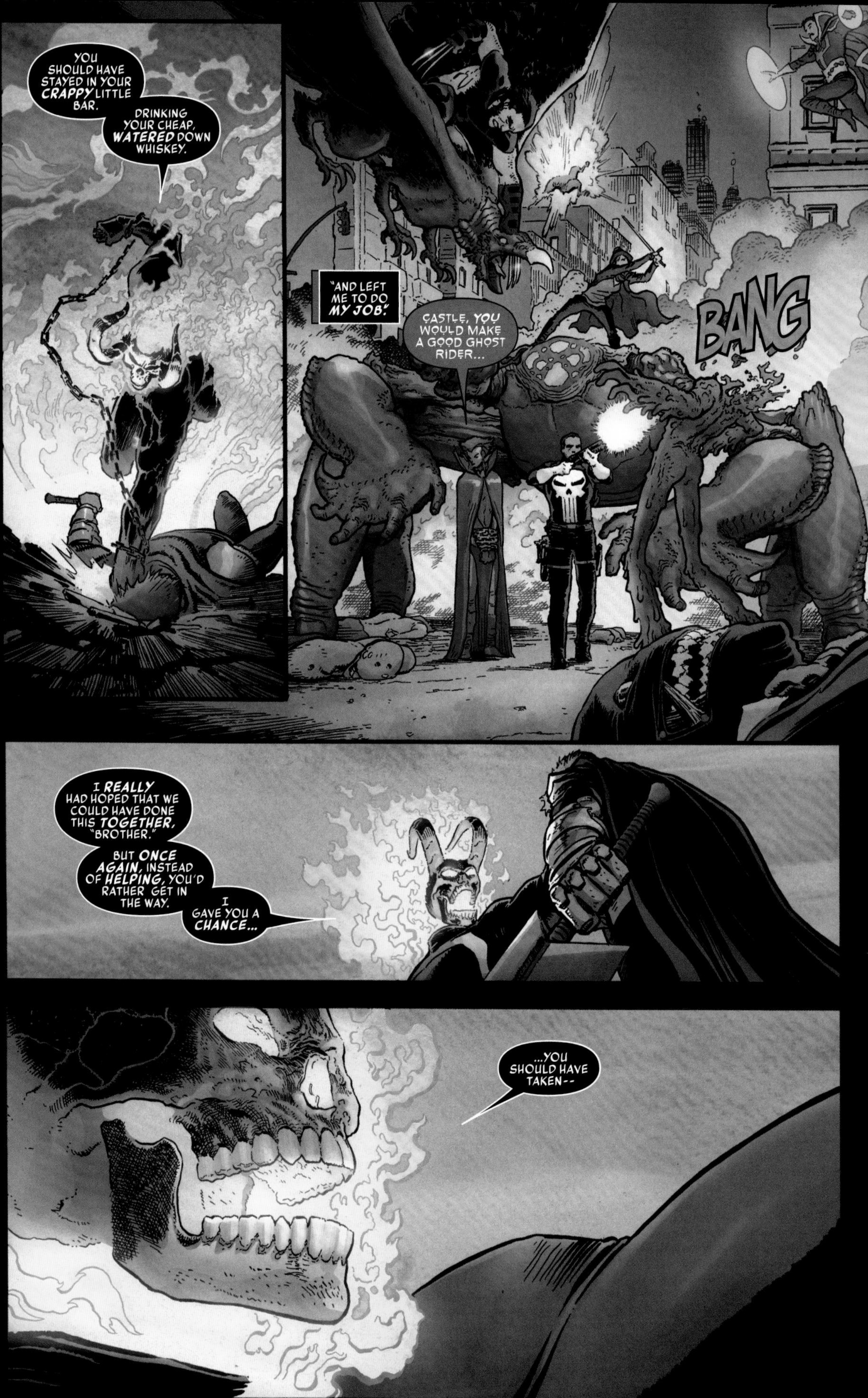
YOU SHOULD HAVE STAYED IN YOUR CRAPPY LITTLE BAR.
DRINKING YOUR CHEAP, WATERED DOWN WHISKEY.
"AND LEFT ME TO DO MY JOB."
CASTLE, YOU WOULD MAKE A GOOD GHOST RIDER...
BANG
I REALLY HAD HOPED THAT WE COULD HAVE DONE THIS TOGETHER, "BROTHER."
BUT ONCE AGAIN, INSTEAD OF HELPING, YOU'D RATHER GET IN THE WAY.
I GAVE YOU A CHANCE...
...YOU SHOULD HAVE TAKEN--

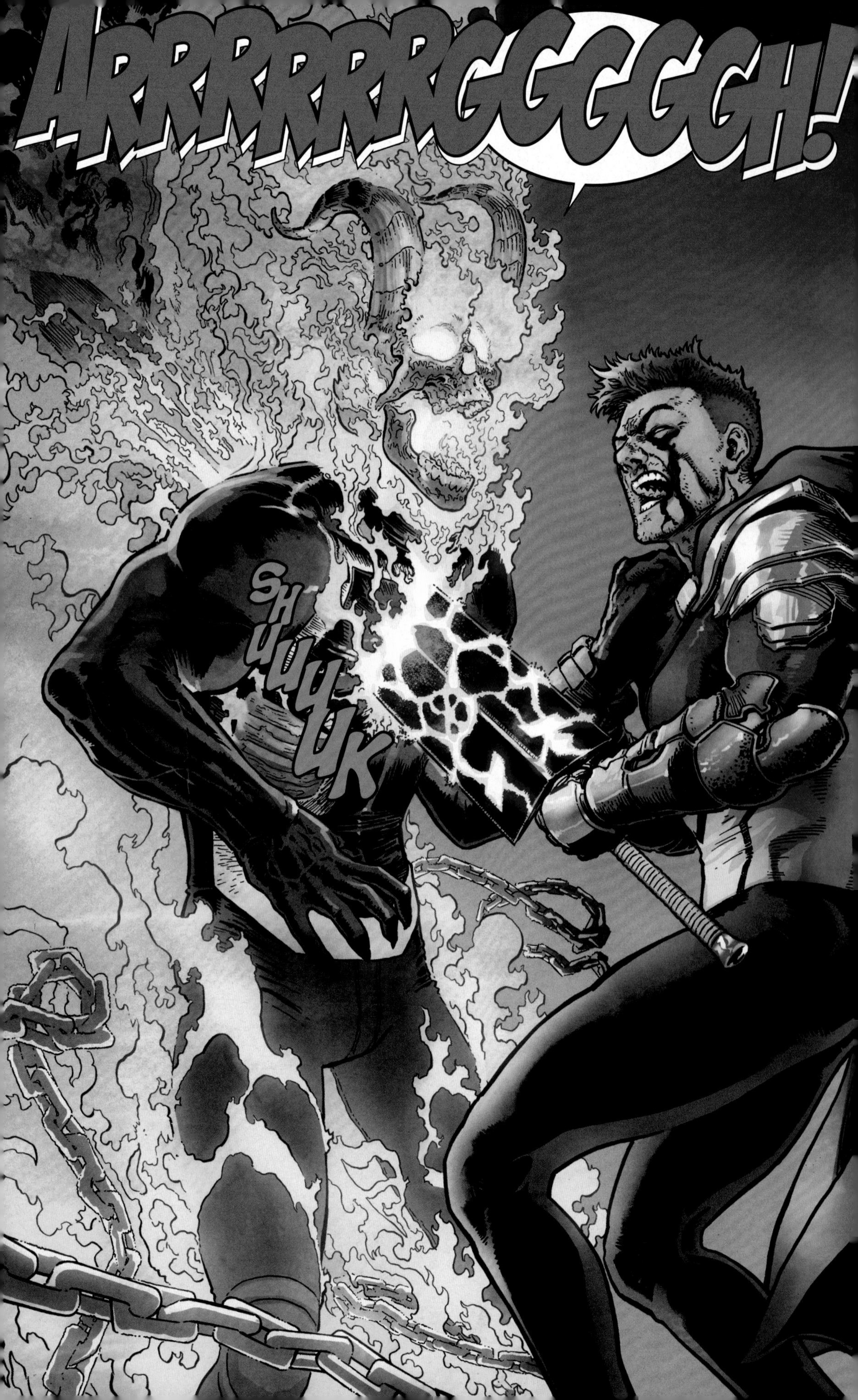
ARRRRRRGGGGGH!
SHUUUUK

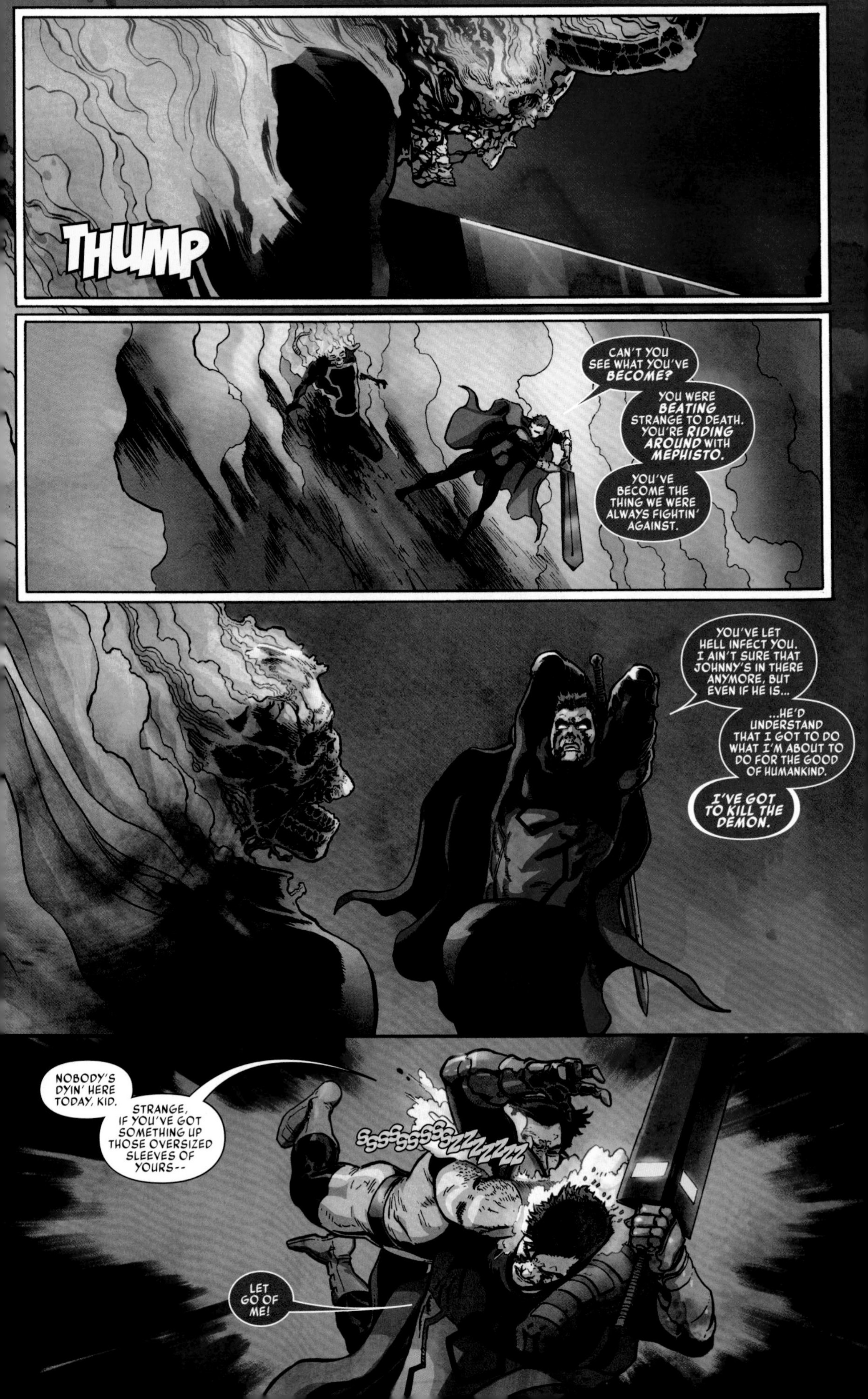
THUMP
CAN'T YOU SEE WHAT YOU'VE BECOME?
YOU WERE BEATING STRANGE TO DEATH. YOU'RE RIDING AROUND WITH MEPHISTO.
YOU'VE BECOME THE THING WE WERE ALWAYS FIGHTIN' AGAINST.
YOU'VE LET HELL INFECT YOU. I AIN'T SURE THAT JOHNNY'S IN THERE ANYMORE, BUT EVEN IF HE IS...
...HE'D UNDERSTAND THAT I GOT TO DO WHAT I'M ABOUT TO DO FOR THE GOOD OF HUMANKIND.
I'VE GOT TO KILL THE DEMON.
NOBODY'S DYIN' HERE TODAY, KID.
STRANGE, IF YOU'VE GOT SOMETHING UP THOSE OVERSIZED SLEEVES OF YOURS--
SSSSSSSSSZZZZZZZZ
LET GO OF ME!

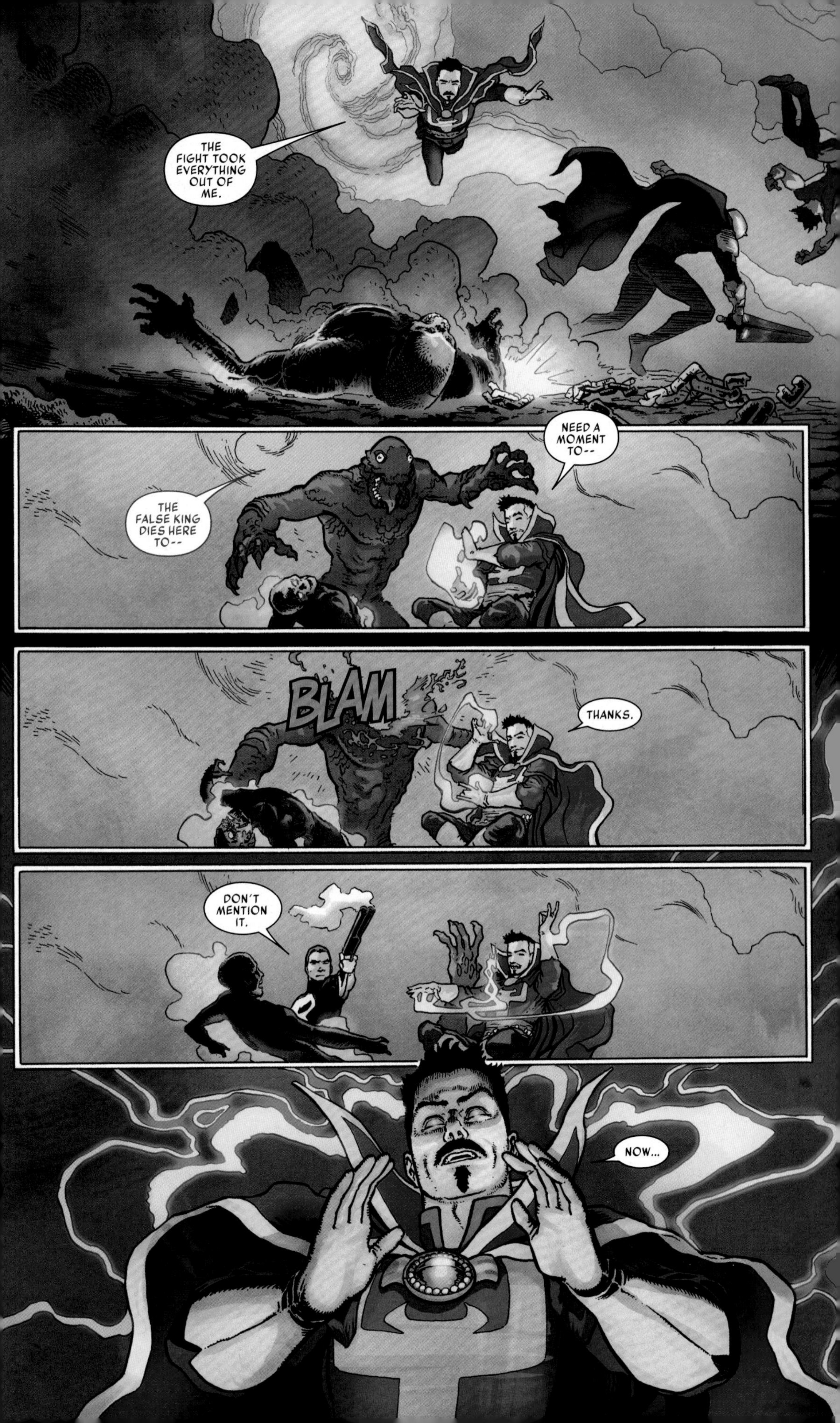
THE FIGHT TOOK EVERYTHING OUT OF ME.
NEED A MOMENT TO--
THE FALSE KING DIES HERE TO--
BLAM
THANKS.
DON'T MENTION IT.
NOW...

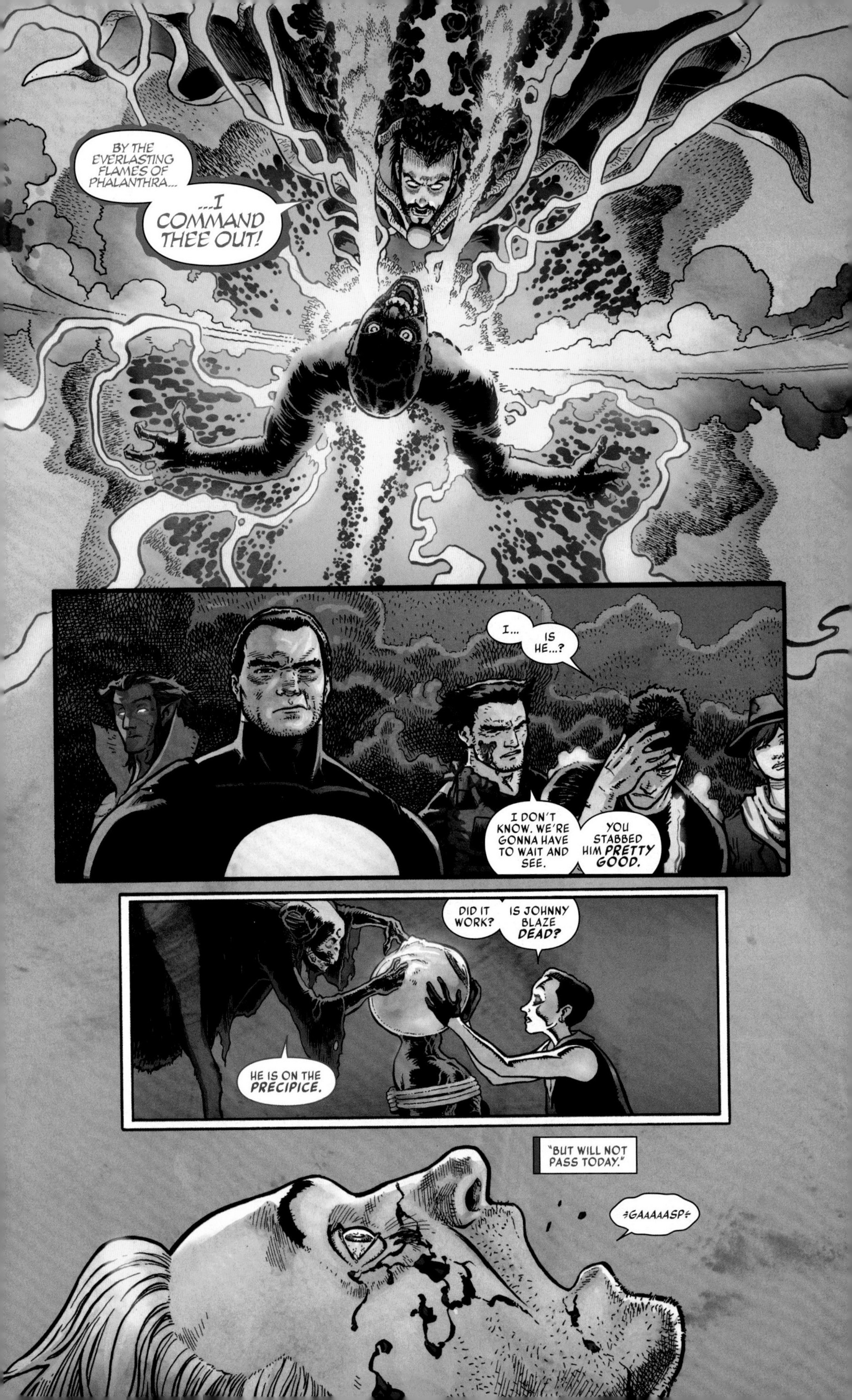
BY THE EVERLASTING FLAMES OF PHALANTHRA...
...I COMMAND THEE OUT!
I...
IS HE...?
I DON'T KNOW. WE'RE GONNA HAVE TO WAIT AND SEE.
YOU STABBED HIM PRETTY GOOD.
DID IT WORK?
IS JOHNNY BLAZE DEAD?
HE IS ON THE PRECIPICE.
"BUT WILL NOT PASS TODAY."
GAAAAASP

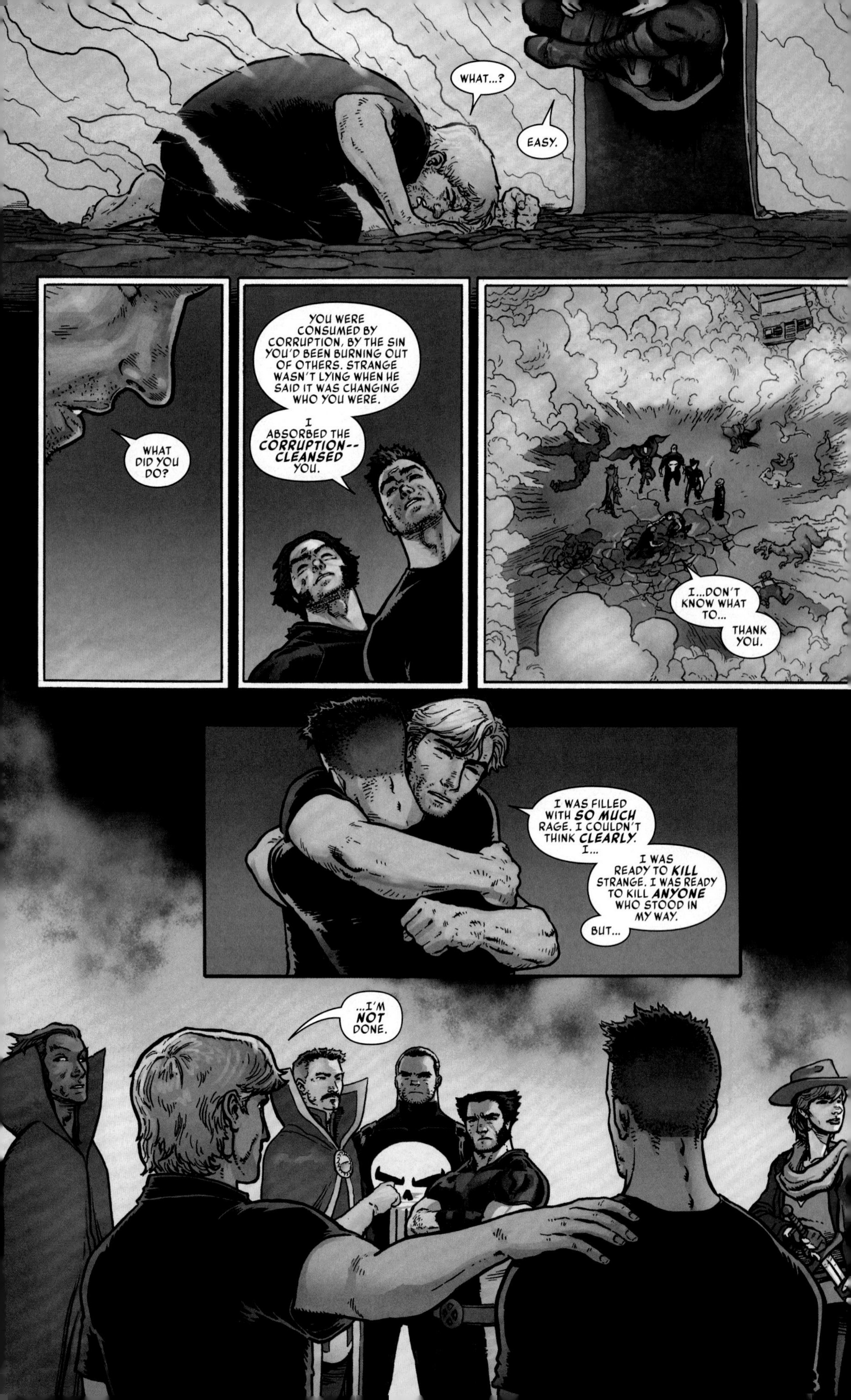
WHAT...?
EASY.
WHAT DID YOU DO?
YOU WERE CONSUMED BY CORRUPTION, BY THE SIN YOU'D BEEN BURNING OUT OF OTHERS. STRANGE WASN'T LYING WHEN HE SAID IT WAS CHANGING WHO YOU WERE.
I ABSORBED THE CORRUPTION-- CLEANSED YOU.
I...DON'T KNOW WHAT TO...
THANK YOU.
I WAS FILLED WITH SO MUCH RAGE. I COULDN'T THINK CLEARLY. I...
I WAS READY TO KILL STRANGE. I WAS READY TO KILL ANYONE WHO STOOD IN MY WAY.
BUT...
...I'M NOT DONE.

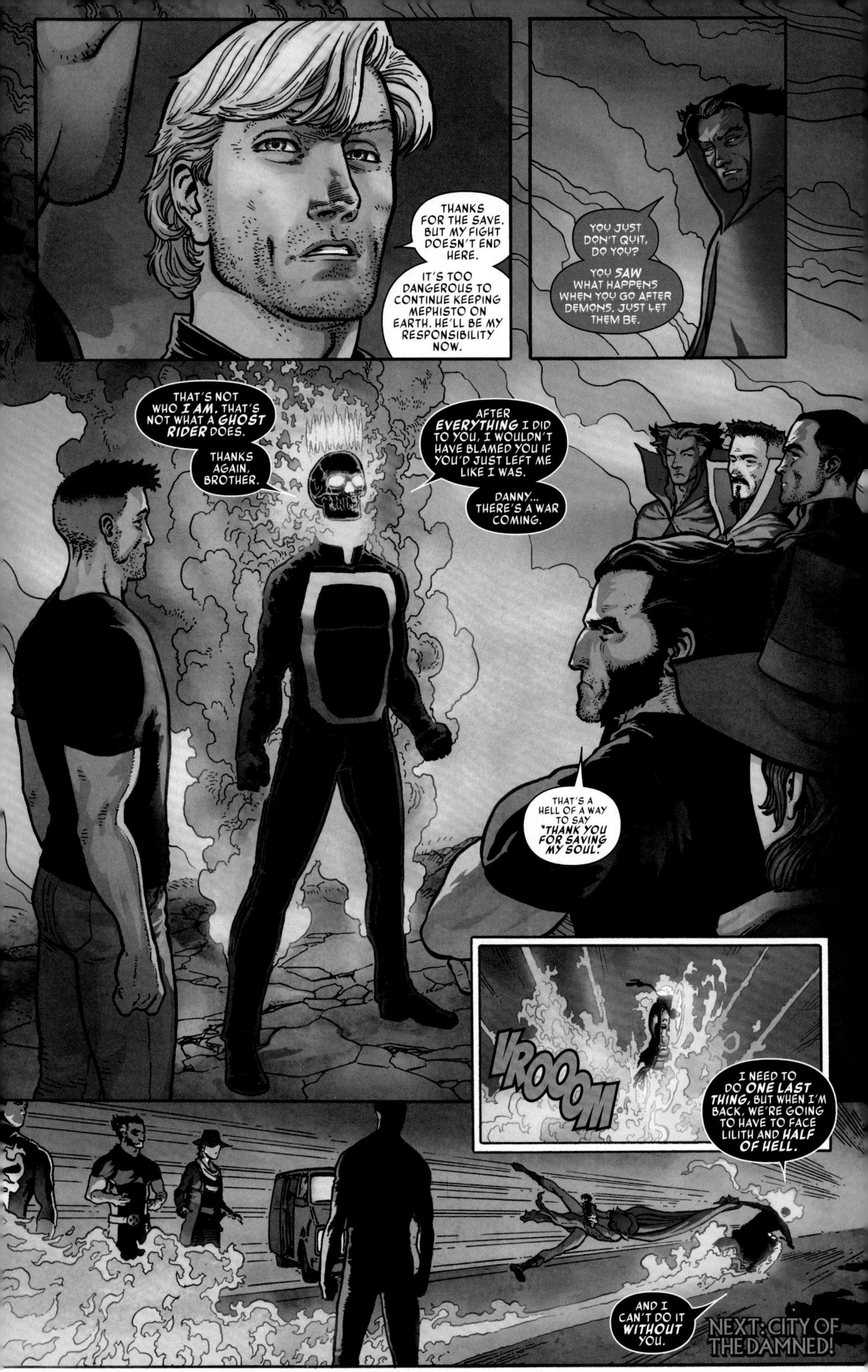
THANKS FOR THE SAVE. BUT MY FIGHT DOESN'T END HERE.
IT'S TOO DANGEROUS TO CONTINUE KEEPING MEPHISTO ON EARTH. HE'LL BE MY RESPONSIBILITY NOW.
YOU JUST DON'T QUIT, DO YOU?
YOU SAW WHAT HAPPENS WHEN YOU GO AFTER DEMONS. JUST LET THEM BE.
THAT'S NOT WHO I AM. THAT'S NOT WHAT A GHOST RIDER DOES.
THANKS AGAIN, BROTHER.
AFTER EVERYTHING I DID TO YOU, I WOULDN'T HAVE BLAMED YOU IF YOU'D JUST LEFT ME LIKE I WAS.
DANNY... THERE'S A WAR COMING.
THAT'S A HELL OF A WAY TO SAY "THANK YOU FOR SAVING MY SOUL."
VROOOOM
I NEED TO DO ONE LAST THING, BUT WHEN I'M BACK, WE'RE GOING TO HAVE TO FACE LILITH AND HALF OF HELL.
AND I CAN'T DO IT WITHOUT YOU.
NEXT: CITY OF THE DAMNED!

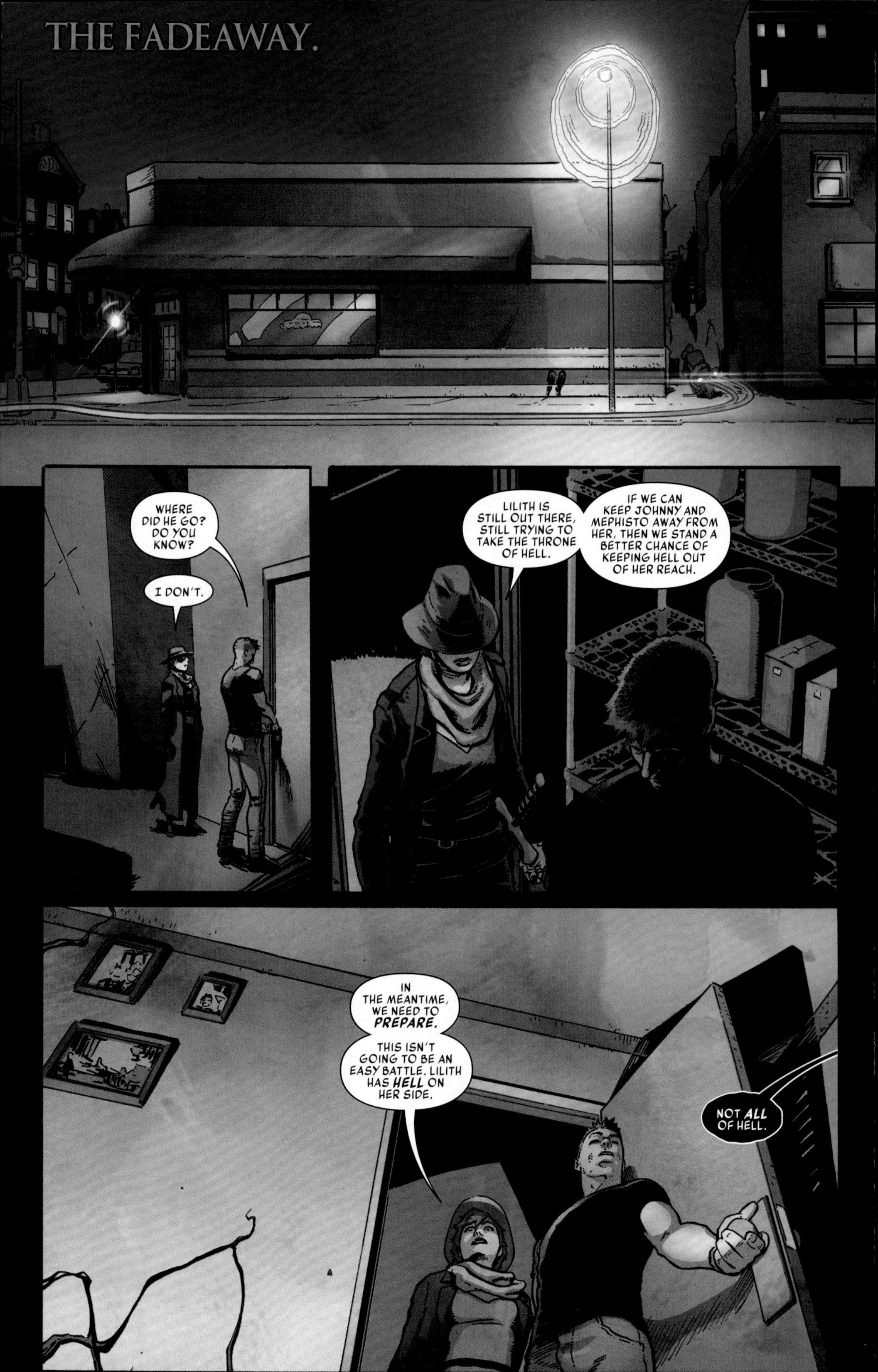
THE FADEAWAY.
WHERE DID HE GO? DO YOU KNOW?
I DON'T.
LILITH IS STILL OUT THERE, STILL TRYING TO TAKE THE THRONE OF HELL.
IF WE CAN KEEP JOHNNY AND MEPHISTO AWAY FROM HER, THEN WE STAND A BETTER CHANCE OF KEEPING HELL OUT OF HER REACH.
IN THE MEANTIME, WE NEED TO PREPARE.
THIS ISN'T GOING TO BE AN EASY BATTLE. LILITH HAS HELL ON HER SIDE.
NOT ALL OF HELL.

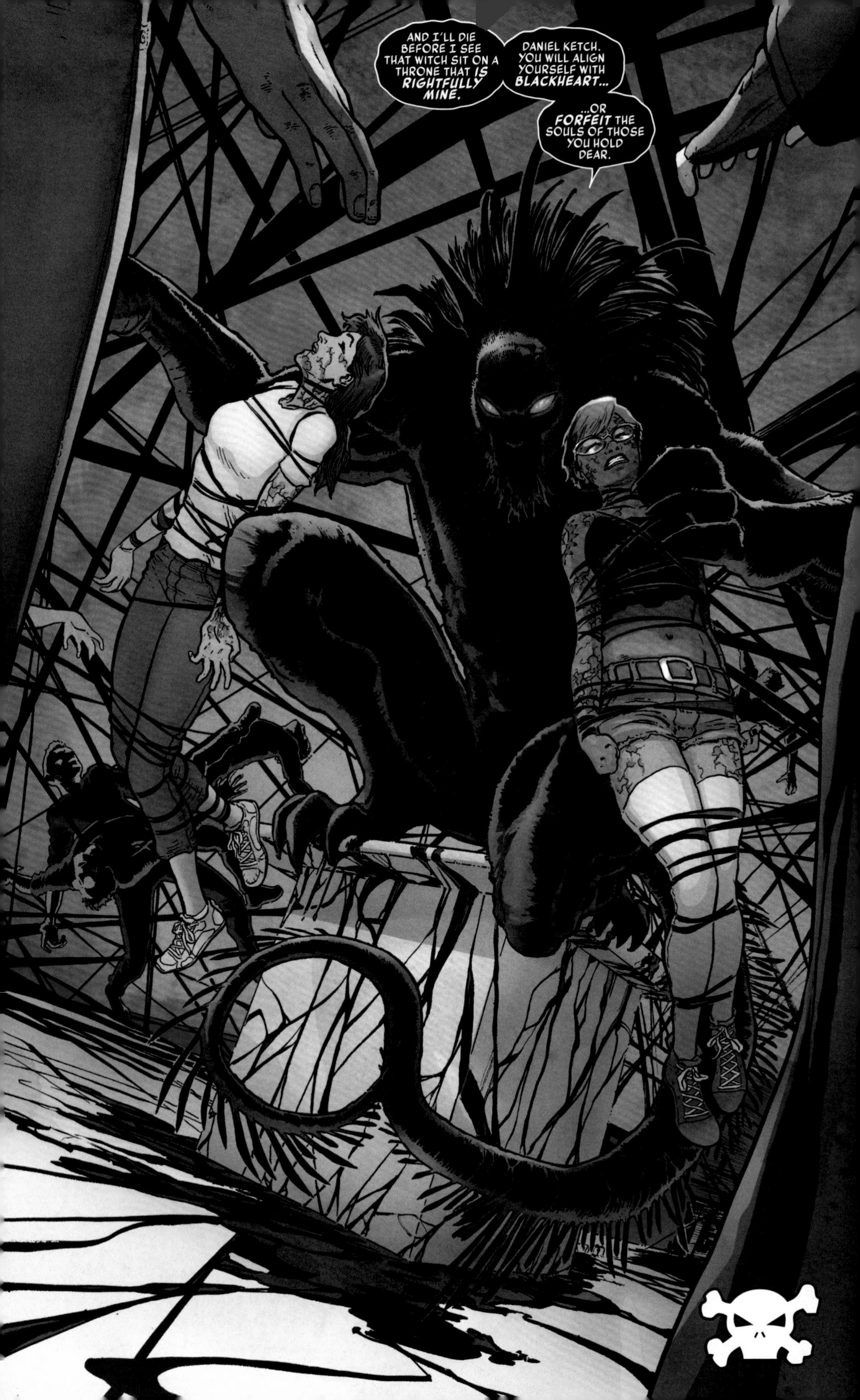
AND I'LL DIE BEFORE I SEE THAT WITCH SIT ON A THRONE THAT IS RIGHTFULLY MINE.
DANIEL KETCH. YOU WILL ALIGN YOURSELF WITH BLACKHEART...
...OR FORFEIT THE SOULS OF THOSE YOU HOLD DEAR.

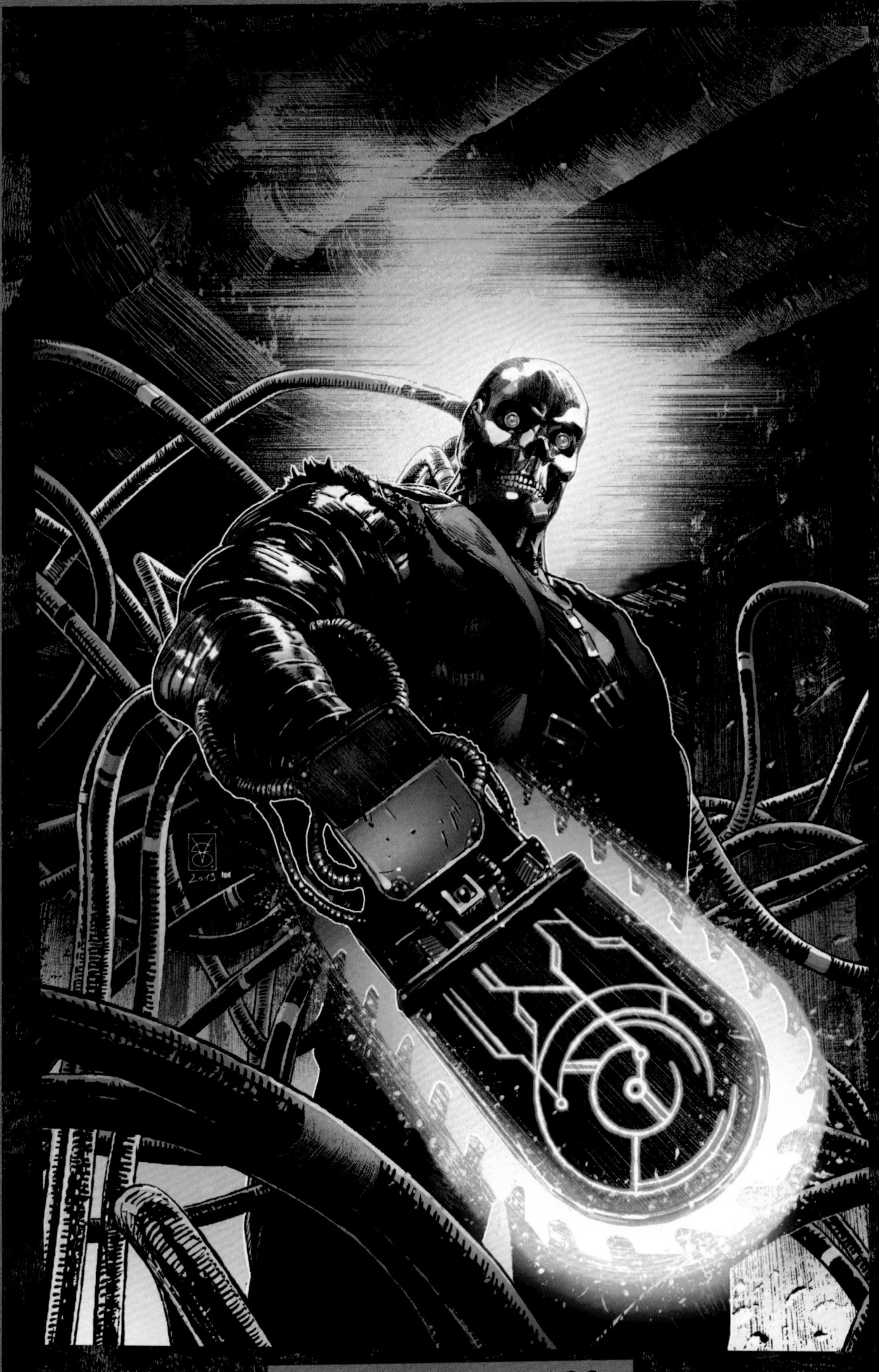

Ghost Rider 2099

YEARS AGO, a catastrophic event brought the age of heroes to an abrupt end. Now, several mega-corporations rule over humanity with the help of their private police force: the Public Eye. And above them Doom rules all. But still, there are those who would threaten to buck the system. This is the future. This is...

2099

GHOST RIDER

ED BRISSON
WRITER

DAMIAN COUCEIRO
ARTIST

DONO SÁNCHEZ-ALMARA
COLORIST

VC's JOE CARAMAGNA
LETTERER

VALERIO GIANGIORDANO & FRANK D'ARMATA
COVER

KYLE HOTZ & DAN BROWN; RON LIM & ISRAEL SILVA
VARIANT COVERS

JAY BOWEN
DESIGN

CHRIS ROBINSON
EDITOR

JORDAN D. WHITE
SENIOR EDITOR

EDITOR IN CHIEF **C.B. CEBULSKI** CHIEF CREATIVE OFFICER **JOE QUESADA**
PRESIDENT **DAN BUCKLEY** EXECUTIVE PRODUCER **ALAN FINE**

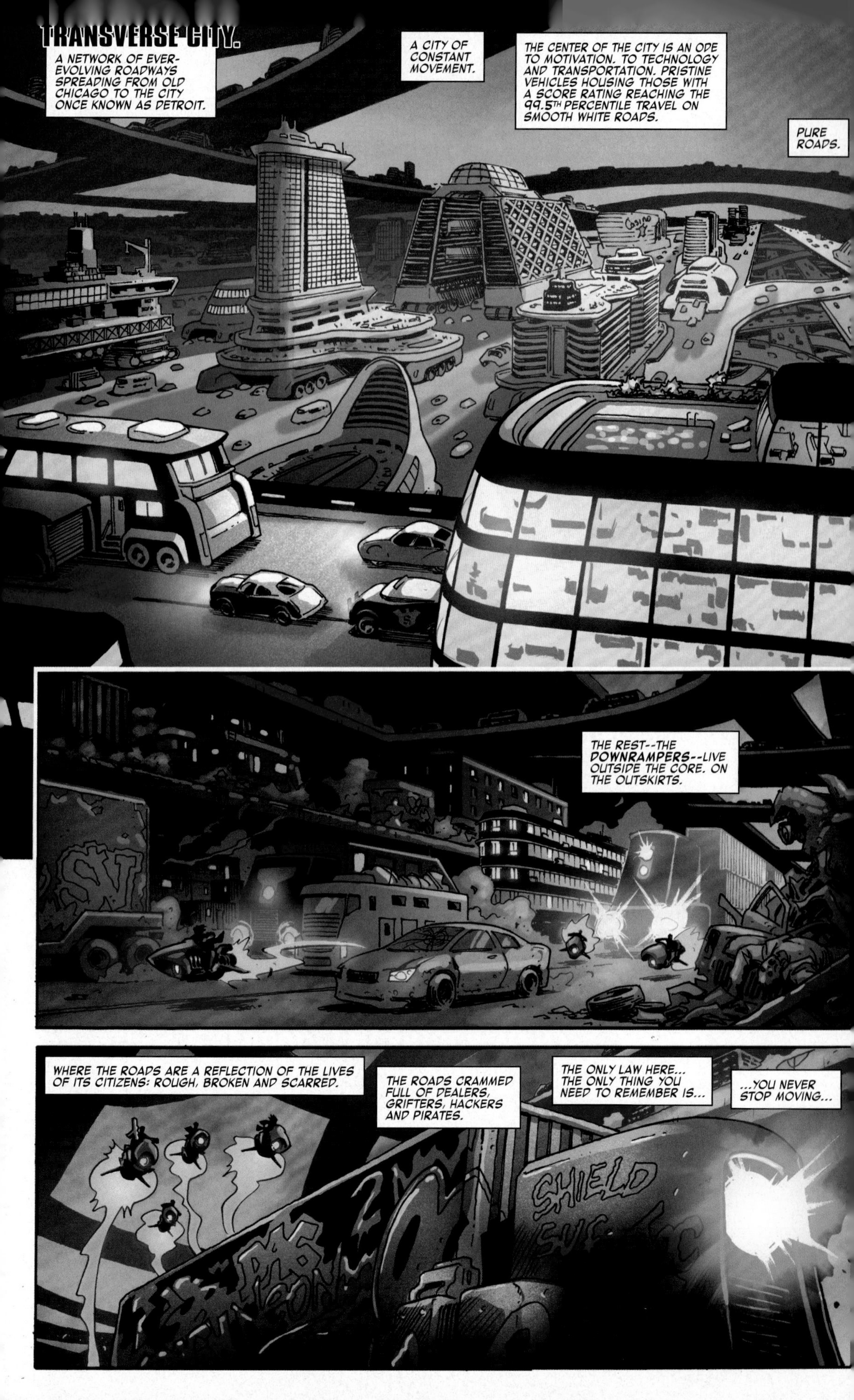
TRANSVERSE CITY.
A NETWORK OF EVER-EVOLVING ROADWAYS SPREADING FROM OLD CHICAGO TO THE CITY ONCE KNOWN AS DETROIT.
A CITY OF CONSTANT MOVEMENT.
THE CENTER OF THE CITY IS AN ODE TO MOTIVATION. TO TECHNOLOGY AND TRANSPORTATION. PRISTINE VEHICLES HOUSING THOSE WITH A SCORE RATING REACHING THE 99.5TH PERCENTILE TRAVEL ON SMOOTH WHITE ROADS.
PURE ROADS.
THE REST--THE DOWNRAMPERS--LIVE OUTSIDE THE CORE. ON THE OUTSKIRTS.
WHERE THE ROADS ARE A REFLECTION OF THE LIVES OF ITS CITIZENS: ROUGH, BROKEN AND SCARRED.
THE ROADS CRAMMED FULL OF DEALERS, GRIFTERS, HACKERS AND PIRATES.
THE ONLY LAW HERE... THE ONLY THING YOU NEED TO REMEMBER IS...
...YOU NEVER STOP MOVING...
SHIELD

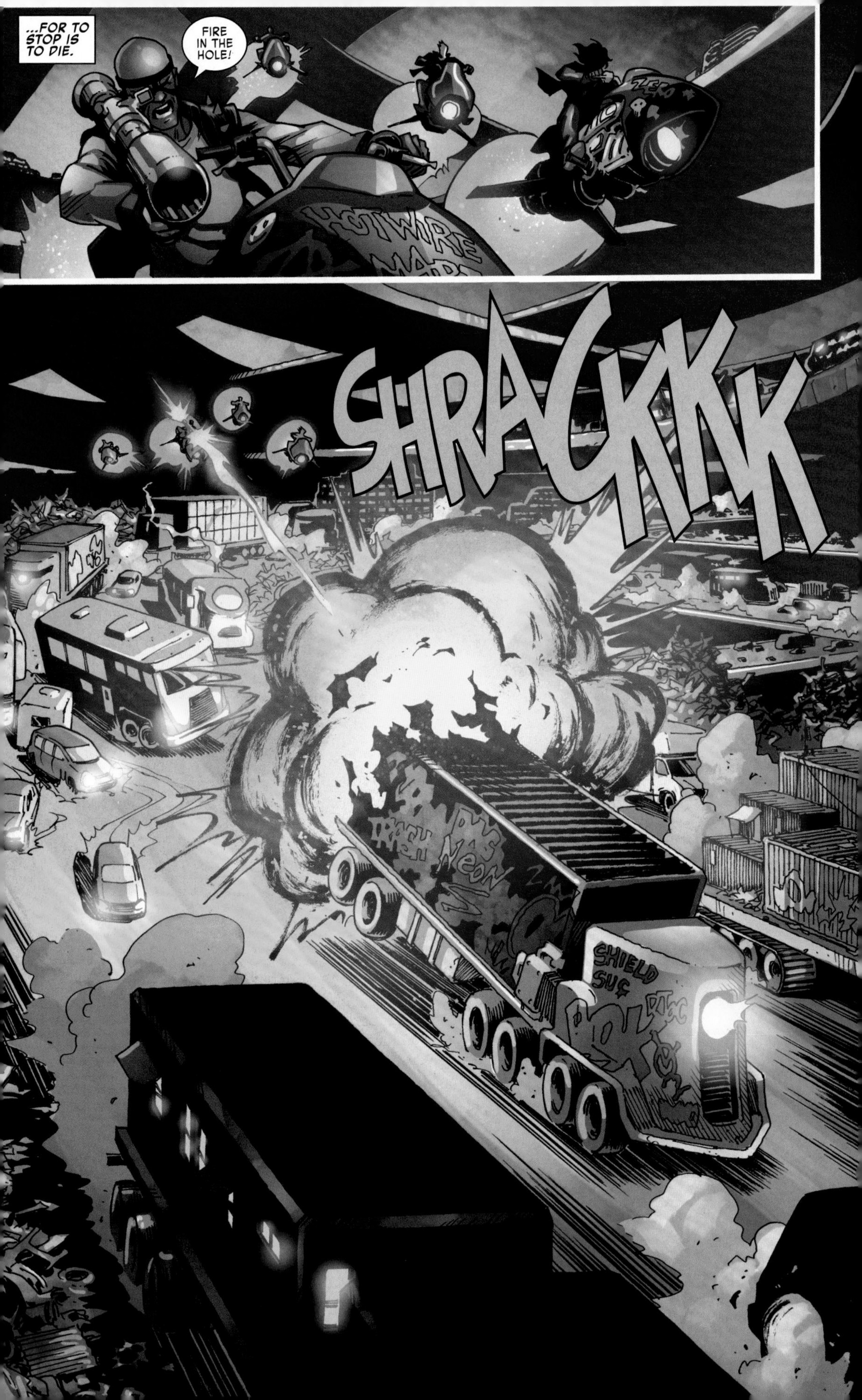

...FOR TO STOP IS TO DIE.
FIRE IN THE HOLE!
SHRACKKK

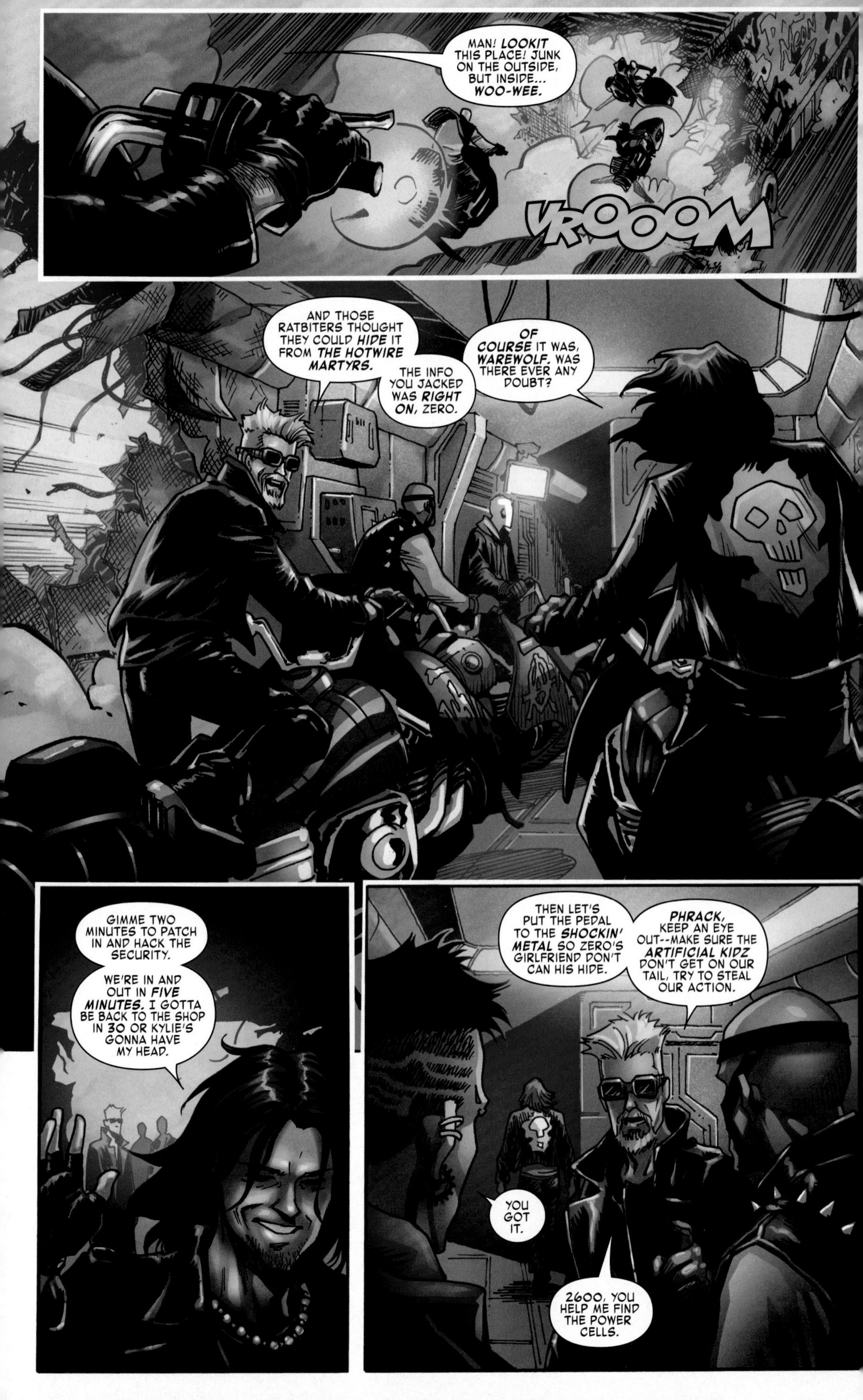
MAN! LOOKIT THIS PLACE! JUNK ON THE OUTSIDE, BUT INSIDE... WOO-WEE.
VROOOM
AND THOSE RATBITERS THOUGHT THEY COULD HIDE IT FROM THE HOTWIRE MARTYRS.
THE INFO YOU JACKED WAS RIGHT ON, ZERO.
OF COURSE IT WAS, WAREWOLF. WAS THERE EVER ANY DOUBT?
GIMME TWO MINUTES TO PATCH IN AND HACK THE SECURITY.
WE'RE IN AND OUT IN FIVE MINUTES. I GOTTA BE BACK TO THE SHOP IN 30 OR KYLIE'S GONNA HAVE MY HEAD.
THEN LET'S PUT THE PEDAL TO THE SHOCKIN' METAL SO ZERO'S GIRLFRIEND DON'T CAN HIS HIDE.
PHRACK, KEEP AN EYE OUT--MAKE SURE THE ARTIFICIAL KIDZ DON'T GET ON OUR TAIL, TRY TO STEAL OUR ACTION.
YOU GOT IT.
2600, YOU HELP ME FIND THE POWER CELLS.

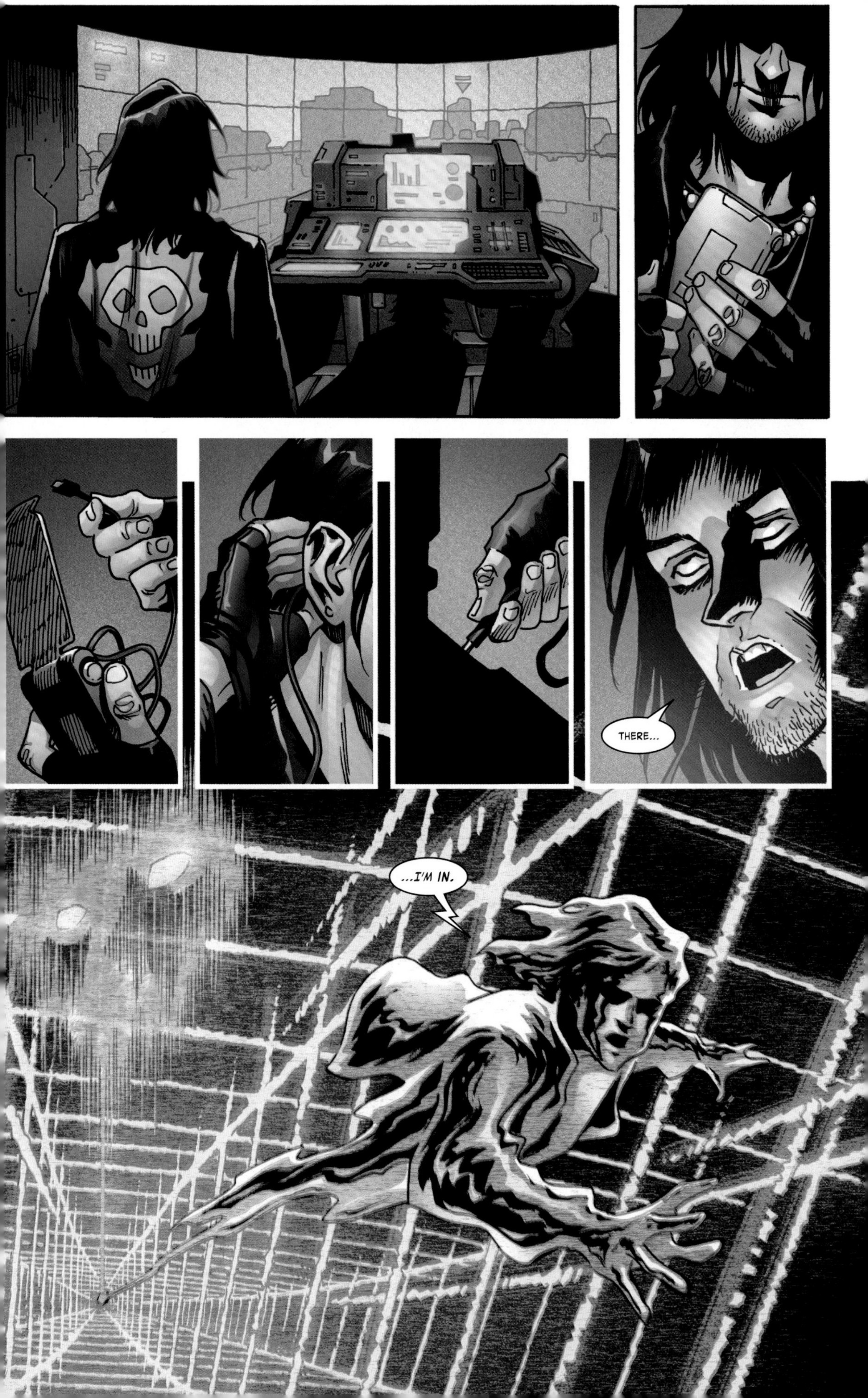
THERE...
...I'M IN.

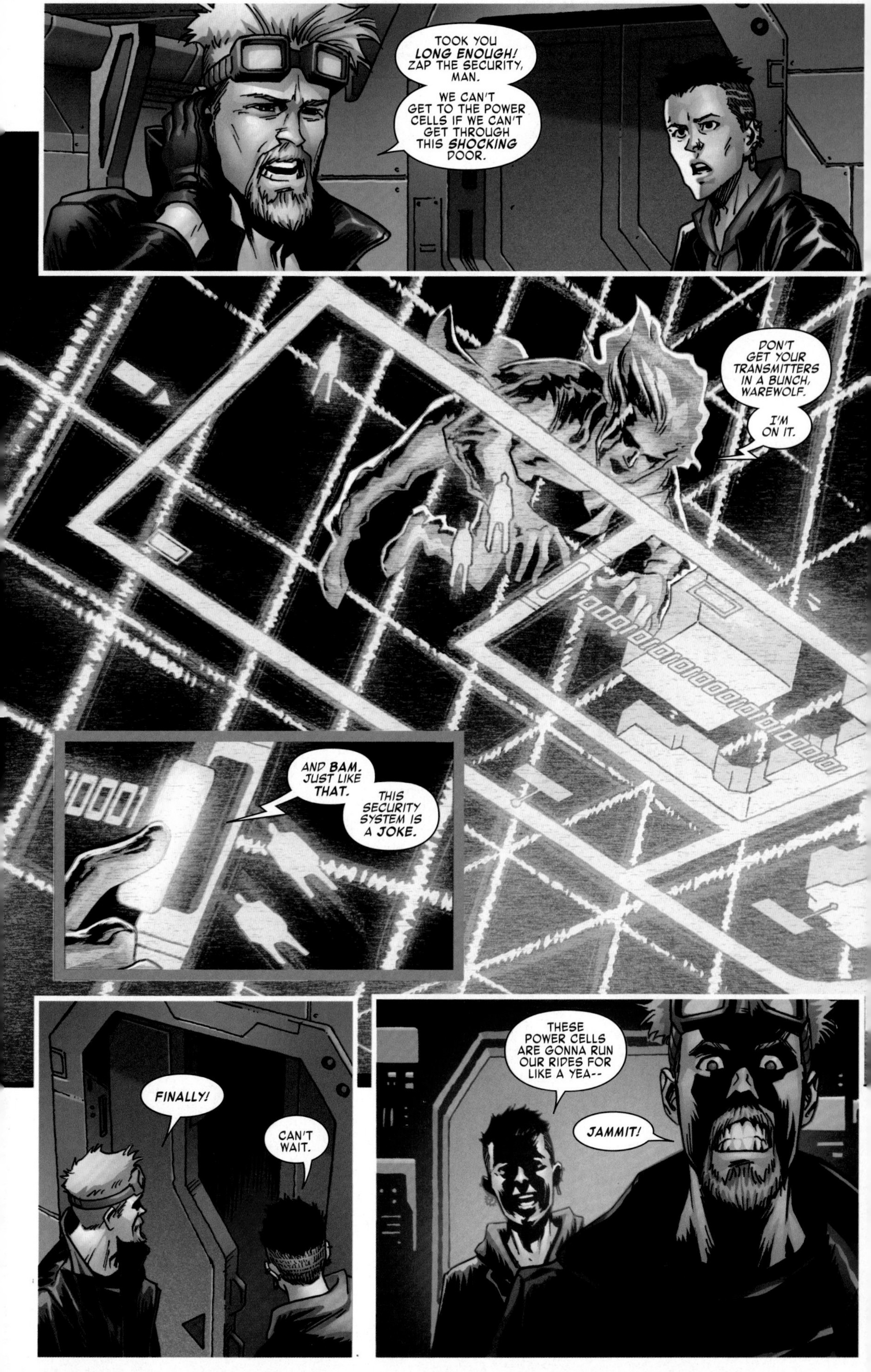
TOOK YOU LONG ENOUGH! ZAP THE SECURITY, MAN.
WE CAN'T GET TO THE POWER CELLS IF WE CAN'T GET THROUGH THIS SHOCKING DOOR.
DON'T GET YOUR TRANSMITTERS IN A BUNCH, WAREWOLF.
I'M ON IT.
AND BAM. JUST LIKE THAT.
THIS SECURITY SYSTEM IS A JOKE.
FINALLY!
CAN'T WAIT.
THESE POWER CELLS ARE GONNA RUN OUR RIDES FOR LIKE A YEA--
JAMMIT!

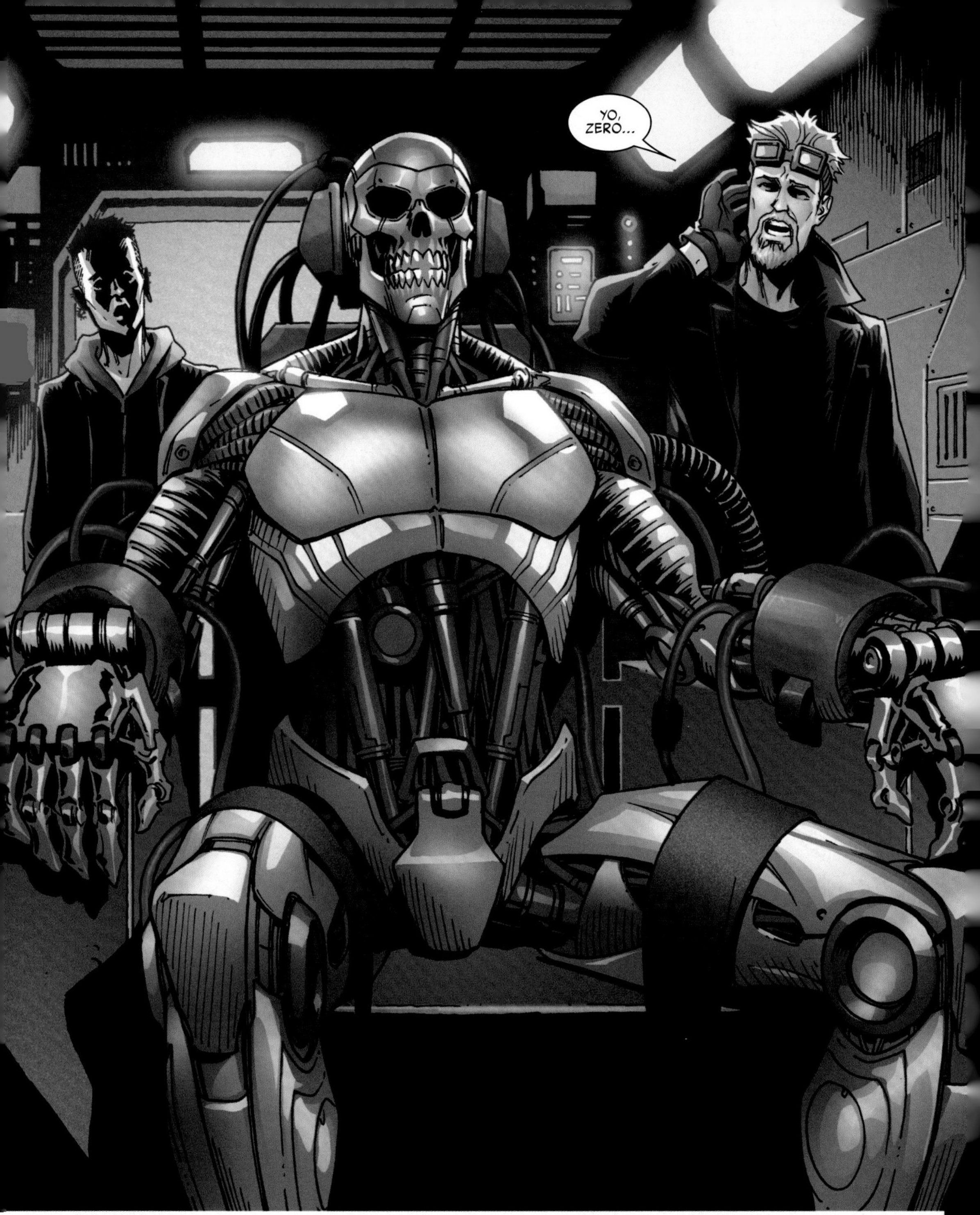
YO, ZERO...

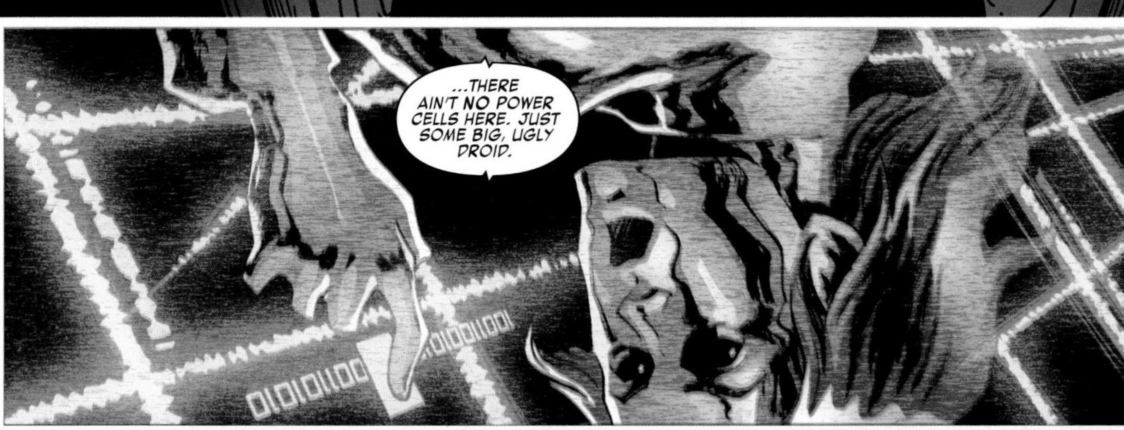
...THERE AIN'T NO POWER CELLS HERE. JUST SOME BIG, UGLY DROID.

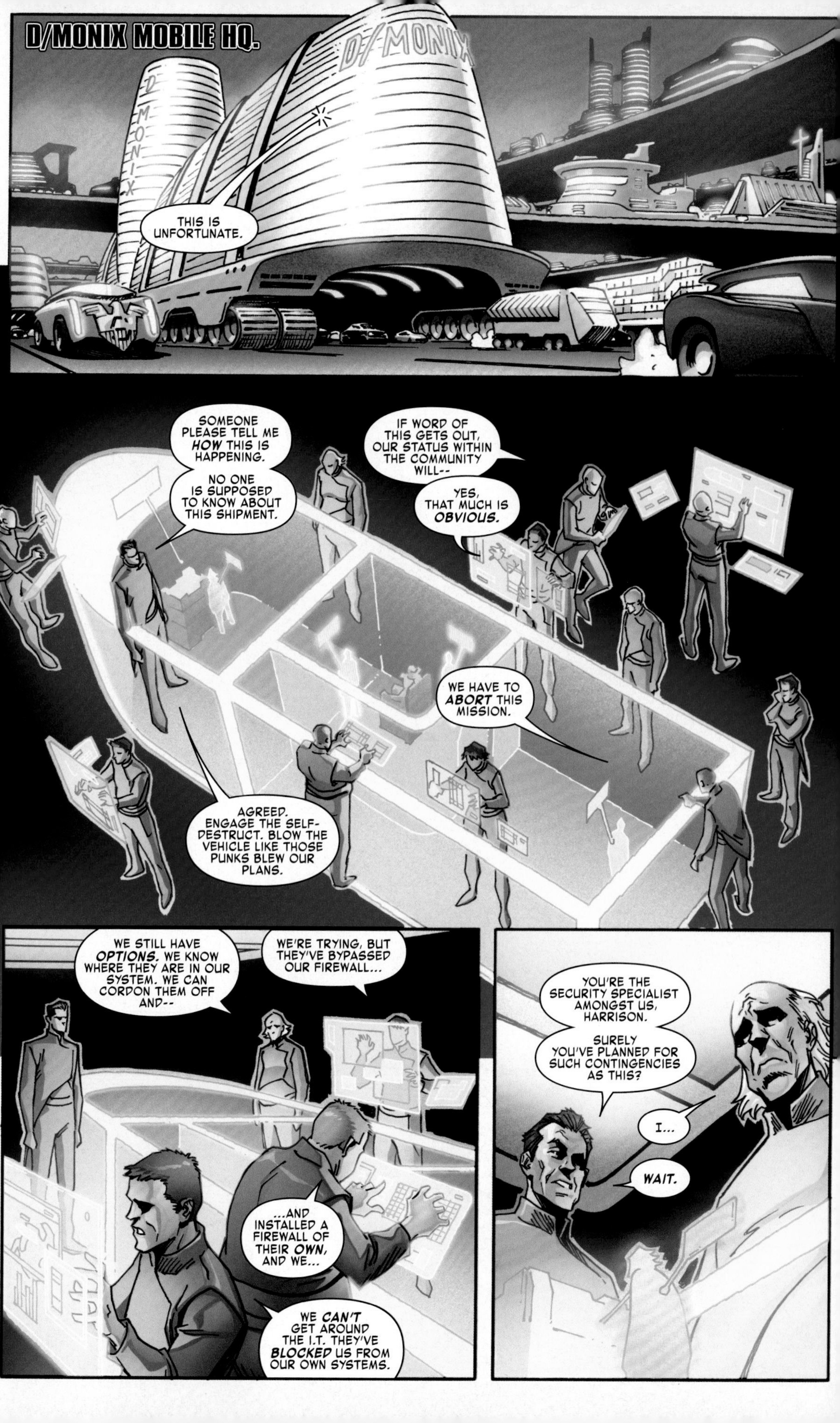
D/MONIX MOBILE HQ.
D/MONIX
THIS IS UNFORTUNATE.
SOMEONE PLEASE TELL ME HOW THIS IS HAPPENING.
NO ONE IS SUPPOSED TO KNOW ABOUT THIS SHIPMENT.
IF WORD OF THIS GETS OUT, OUR STATUS WITHIN THE COMMUNITY WILL--
YES, THAT MUCH IS OBVIOUS.
WE HAVE TO ABORT THIS MISSION.
AGREED. ENGAGE THE SELF-DESTRUCT. BLOW THE VEHICLE LIKE THOSE PUNKS BLEW OUR PLANS.
WE STILL HAVE OPTIONS. WE KNOW WHERE THEY ARE IN OUR SYSTEM. WE CAN CORDON THEM OFF AND--
WE'RE TRYING, BUT THEY'VE BYPASSED OUR FIREWALL...
...AND INSTALLED A FIREWALL OF THEIR OWN, AND WE...
WE CAN'T GET AROUND THE I.T. THEY'VE BLOCKED US FROM OUR OWN SYSTEMS.
YOU'RE THE SECURITY SPECIALIST AMONGST US, HARRISON.
SURELY YOU'VE PLANNED FOR SUCH CONTINGENCIES AS THIS?
I...
WAIT.

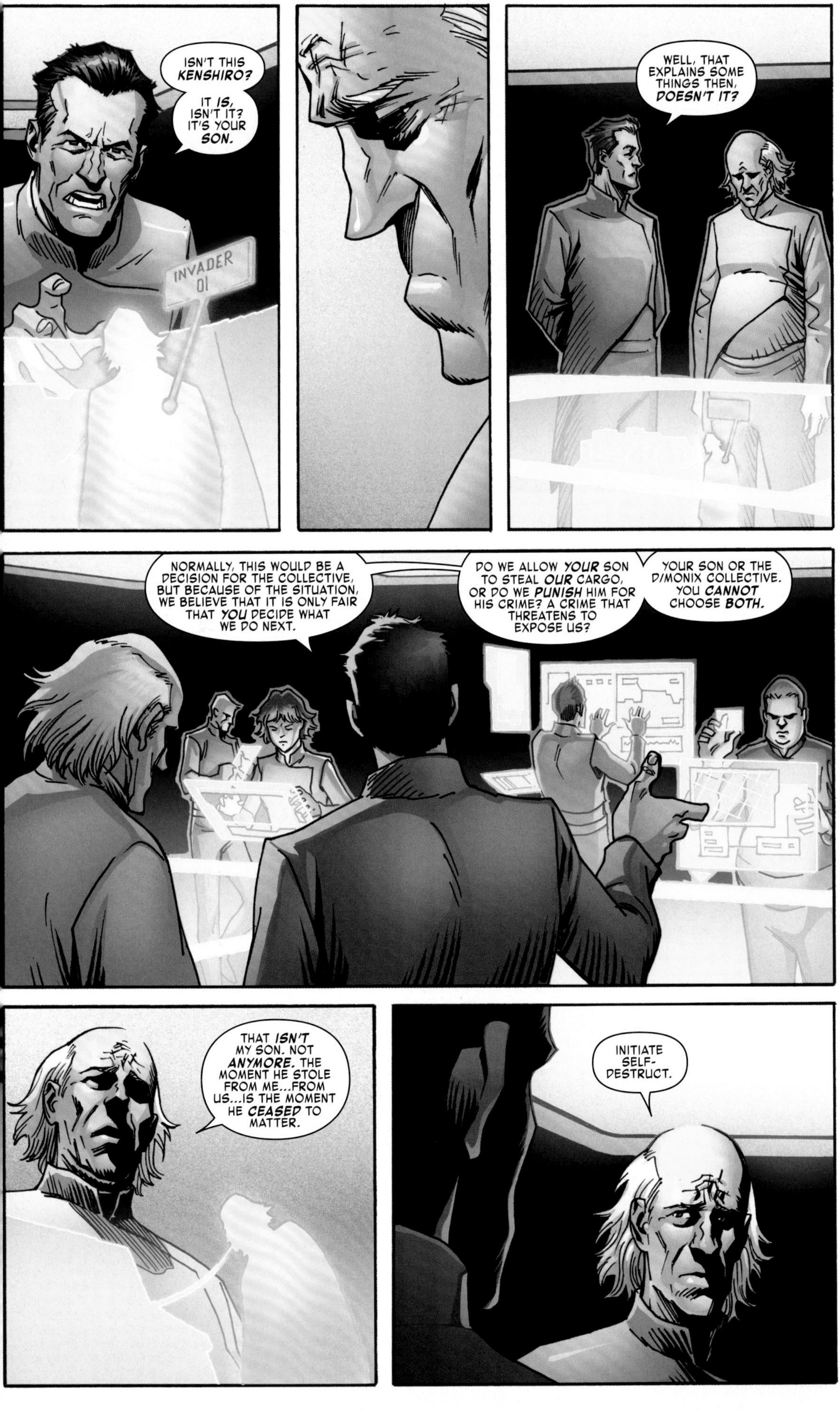
ISN'T THIS KENSHIRO?
IT IS, ISN'T IT? IT'S YOUR SON.
INVADER 01
WELL, THAT EXPLAINS SOME THINGS THEN, DOESN'T IT?
NORMALLY, THIS WOULD BE A DECISION FOR THE COLLECTIVE, BUT BECAUSE OF THE SITUATION, WE BELIEVE THAT IT IS ONLY FAIR THAT YOU DECIDE WHAT WE DO NEXT.
DO WE ALLOW YOUR SON TO STEAL OUR CARGO, OR DO WE PUNISH HIM FOR HIS CRIME? A CRIME THAT THREATENS TO EXPOSE US?
YOUR SON OR THE D/MONIX COLLECTIVE. YOU CANNOT CHOOSE BOTH.
THAT ISN'T MY SON. NOT ANYMORE. THE MOMENT HE STOLE FROM ME...FROM US...IS THE MOMENT HE CEASED TO MATTER.
INITIATE SELF-DESTRUCT.

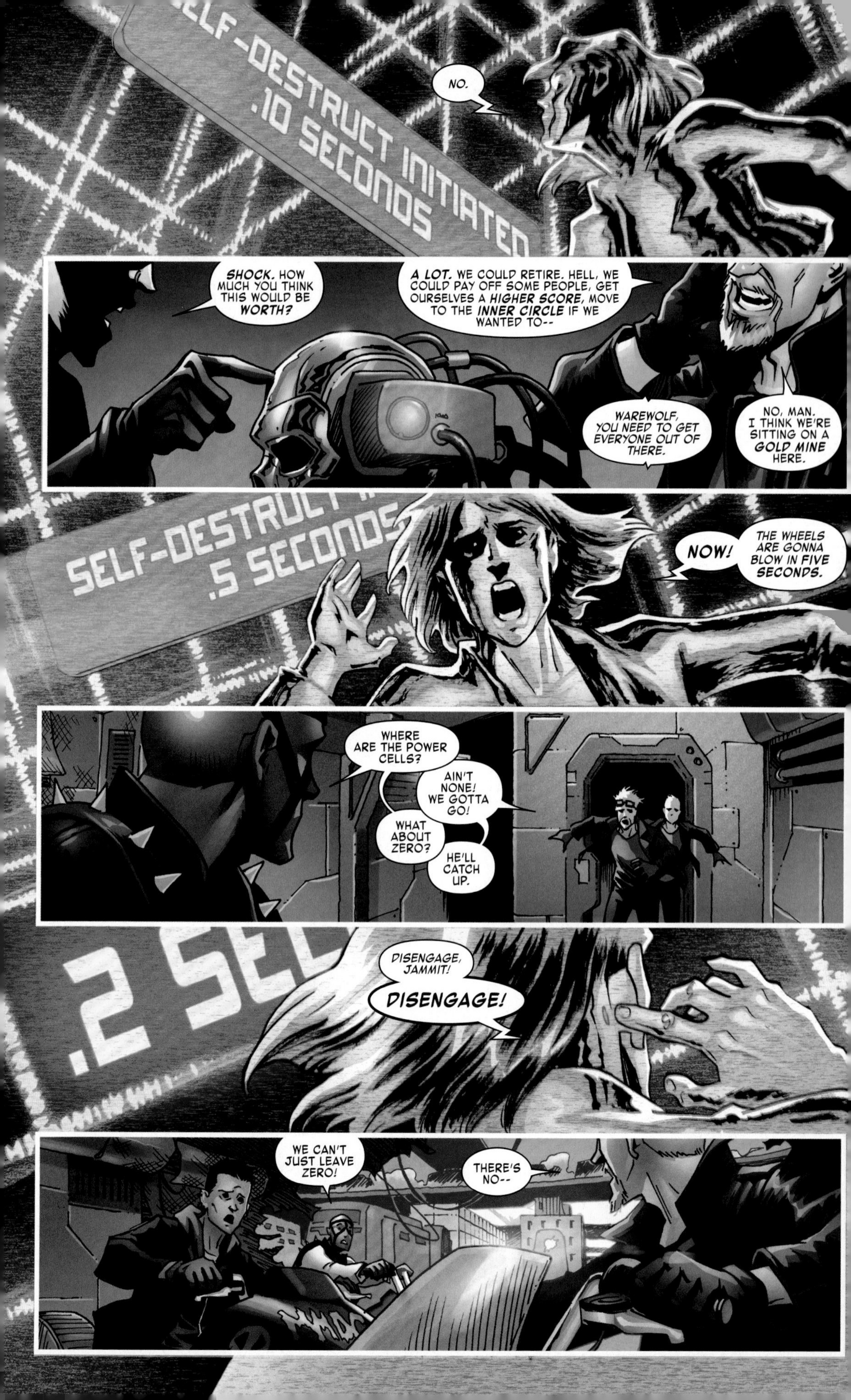
SELF-DESTRUCT INITIATED
.10 SECONDS
NO.
SHOCK. HOW MUCH YOU THINK THIS WOULD BE WORTH?
A LOT. WE COULD RETIRE. HELL, WE COULD PAY OFF SOME PEOPLE, GET OURSELVES A HIGHER SCORE, MOVE TO THE INNER CIRCLE IF WE WANTED TO--
WAREWOLF, YOU NEED TO GET EVERYONE OUT OF THERE.
NO, MAN. I THINK WE'RE SITTING ON A GOLD MINE HERE.
.5 SECONDS
NOW!
THE WHEELS ARE GONNA BLOW IN FIVE SECONDS.
WHERE ARE THE POWER CELLS?
AIN'T NONE! WE GOTTA GO!
WHAT ABOUT ZERO?
HE'LL CATCH UP.
DISENGAGE, JAMMIT!
DISENGAGE!
WE CAN'T JUST LEAVE ZERO!
THERE'S NO--

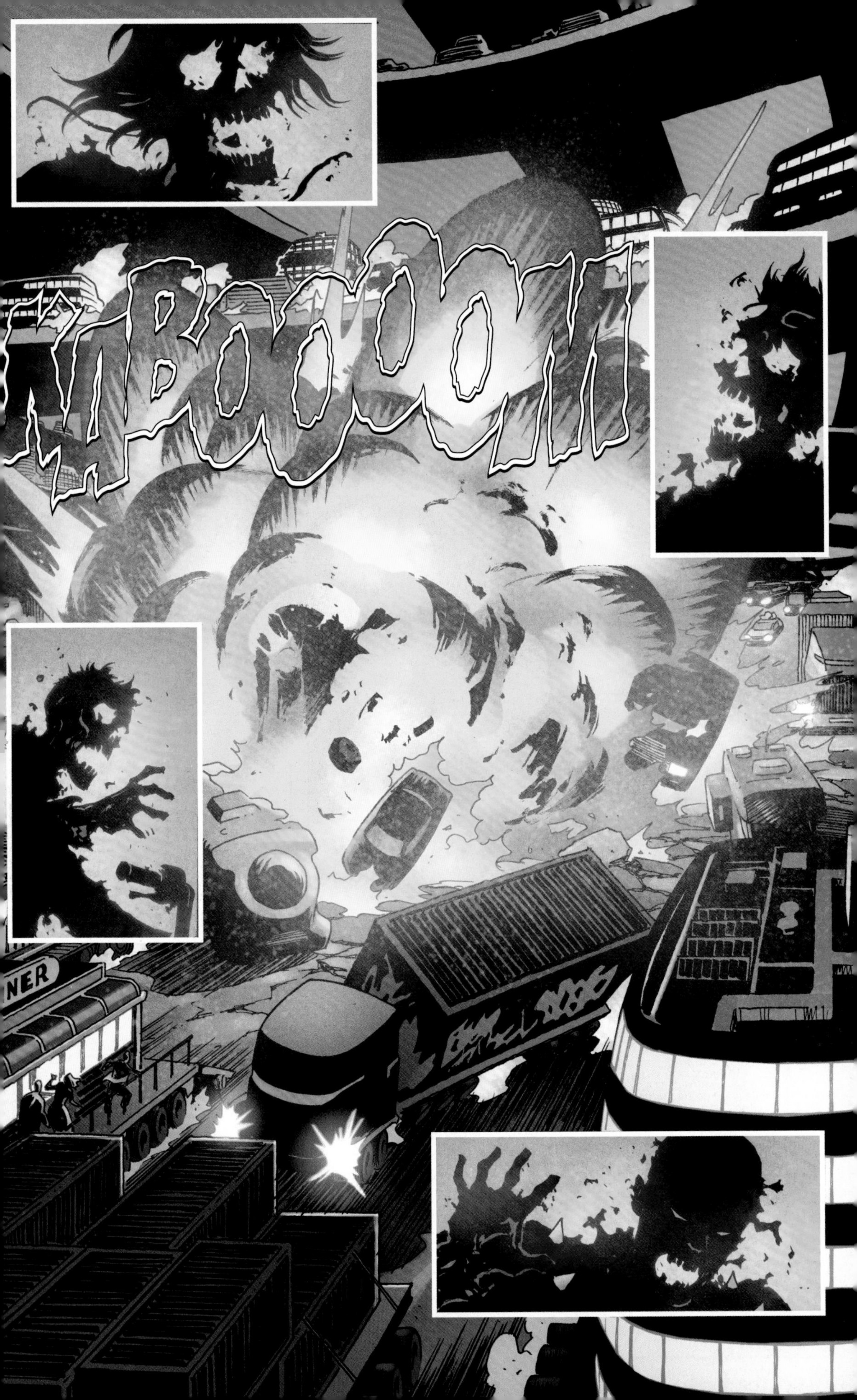
KABOOOOM
NER

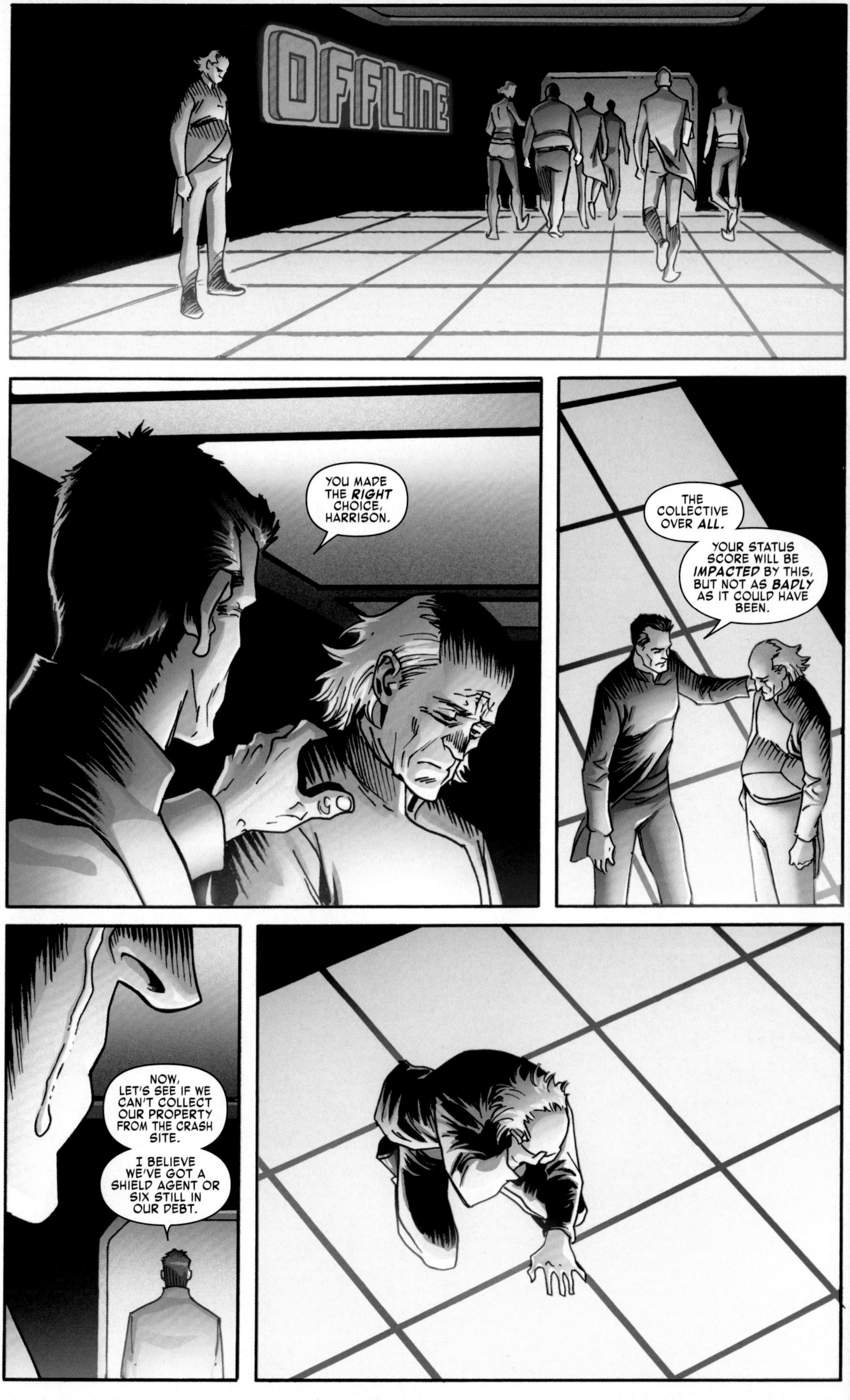
OFFLINE
YOU MADE THE RIGHT CHOICE, HARRISON.
THE COLLECTIVE OVER ALL.
YOUR STATUS SCORE WILL BE IMPACTED BY THIS, BUT NOT AS BADLY AS IT COULD HAVE BEEN.
NOW, LET'S SEE IF WE CAN'T COLLECT OUR PROPERTY FROM THE CRASH SITE.
I BELIEVE WE'VE GOT A SHIELD AGENT OR SIX STILL IN OUR DEBT.

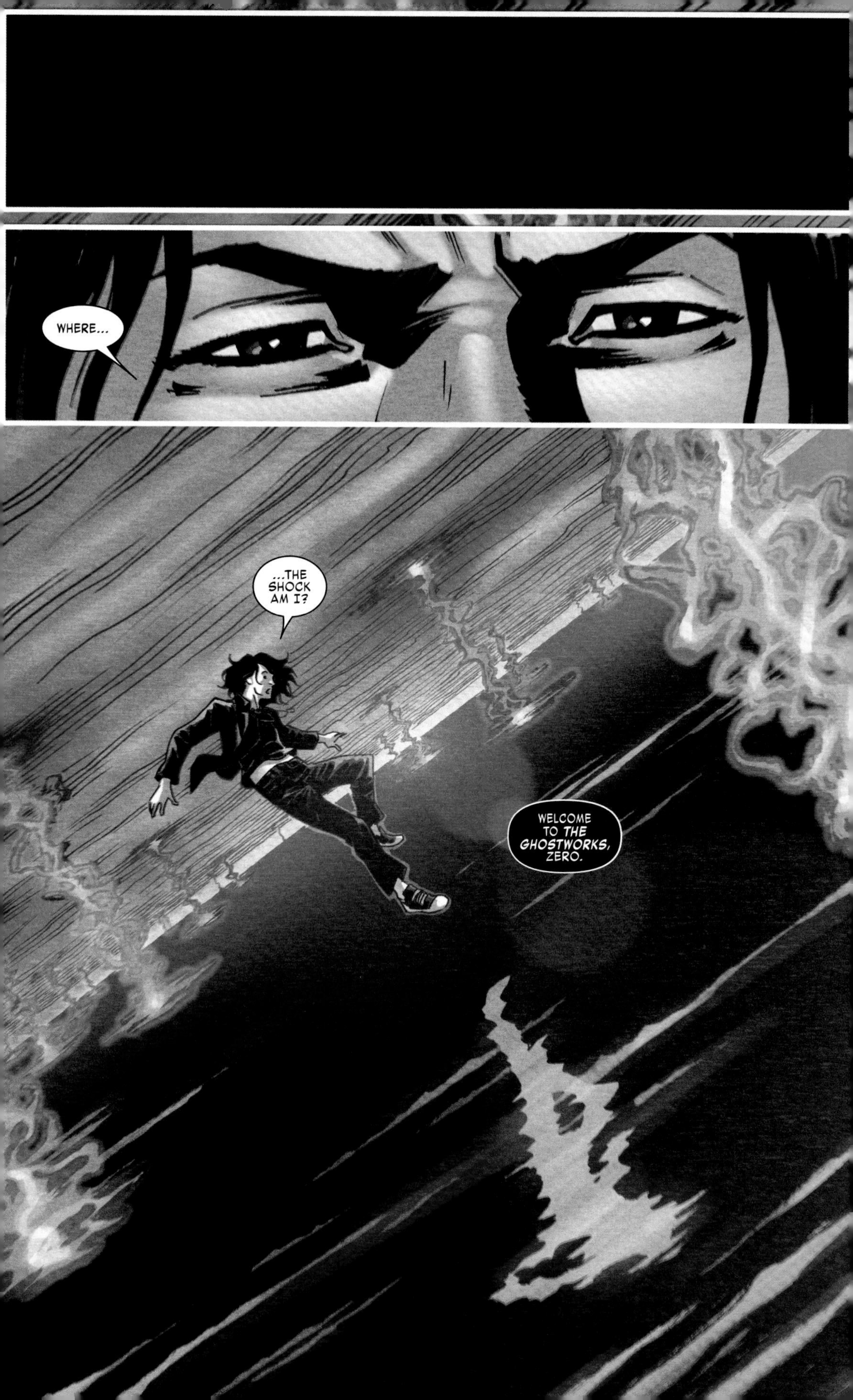
WHERE...
...THE SHOCK AM I?
WELCOME TO THE GHOSTWORKS, ZERO.

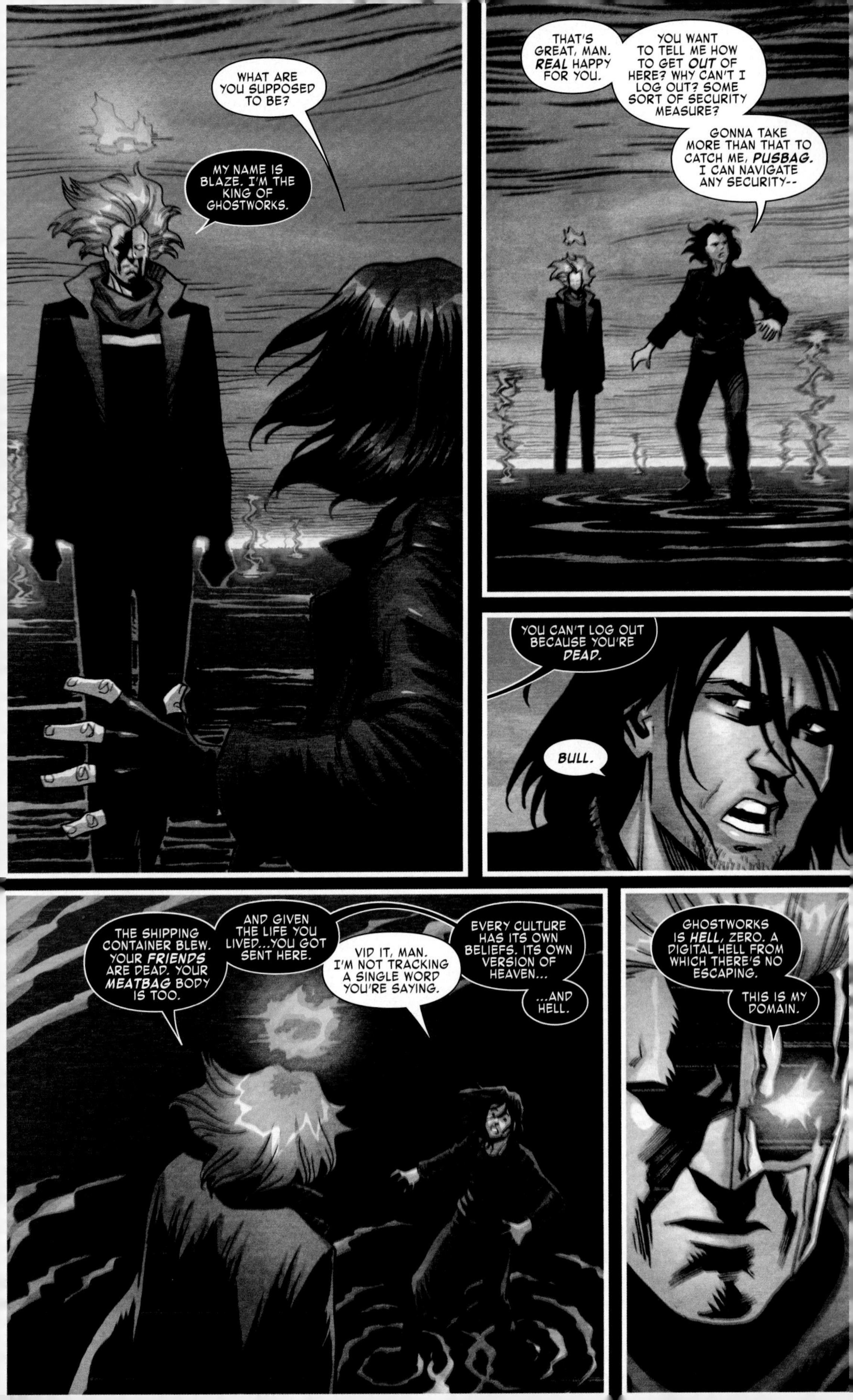
WHAT ARE YOU SUPPOSED TO BE?
MY NAME IS BLAZE. I'M THE KING OF GHOSTWORKS.
THAT'S GREAT, MAN. REAL HAPPY FOR YOU.
YOU WANT TO TELL ME HOW TO GET OUT OF HERE? WHY CAN'T I LOG OUT? SOME SORT OF SECURITY MEASURE?
GONNA TAKE MORE THAN THAT TO CATCH ME, PUSBAG. I CAN NAVIGATE ANY SECURITY--
YOU CAN'T LOG OUT BECAUSE YOU'RE DEAD.
BULL.
THE SHIPPING CONTAINER BLEW. YOUR FRIENDS ARE DEAD. YOUR MEATBAG BODY IS TOO.
AND GIVEN THE LIFE YOU LIVED...YOU GOT SENT HERE.
VID IT, MAN. I'M NOT TRACKING A SINGLE WORD YOU'RE SAYING.
EVERY CULTURE HAS ITS OWN BELIEFS. ITS OWN VERSION OF HEAVEN...
...AND HELL.
GHOSTWORKS IS HELL, ZERO. A DIGITAL HELL FROM WHICH THERE'S NO ESCAPING.
THIS IS MY DOMAIN.

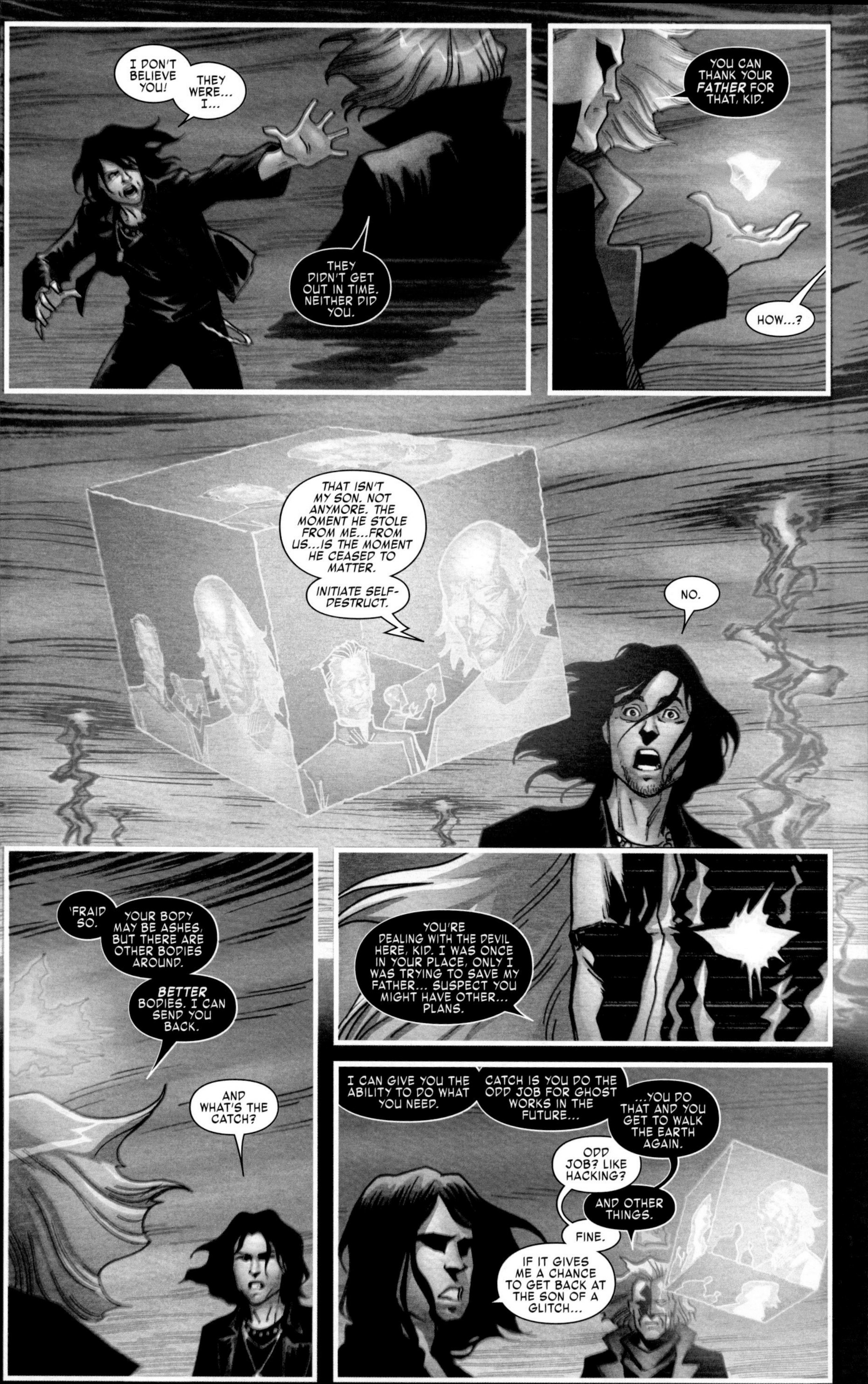
I DON'T BELIEVE YOU!
THEY WERE... I...
THEY DIDN'T GET OUT IN TIME. NEITHER DID YOU.
YOU CAN THANK YOUR FATHER FOR THAT, KID.
HOW...?
THAT ISN'T MY SON. NOT ANYMORE. THE MOMENT HE STOLE FROM ME...FROM US...IS THE MOMENT HE CEASED TO MATTER.
INITIATE SELF-DESTRUCT.
NO.
'FRAID SO.
YOUR BODY MAY BE ASHES, BUT THERE ARE OTHER BODIES AROUND.
BETTER BODIES. I CAN SEND YOU BACK.
AND WHAT'S THE CATCH?
YOU'RE DEALING WITH THE DEVIL HERE, KID. I WAS ONCE IN YOUR PLACE, ONLY I WAS TRYING TO SAVE MY FATHER... SUSPECT YOU MIGHT HAVE OTHER... PLANS.
I CAN GIVE YOU THE ABILITY TO DO WHAT YOU NEED.
CATCH IS YOU DO THE ODD JOB FOR GHOST WORKS IN THE FUTURE...
...YOU DO THAT AND YOU GET TO WALK THE EARTH AGAIN.
ODD JOB? LIKE HACKING?
AND OTHER THINGS.
FINE.
IF IT GIVES ME A CHANCE TO GET BACK AT THE SON OF A GLITCH...

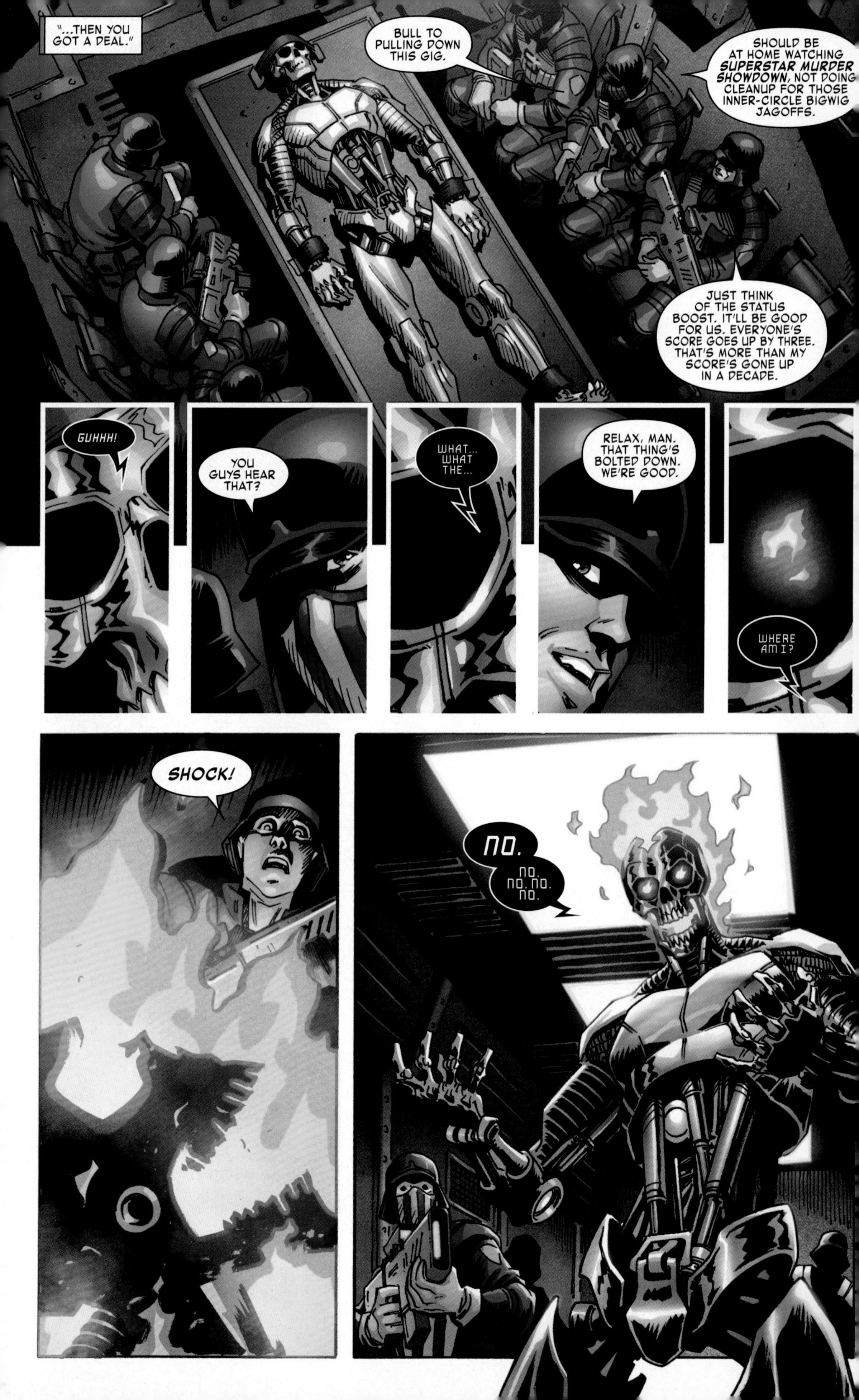
"...THEN YOU GOT A DEAL."
BULL TO PULLING DOWN THIS GIG.
SHOULD BE AT HOME WATCHING SUPERSTAR MURDER SHOWDOWN, NOT DOING CLEANUP FOR THOSE INNER-CIRCLE BIGWIG JAGOFFS.
JUST THINK OF THE STATUS BOOST. IT'LL BE GOOD FOR US. EVERYONE'S SCORE GOES UP BY THREE. THAT'S MORE THAN MY SCORE'S GONE UP IN A DECADE.
GUHHH!
YOU GUYS HEAR THAT?
WHAT... WHAT THE...
RELAX, MAN. THAT THING'S BOLTED DOWN. WE'RE GOOD.
WHERE AM I?
SHOCK!
NO.
NO. NO. NO. NO.

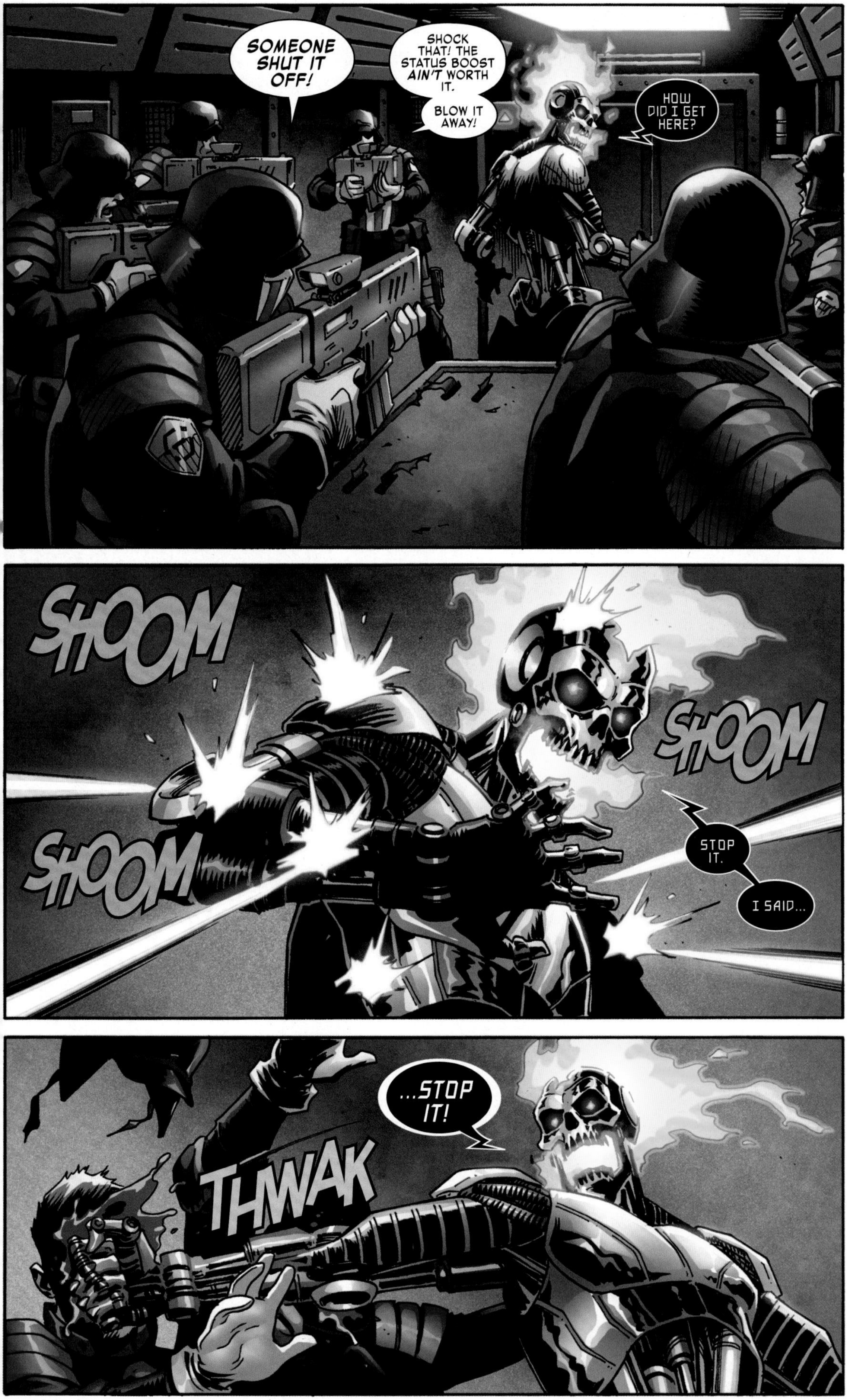
SOMEONE SHUT IT OFF!
SHOCK THAT! THE STATUS BOOST AIN'T WORTH IT.
BLOW IT AWAY!
HOW DID I GET HERE?
SHOOM
SHOOM
SHOOM
STOP IT.
I SAID...
...STOP IT!
THWAK

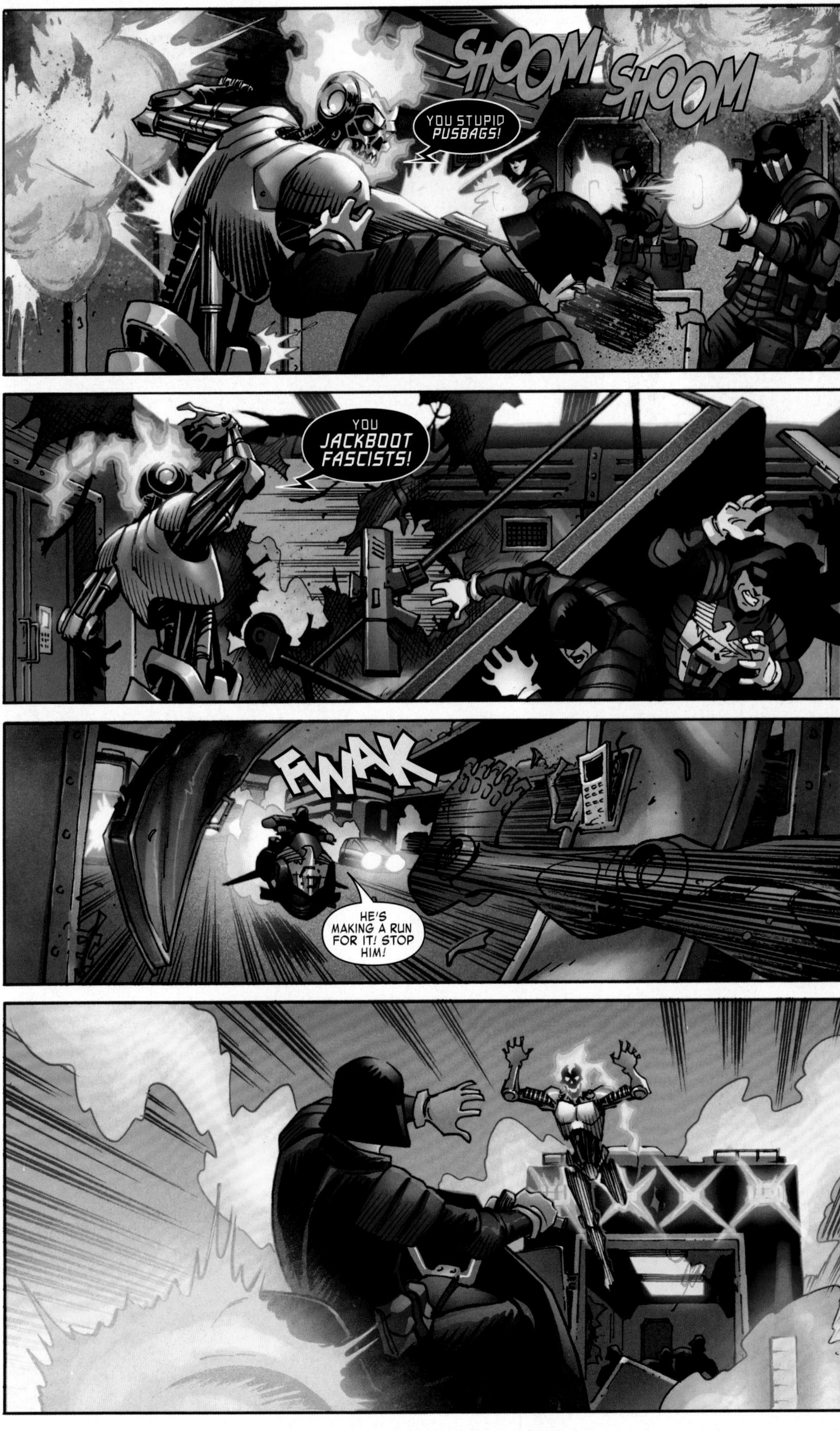
SHOOM SHOOM
YOU STUPID PUSBAGS!
YOU JACKBOOT FASCISTS!
FWAK
HE'S MAKING A RUN FOR IT! STOP HIM!

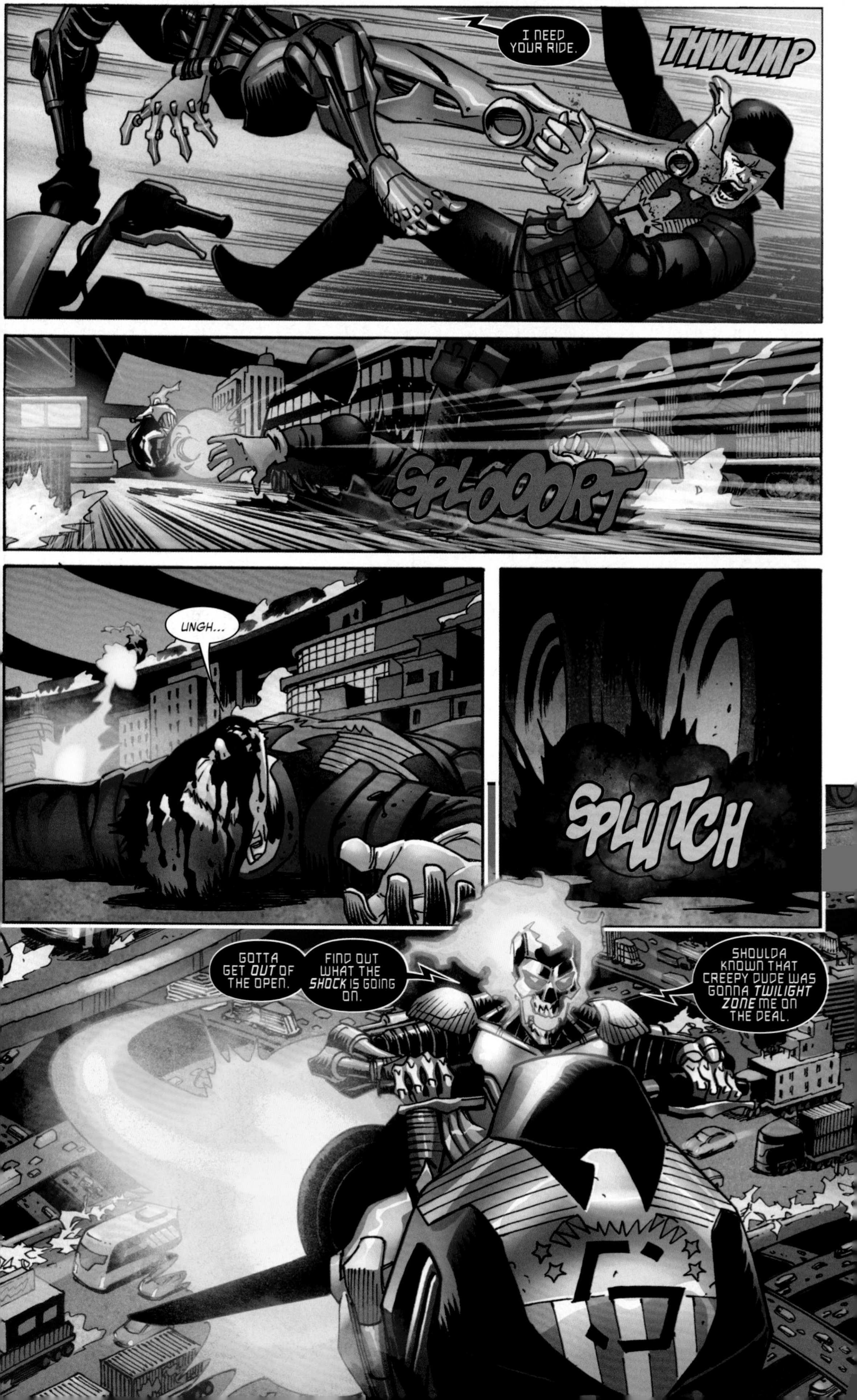
I NEED YOUR RIDE.
THWUMP
SPLOOORT
UNGH...
SPLUTCH
GOTTA GET OUT OF THE OPEN.
FIND OUT WHAT THE SHOCK IS GOING ON.
SHOULDA KNOWN THAT CREEPY DUDE WAS GONNA TWILIGHT ZONE ME ON THE DEAL.

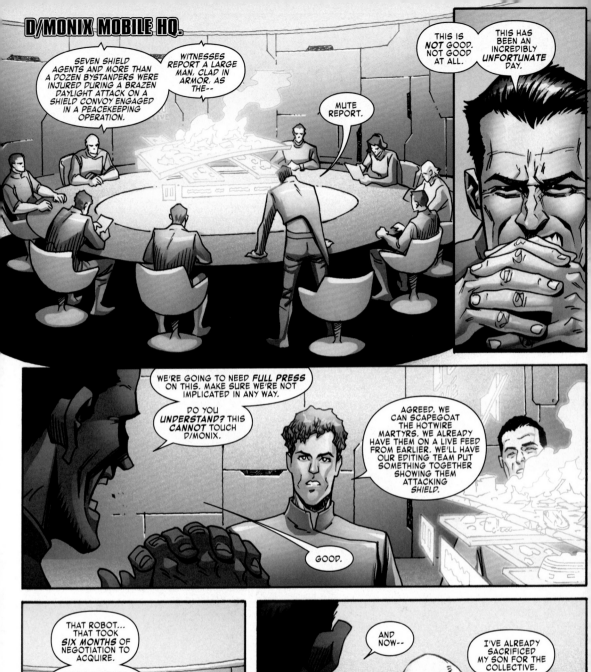

SEVEN SHIELD AGENTS AND MORE THAN A DOZEN BYSTANDERS WERE INJURED DURING A BRAZEN DAYLIGHT ATTACK ON A SHIELD CONVOY ENGAGED IN A PEACEKEEPING OPERATION.

WITNESSES REPORT A LARGE MAN, CLAD IN ARMOR, AS THE--

MUTE REPORT.

THIS IS *NOT GOOD.* NOT GOOD AT ALL.

THIS HAS BEEN AN INCREDIBLY *UNFORTUNATE* DAY.

WE'RE GOING TO NEED *FULL PRESS* ON THIS. MAKE SURE WE'RE NOT IMPLICATED IN ANY WAY.

DO YOU *UNDERSTAND?* THIS *CANNOT* TOUCH D/MONIX.

AGREED. WE CAN SCAPEGOAT THE HOTWIRE MARTYRS. WE ALREADY HAVE THEM ON A LIVE FEED FROM EARLIER. WE'LL HAVE OUR EDITING TEAM PUT SOMETHING TOGETHER SHOWING THEM ATTACKING SHIELD.

GOOD.

THAT ROBOT... THAT TOOK *SIX MONTHS* OF NEGOTIATION TO ACQUIRE.

WE'RE ALREADY TWO MONTHS BEHIND ON DEVELOPMENT OF MORE ROAD--ROAD WE NEEDED THAT ROBOT TO CLEAR OF DOWNRAMPERS.

AND NOW--

I'VE ALREADY SACRIFICED MY SON FOR THE COLLECTIVE.

HOW MUCH *MORE* MUST I GIVE TO EARN FORGIVENESS?

WE'VE BEEN WONDERING *THE SAME.*

THE COUNCIL HAS SCHEDULED A DISCIPLINARY TRIAL FOR THIS EVENING TO DECIDE ON THE ANSWER.

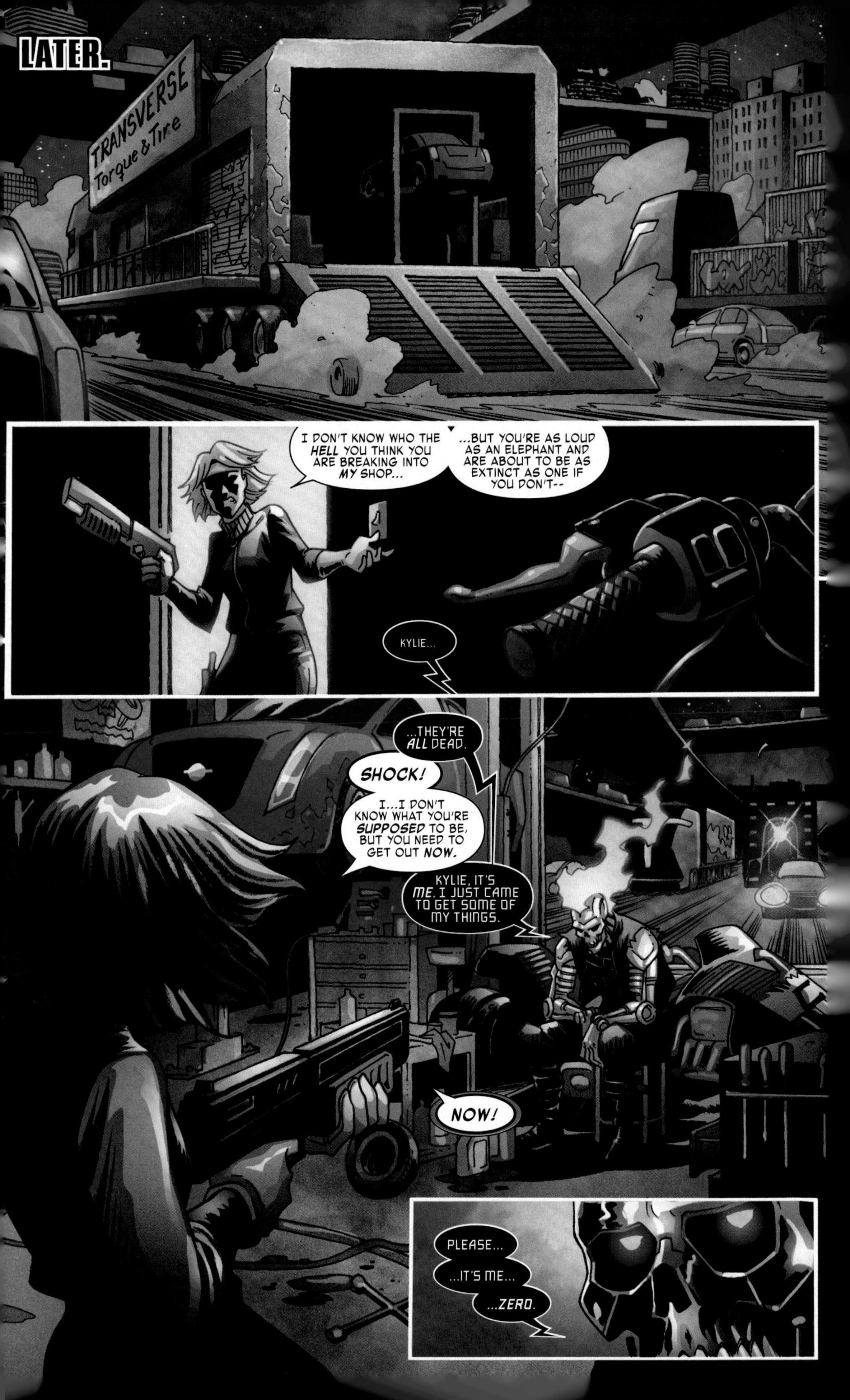
LATER.
TRANSVERSE
Torque & Tire
I DON'T KNOW WHO THE HELL YOU THINK YOU ARE BREAKING INTO MY SHOP...
...BUT YOU'RE AS LOUD AS AN ELEPHANT AND ARE ABOUT TO BE AS EXTINCT AS ONE IF YOU DON'T--
KYLIE...
...THEY'RE ALL DEAD.
SHOCK!
I...I DON'T KNOW WHAT YOU'RE SUPPOSED TO BE, BUT YOU NEED TO GET OUT NOW.
KYLIE, IT'S ME. I JUST CAME TO GET SOME OF MY THINGS.
NOW!
PLEASE...
...IT'S ME...
...ZERO.

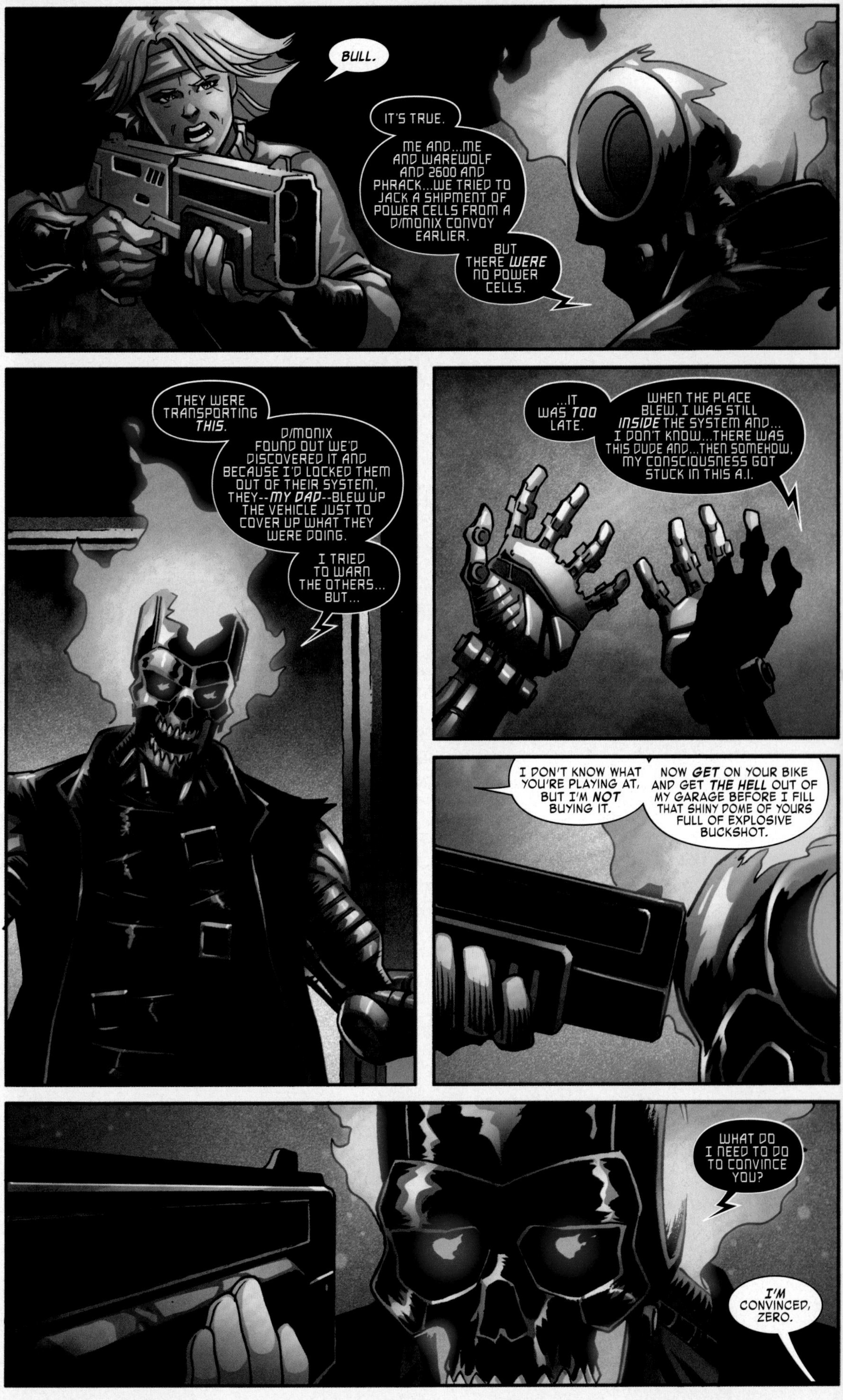
BULL.
IT'S TRUE.
ME AND...ME AND WAREWOLF AND 2600 AND PHRACK...WE TRIED TO JACK A SHIPMENT OF POWER CELLS FROM A D/MONIX CONVOY EARLIER.
BUT THERE WERE NO POWER CELLS.
THEY WERE TRANSPORTING THIS.
D/MONIX FOUND OUT WE'D DISCOVERED IT AND BECAUSE I'D LOCKED THEM OUT OF THEIR SYSTEM, THEY--MY DAD--BLEW UP THE VEHICLE JUST TO COVER UP WHAT THEY WERE DOING.
I TRIED TO WARN THE OTHERS... BUT...
...IT WAS TOO LATE.
WHEN THE PLACE BLEW, I WAS STILL INSIDE THE SYSTEM AND... I DON'T KNOW...THERE WAS THIS DUDE AND...THEN SOMEHOW, MY CONSCIOUSNESS GOT STUCK IN THIS A.I.
I DON'T KNOW WHAT YOU'RE PLAYING AT, BUT I'M NOT BUYING IT.
NOW GET ON YOUR BIKE AND GET THE HELL OUT OF MY GARAGE BEFORE I FILL THAT SHINY DOME OF YOURS FULL OF EXPLOSIVE BUCKSHOT.
WHAT DO I NEED TO DO TO CONVINCE YOU?
I'M CONVINCED, ZERO.

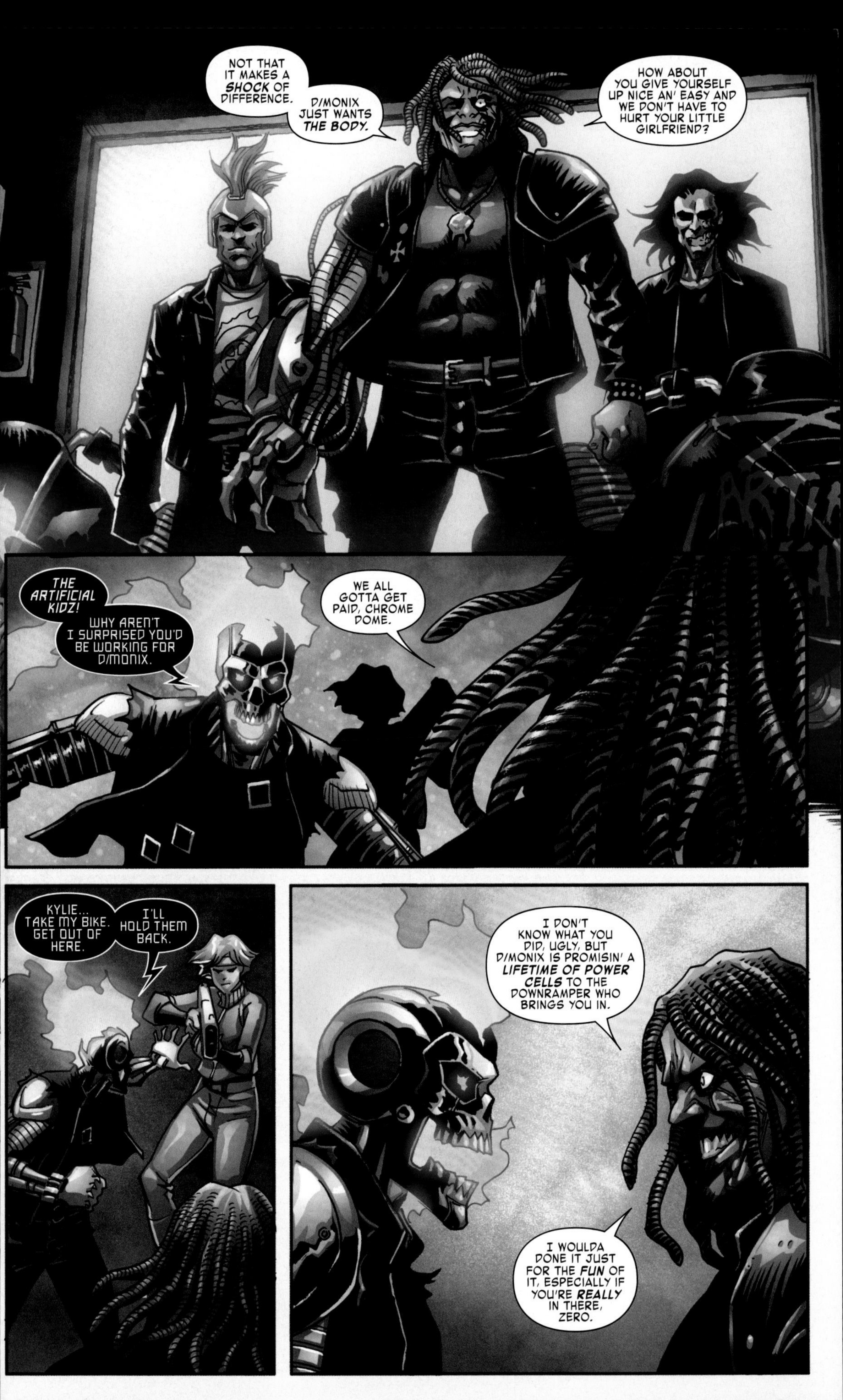

NOT THAT IT MAKES A SHOCK OF DIFFERENCE.
D/MONIX JUST WANTS THE BODY.
HOW ABOUT YOU GIVE YOURSELF UP NICE AN' EASY AND WE DON'T HAVE TO HURT YOUR LITTLE GIRLFRIEND?
THE ARTIFICIAL KIDZ! WHY AREN'T I SURPRISED YOU'D BE WORKING FOR D/MONIX.
WE ALL GOTTA GET PAID, CHROME DOME.
KYLIE... TAKE MY BIKE. GET OUT OF HERE.
I'LL HOLD THEM BACK.
I DON'T KNOW WHAT YOU DID, UGLY, BUT D/MONIX IS PROMISIN' A LIFETIME OF POWER CELLS TO THE DOWNRAMPER WHO BRINGS YOU IN.
I WOULDA DONE IT JUST FOR THE FUN OF IT, ESPECIALLY IF YOU'RE REALLY IN THERE, ZERO.

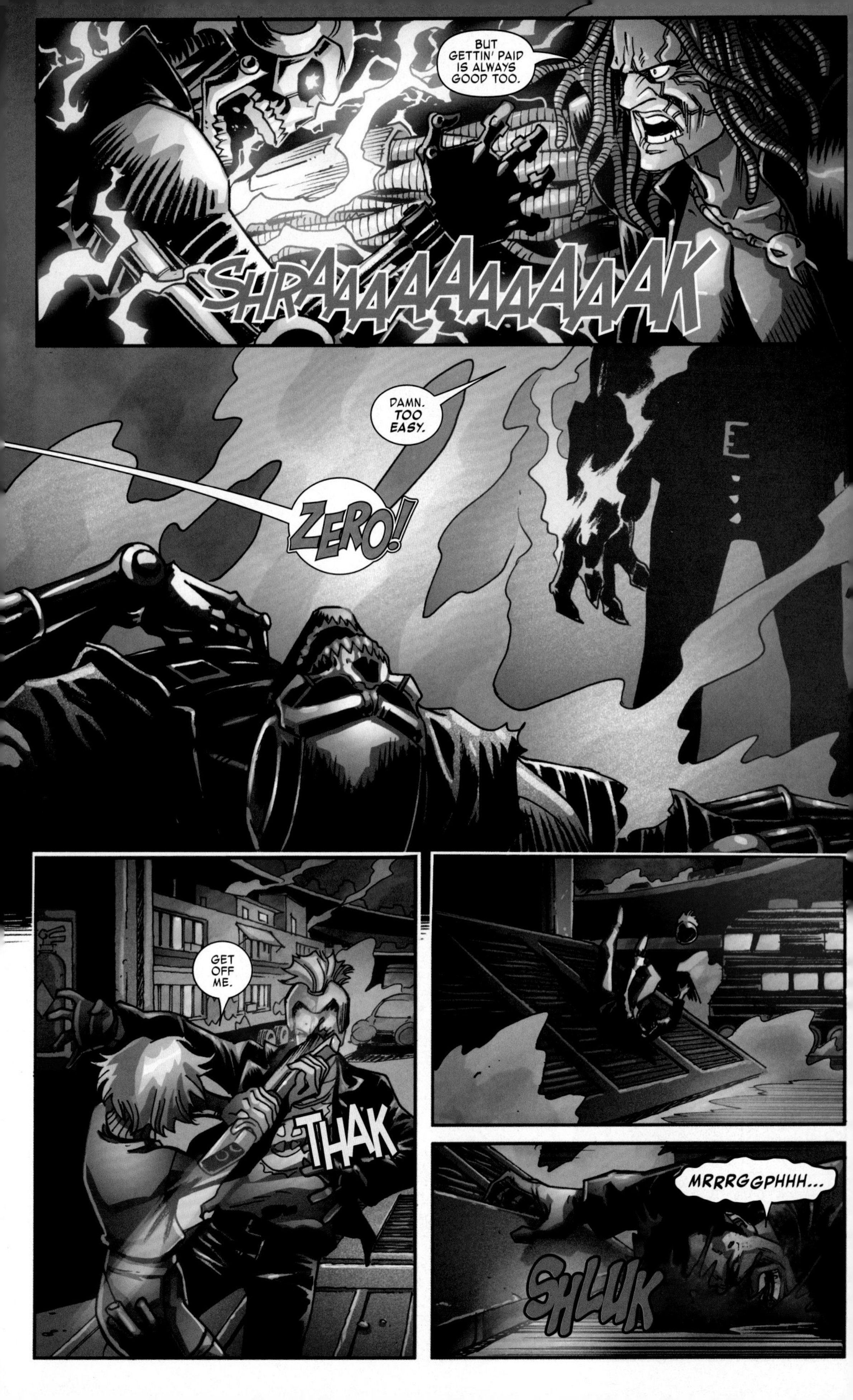
BUT GETTIN' PAID IS ALWAYS GOOD TOO.
SHRAAAAAAAAAAAAK
DAMN. TOO EASY.
ZERO!
GET OFF ME.
THAK
MRRRGGPHHH...
SHLUK

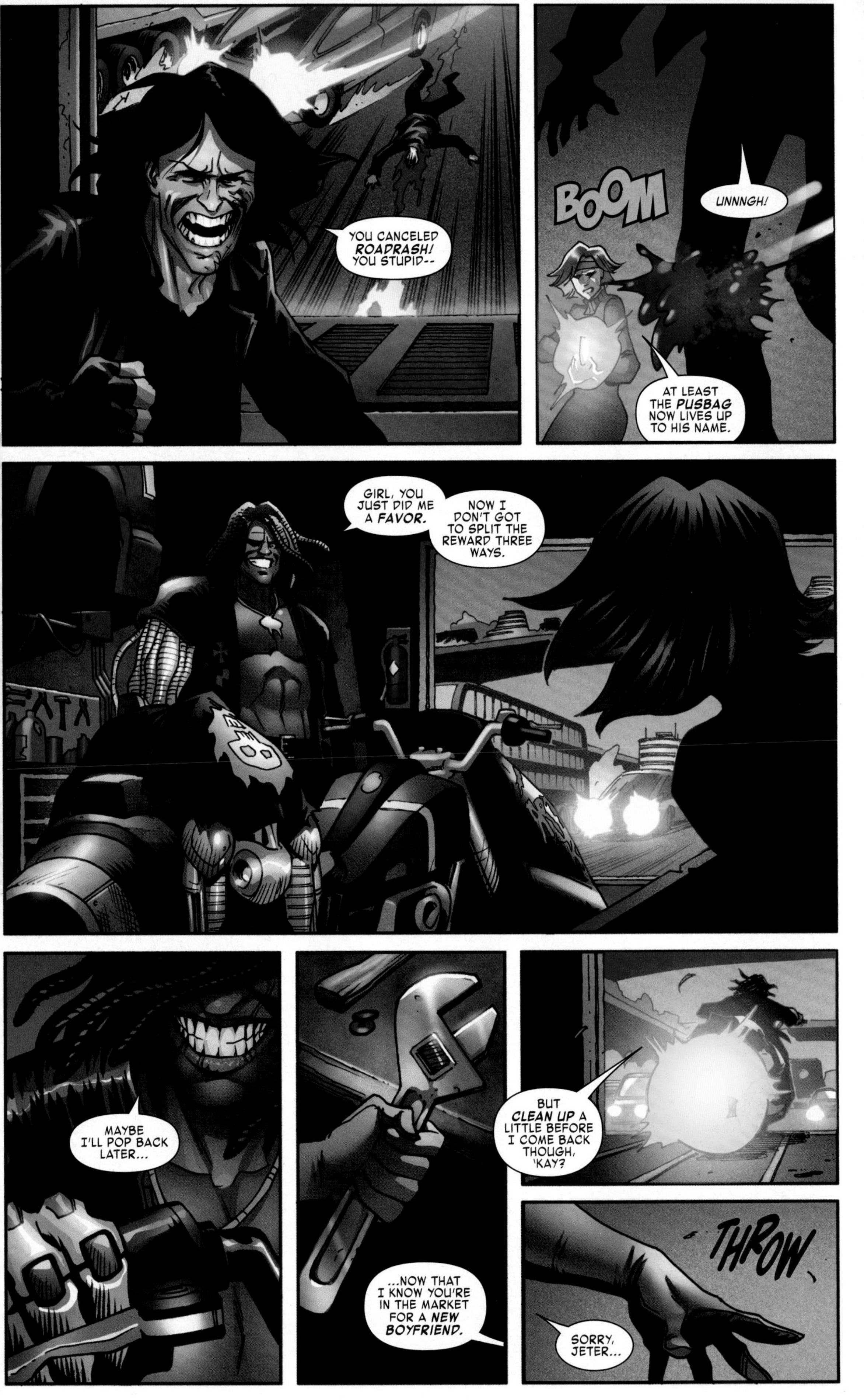
YOU CANCELED ROADRASH! YOU STUPID--
BOOM
UNNNGH!
AT LEAST THE PUSBAG NOW LIVES UP TO HIS NAME.
GIRL, YOU JUST DID ME A FAVOR.
NOW I DON'T GOT TO SPLIT THE REWARD THREE WAYS.
MAYBE I'LL POP BACK LATER...
...NOW THAT I KNOW YOU'RE IN THE MARKET FOR A NEW BOYFRIEND.
BUT CLEAN UP A LITTLE BEFORE I COME BACK THOUGH, 'KAY?
THROW
SORRY, JETER...

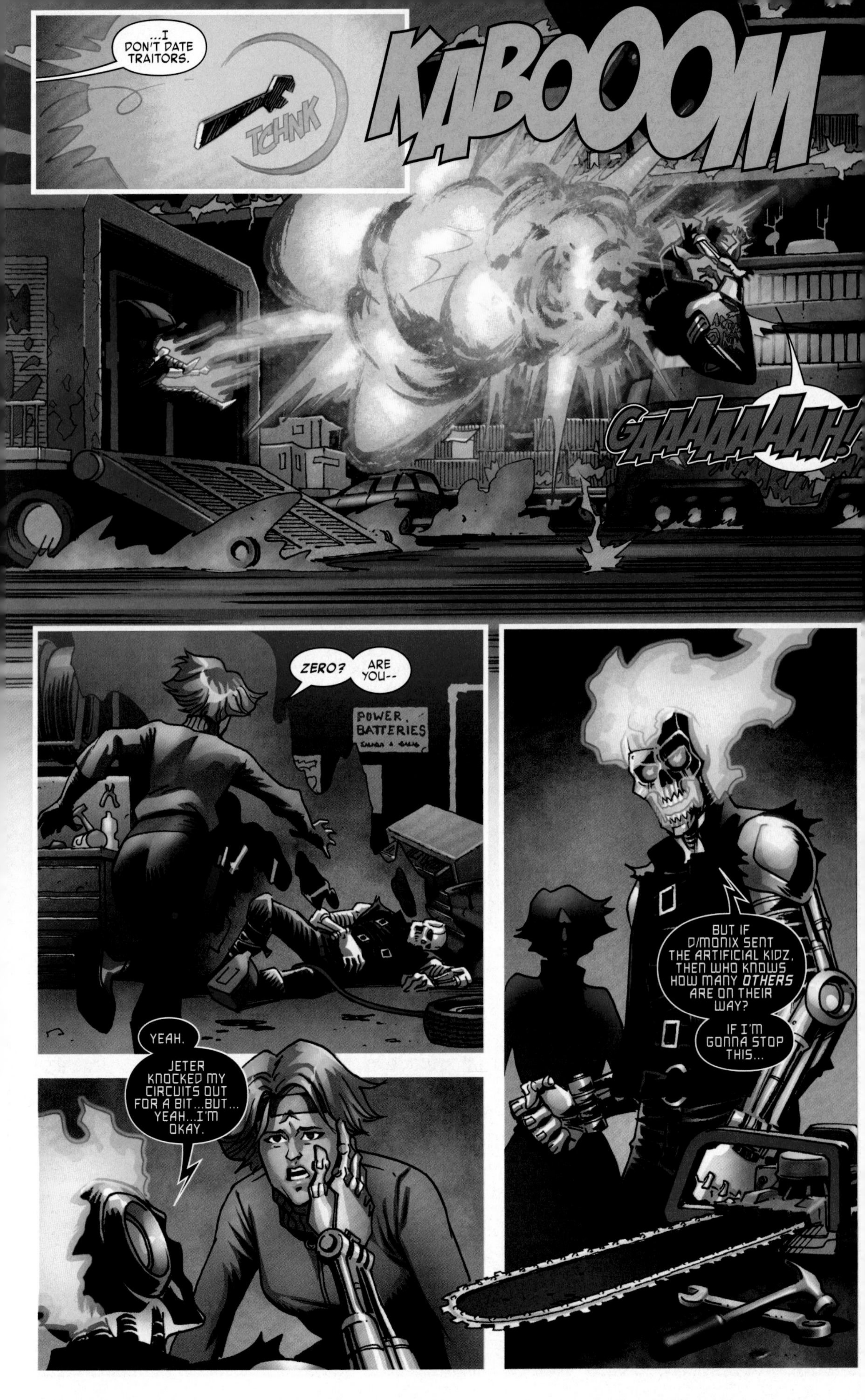

...I DON'T DATE TRAITORS.
TCHNK
KABOOOM
GAAAAAAAH!
ZERO?
ARE YOU--
POWER BATTERIES
YEAH.
JETER KNOCKED MY CIRCUITS OUT FOR A BIT...BUT... YEAH...I'M OKAY.
BUT IF D/MONIX SENT THE ARTIFICIAL KIDZ, THEN WHO KNOWS HOW MANY OTHERS ARE ON THEIR WAY?
IF I'M GONNA STOP THIS...

"...I NEED TO CUT THE HEAD OFF THE SNAKE."

IN THE TRIAL OF *D/MONIX* VS. *HARRISON COCHRANE* FOR HIS CRIMES AGAINST THE COLLECTIVE...

D/MONIX MOBILE HQ.

...FOR HIS PART IN DIVULGING COLLECTIVE SECRETS AND COMPROMISING D/MONIX OPERATIONS THROUGH WILLFUL NEGLECT--

YOU CAN'T DO THIS!

I'VE GIVEN *EVERYTHING* TO D/MONIX!

WITHOUT ME, NONE OF YOU WOULD HAVE THOUGHT TO BRING IN AN A.I. DROID TO WIPE THE *DOWNRAMPERS* FROM OUR ROADS.

THE COLLECTIVE WOULD *STILL* BE TRYING TO FIND OTHER, *LESS-EFFICIENT* METHODS TO EXPAND THE INNER CIRCLE.

THE RESIDENTS OF THE INNER CIRCLE WOULD HAVE GROWN FRUSTRATED AND *DOWNVOTED* US. OUR REPUTATIONS WOULD BE *MUD!*

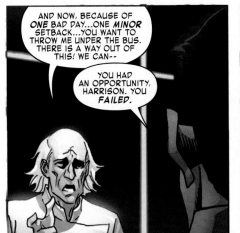

AND NOW, BECAUSE OF *ONE* BAD DAY...ONE *MINOR* SETBACK...YOU WANT TO THROW ME UNDER THE BUS. THERE IS A WAY OUT OF THIS! WE CAN--

YOU HAD AN OPPORTUNITY, HARRISON. YOU *FAILED.*

THE INNER CIRCLE DEMANDS THAT *SOMEONE* TAKE RESPONSIBILITY AND... AS YOU'VE POINTED OUT... THIS WAS YOUR PLAN, SO IT IS ONLY RIGHT THAT YOU FALL ON THE SWORD.

I'VE GOT A *BETTER* IDEA...

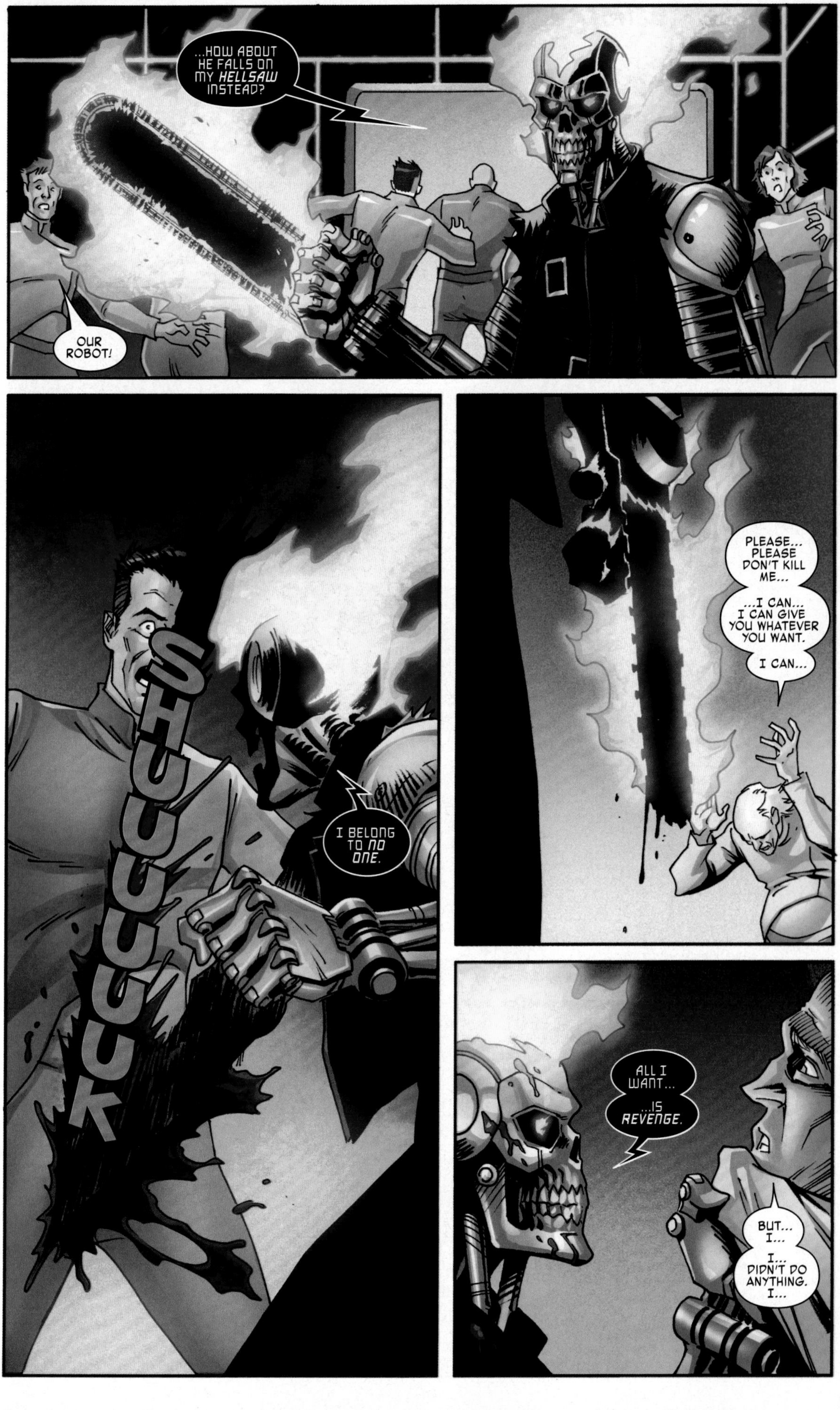
...HOW ABOUT HE FALLS ON MY HELLSAW INSTEAD?
OUR ROBOT!
SHUUUUUUUK
I BELONG TO NO ONE.
PLEASE... PLEASE DON'T KILL ME...
...I CAN... I CAN GIVE YOU WHATEVER YOU WANT.
I CAN...
ALL I WANT...
...IS REVENGE.
BUT... I...
I... DIDN'T DO ANYTHING. I...

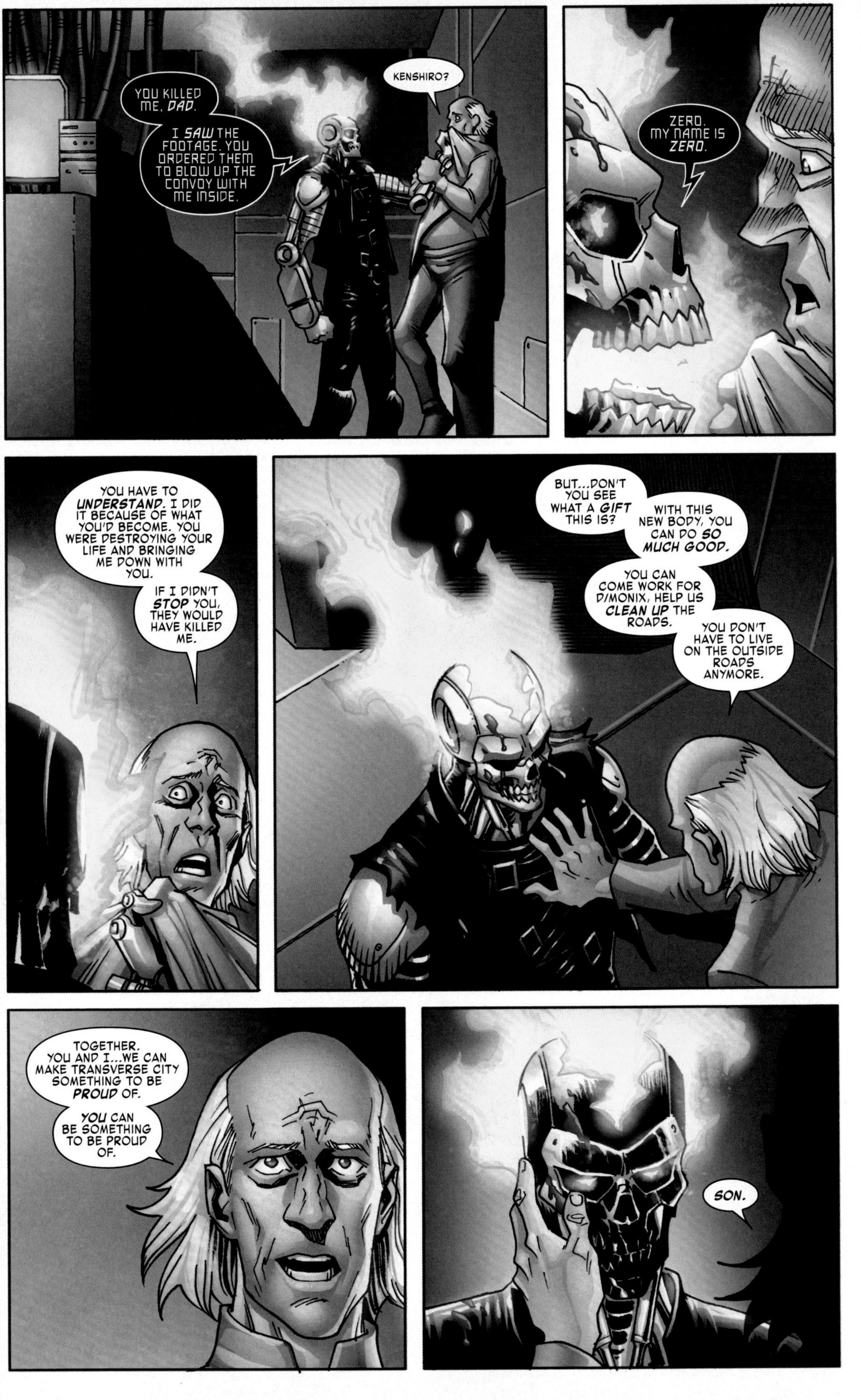
YOU KILLED ME, DAD.
I SAW THE FOOTAGE. YOU ORDERED THEM TO BLOW UP THE CONVOY WITH ME INSIDE.
KENSHIRO?
ZERO. MY NAME IS ZERO.
YOU HAVE TO UNDERSTAND. I DID IT BECAUSE OF WHAT YOU'D BECOME. YOU WERE DESTROYING YOUR LIFE AND BRINGING ME DOWN WITH YOU.
IF I DIDN'T STOP YOU, THEY WOULD HAVE KILLED ME.
BUT...DON'T YOU SEE WHAT A GIFT THIS IS?
WITH THIS NEW BODY, YOU CAN DO SO MUCH GOOD.
YOU CAN COME WORK FOR D/MONIX, HELP US CLEAN UP THE ROADS.
YOU DON'T HAVE TO LIVE ON THE OUTSIDE ROADS ANYMORE.
TOGETHER. YOU AND I...WE CAN MAKE TRANSVERSE CITY SOMETHING TO BE PROUD OF.
YOU CAN BE SOMETHING TO BE PROUD OF.
SON.

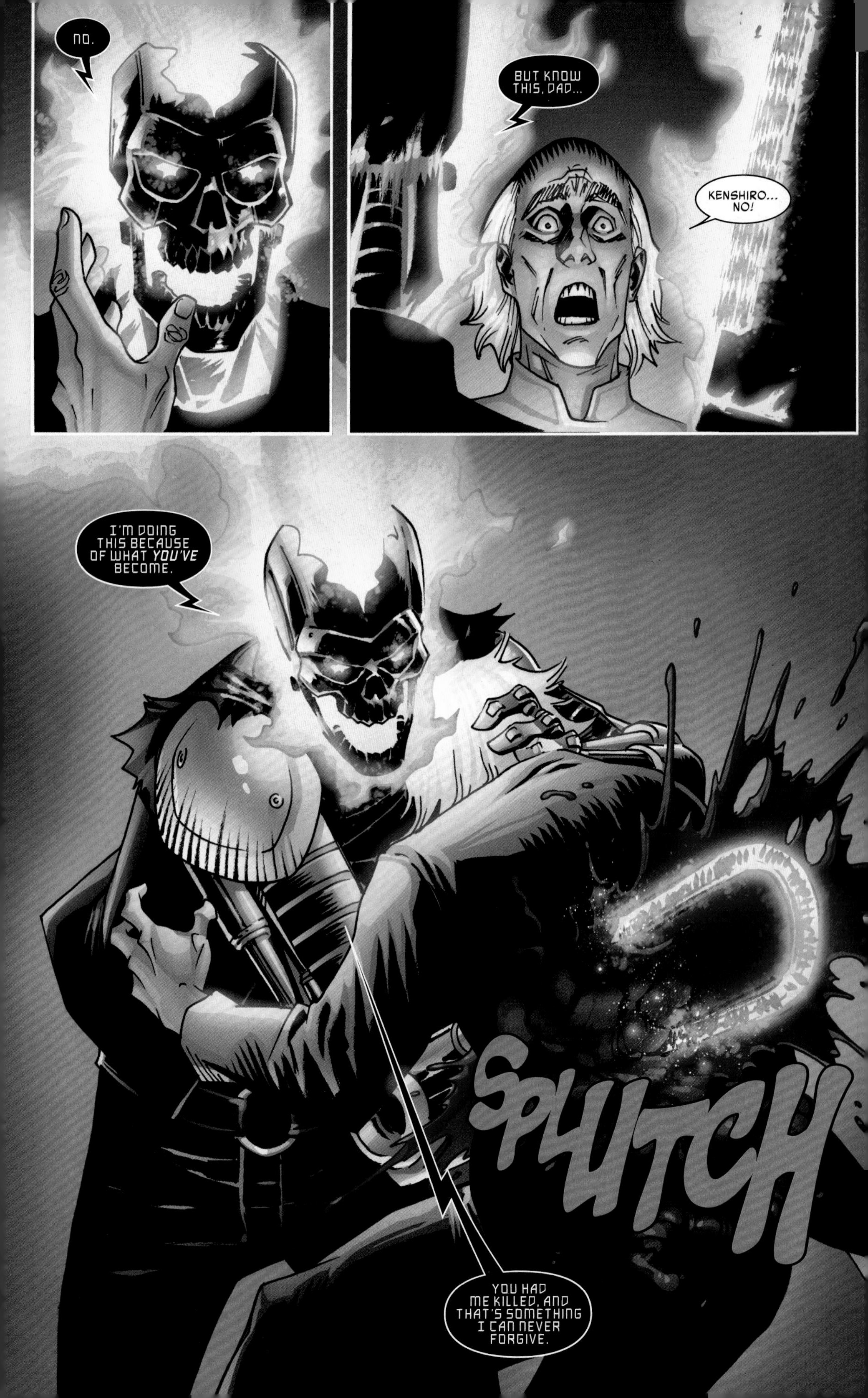
NO.
BUT KNOW THIS, DAD...
KENSHIRO... NO!
I'M DOING THIS BECAUSE OF WHAT *YOU'VE* BECOME.
SPLUTCH
YOU HAD ME KILLED, AND THAT'S SOMETHING I CAN NEVER FORGIVE.

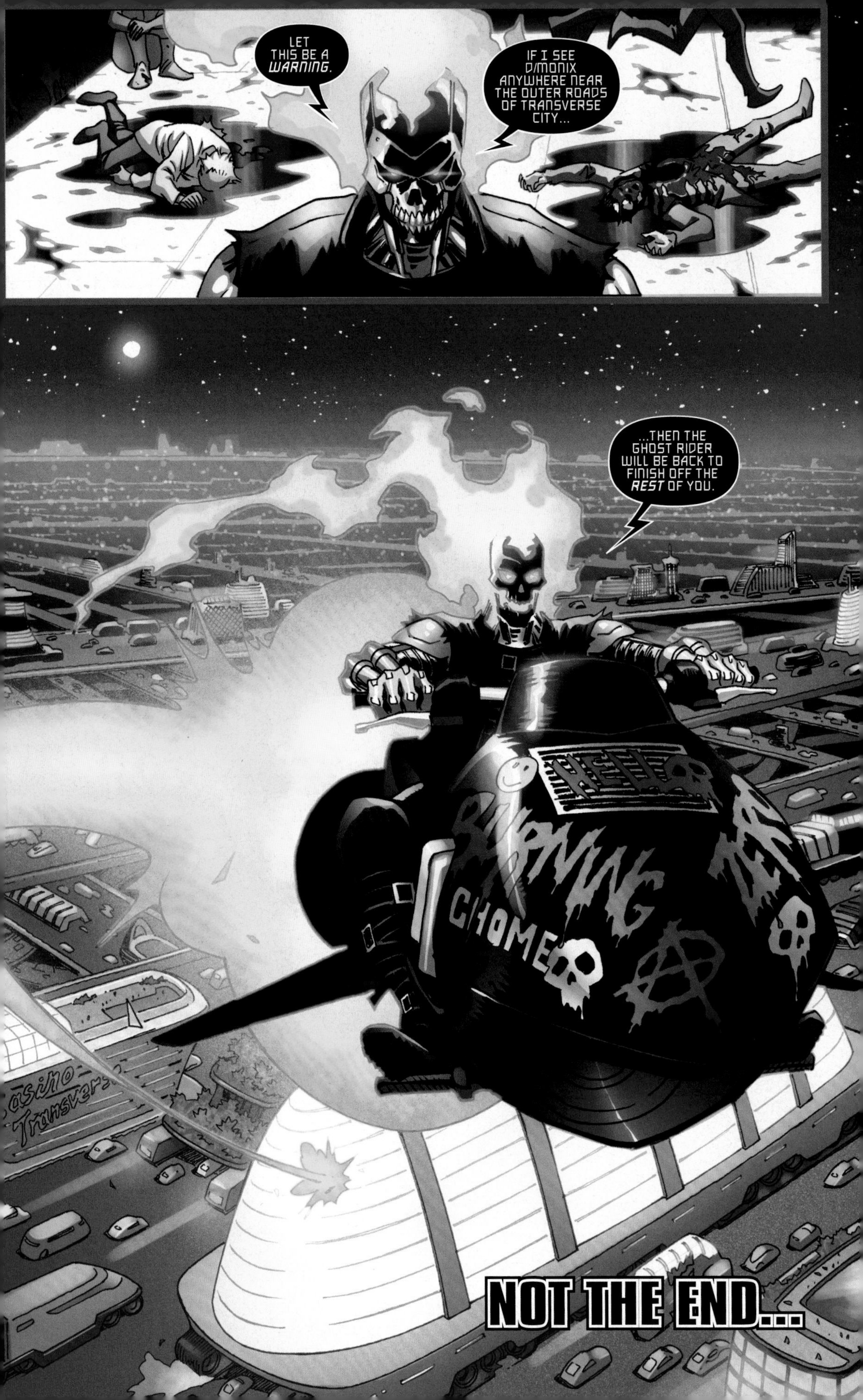
LET THIS BE A *WARNING*.
IF I SEE D/MONIX ANYWHERE NEAR THE OUTER ROADS OF TRANSVERSE CITY...
...THEN THE GHOST RIDER WILL BE BACK TO FINISH OFF THE *REST* OF YOU.
NOT THE END...

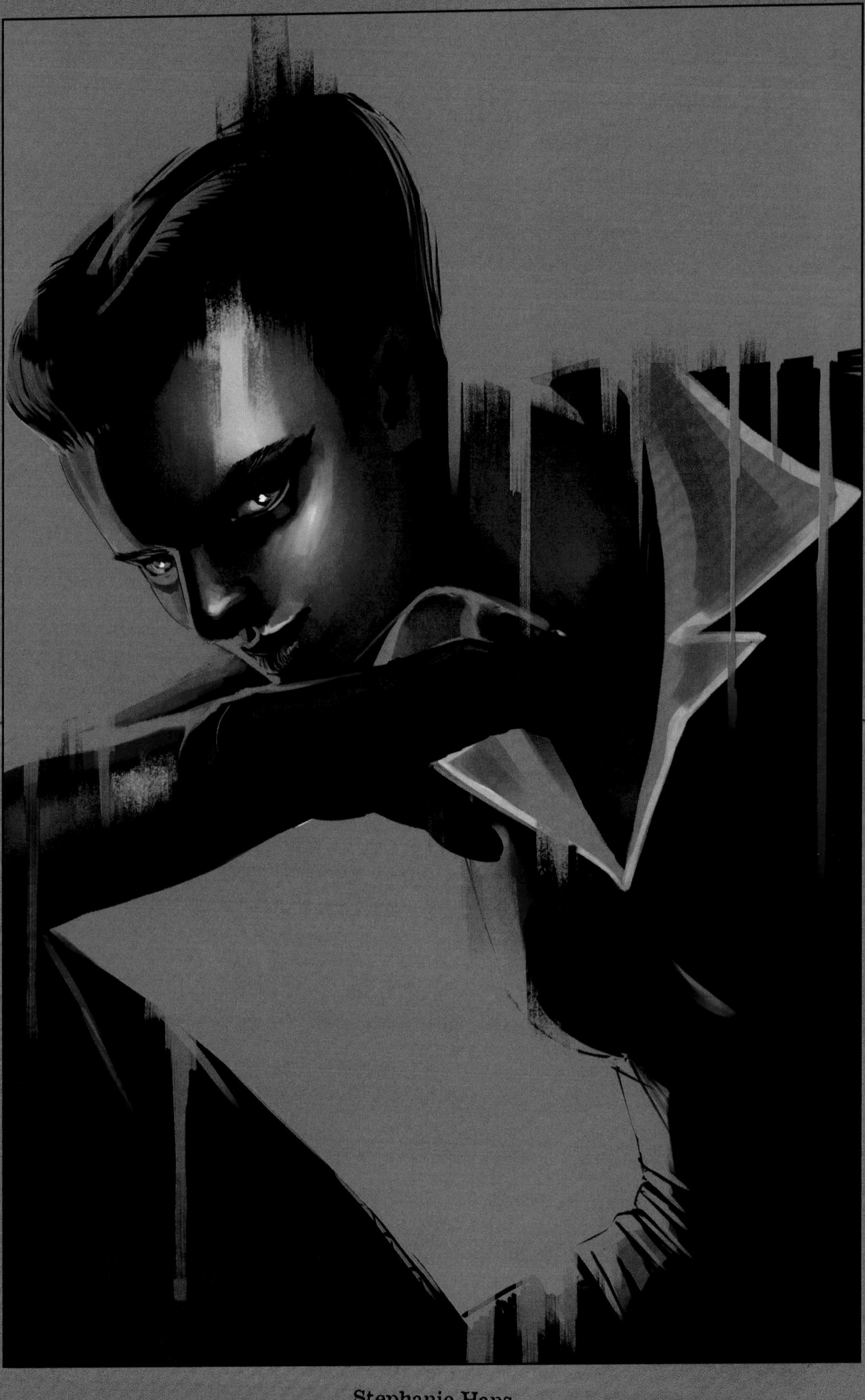

Stephanie Hans
SPIRITS OF GHOST RIDER: MOTHER OF DEMONS VARIANT

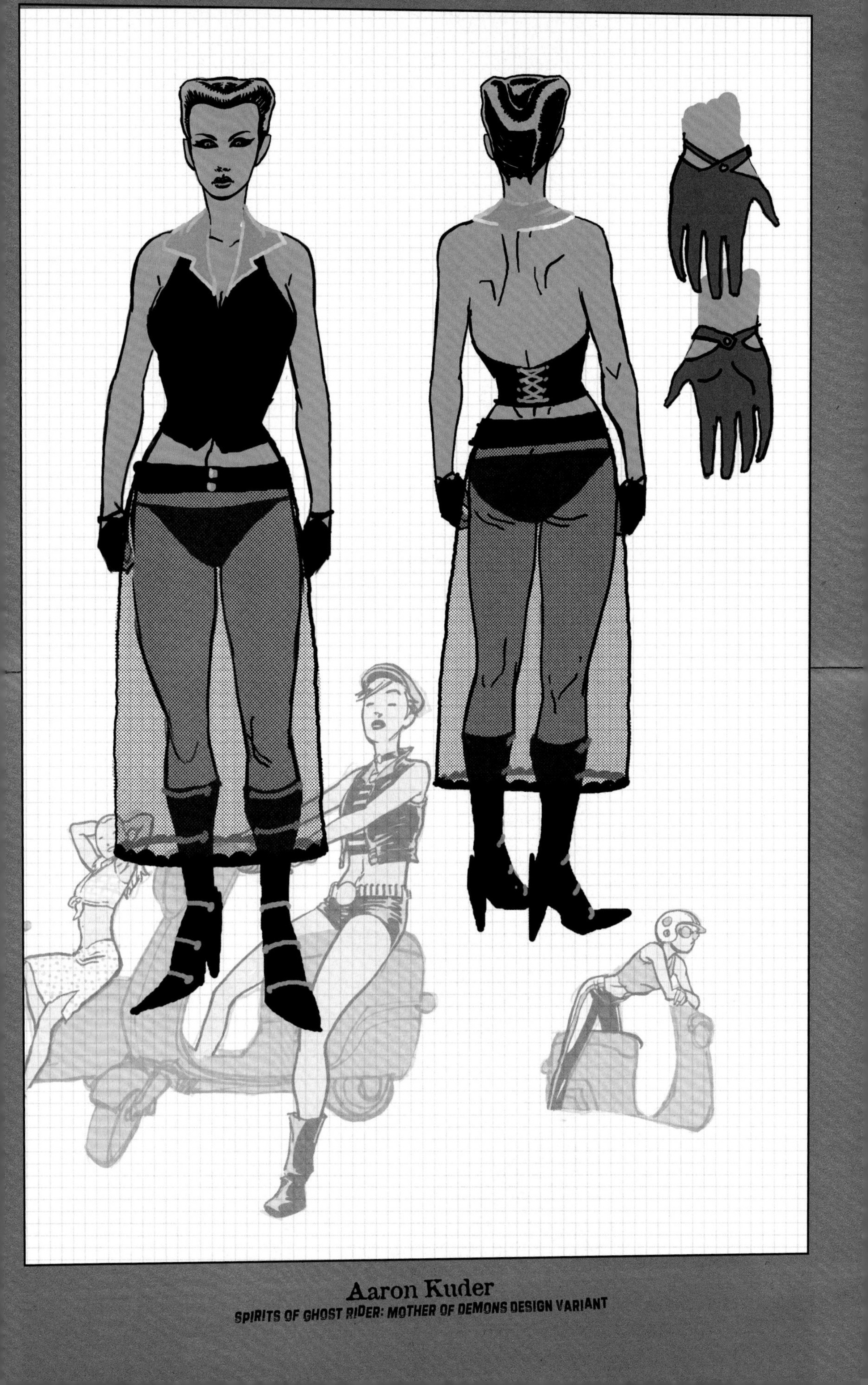

Aaron Kuder

SPIRITS OF GHOST RIDER: MOTHER OF DEMONS DESIGN VARIANT

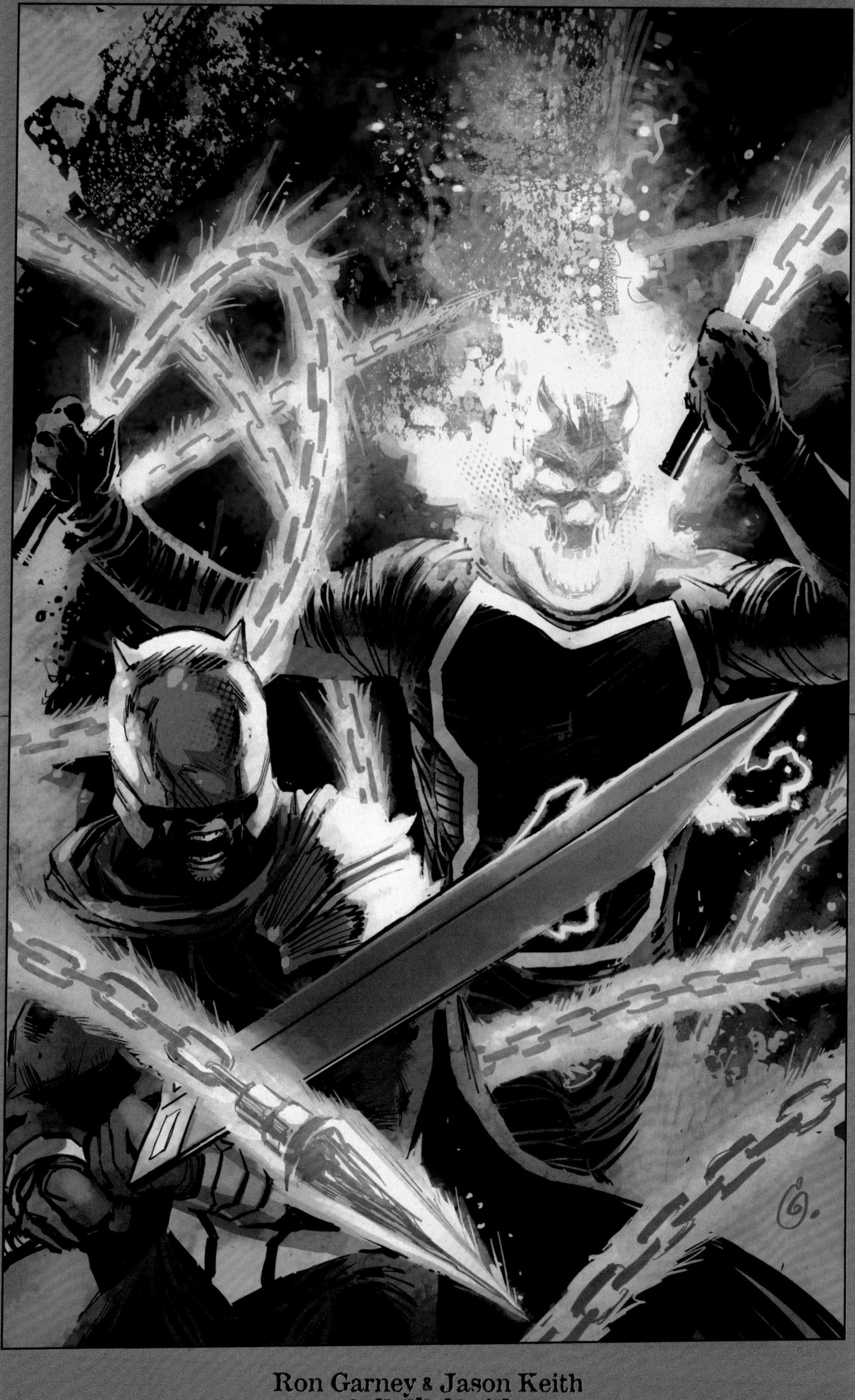

Ron Garney & Jason Keith
GHOST RIDER #5 VARIANT

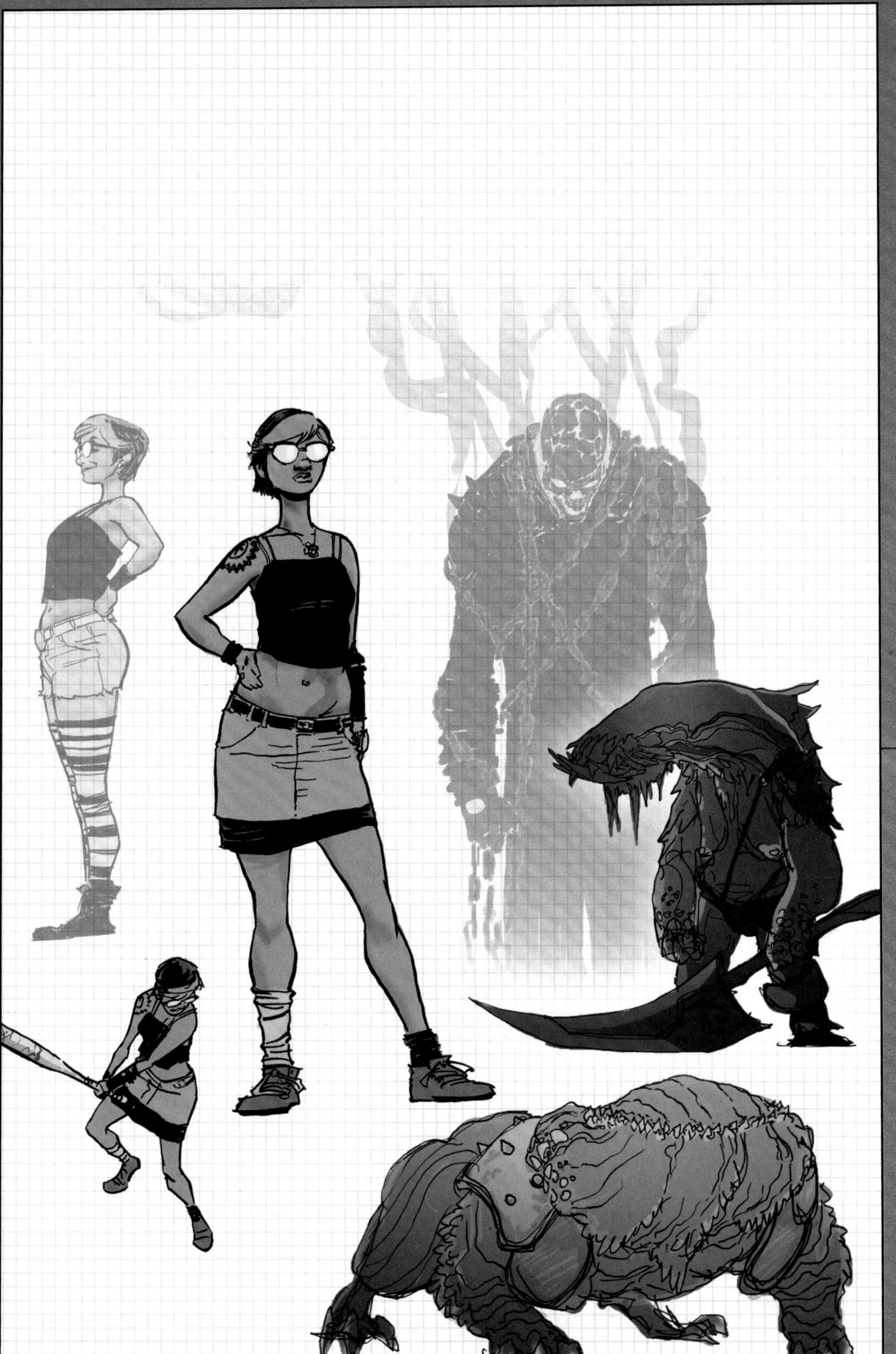

Aaron Kuder
GHOST RIDER #6 DESIGN VARIANT

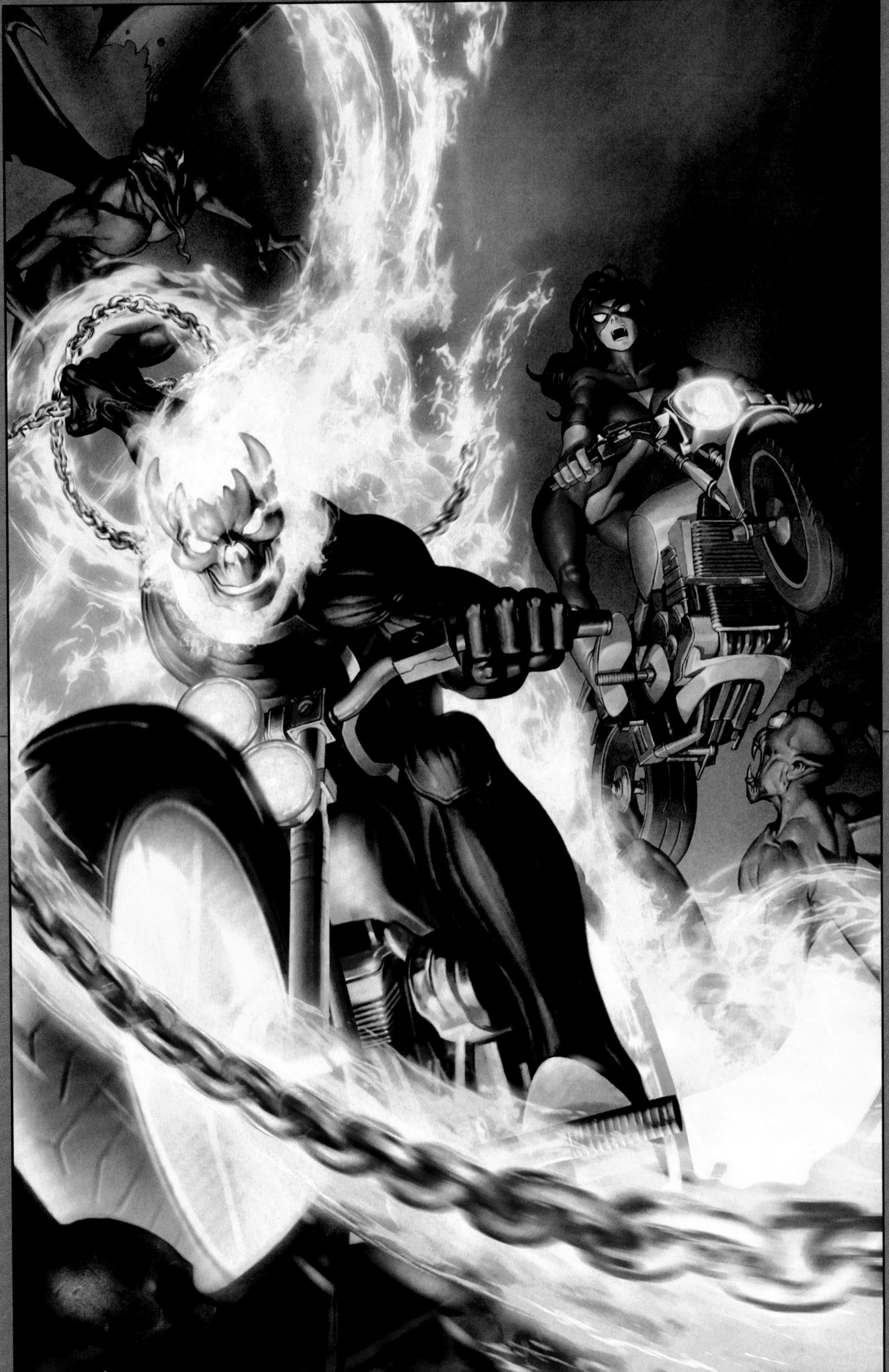

JUNGGEUN YOON

GHOST RIDER #6 SPIDER-WOMAN VARIANT

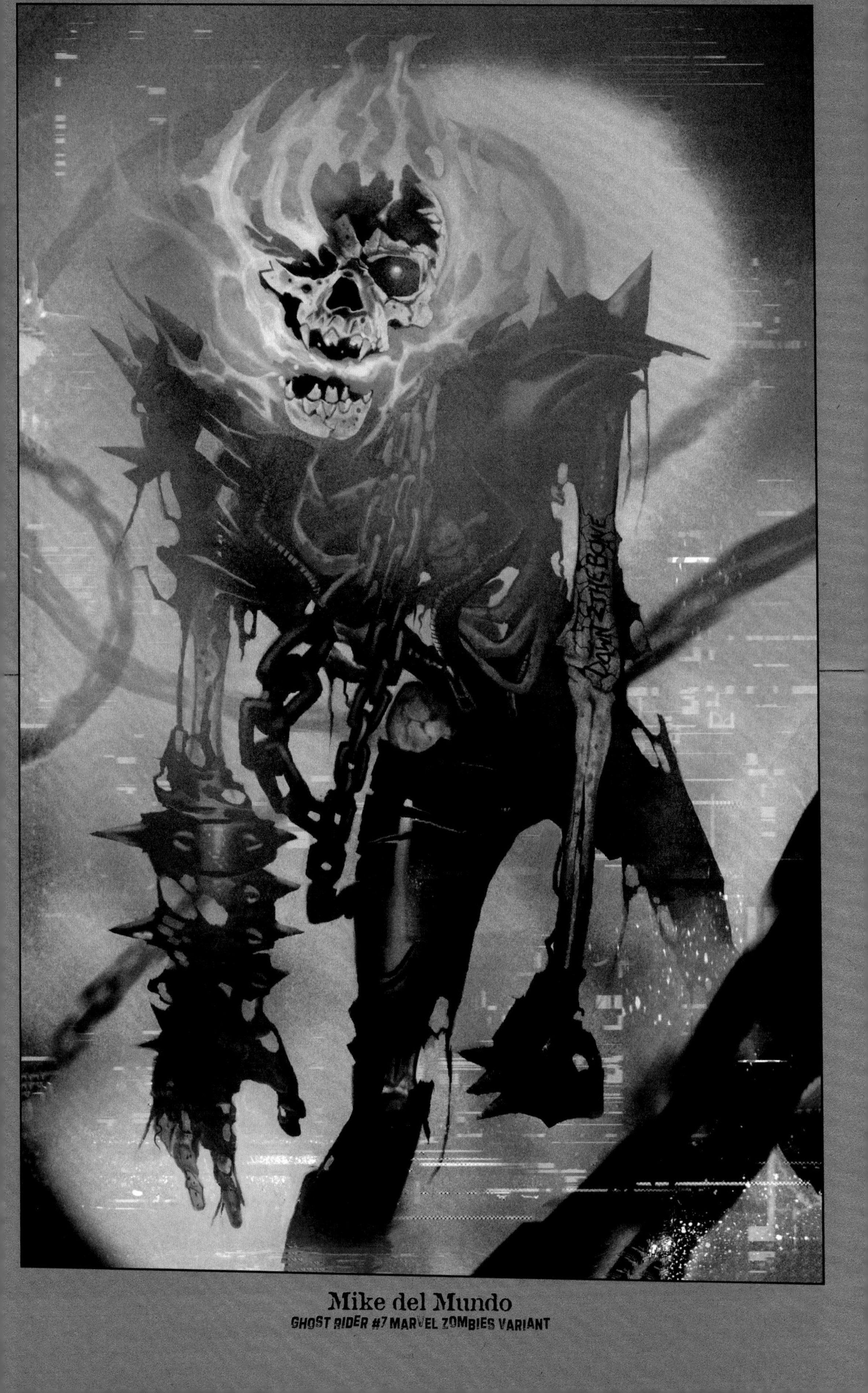
DOWN 2 THE BONE

Mike del Mundo

GHOST RIDER #7 MARVEL ZOMBIES VARIANT

Kyle Hotz & Dan Brown
GHOST RIDER 2099 VARIANT

Ron Lim & Israel Silva
GHOST RIDER 2099 VARIANT